African American Voices

[handwritten annotations:]

Kelly

1) Book
2) PPoint
3) Exam after
   colonial stuff
4) 2GA slavery
        — NA
        — us

AR / 2nd G.A. ——↑   religion

Nec. evil

(·)

AA → religious life
   → ideol. int mislted slavery

Uncovering the Past: Documentary Readers in American History
Series Editors: Steven Lawson and Nancy Hewitt

The books in this series introduce students in American history courses to two important dimensions of historical analysis. They enable students to engage actively in historical interpretation, and they further students' understanding of the interplay between social and political forces in historical developments.

Consisting of primary sources and an introductory essay, these readers are aimed at the major courses in the American history curriculum, as outlined further below. Each book in the series will be approximately 225–50 pages, including a 25–30 page introduction addressing key issues and questions about the subject under consideration, a discussion of sources and methodology, and a bibliography of suggested secondary readings.

Published

Paul G. E. Clemens
The Colonial Era: A Documentary Reader

Sean Patrick Adams
The Early American Republic: A Documentary Reader

Stanley Harrold
The Civil War and Reconstruction: A Documentary Reader

Steven Mintz
African American Voices: A Documentary Reader, 1619–1877

Robert P. Ingalls and David K. Johnson
The United States Since 1945: A Documentary Reader

Camilla Townsend
American Indian History: A Documentary Reader

Steven Mintz
Mexican American Voices: A Documentary Reader

In preparation

Brian Ward
The 1960s: A Documentary Reader

Jeremi Suri
American Foreign Relations Since 1898: A Documentary Reader

Nancy Rosenbloom
Women in Modern America, 1880–Present: A Documentary Reader

African American Voices

Voices

A Documentary Reader, 1619–1877

Edited by
Steven Mintz

WILEY-BLACKWELL
A John Wiley & Sons, Ltd., Publication

This fourth edition first published 2009
Editorial material and organization © 2009 by Steven Mintz
Edition history: Brandywine Press (1e, 1993; 2e, 1999; 3e, 2004)

Blackwell Publishing was acquired by John Wiley & Sons in February 2007. Blackwell's publishing program has been merged with Wiley's global Scientific, Technical, and Medical business to form Wiley-Blackwell.

Registered Office
John Wiley & Sons Ltd, The Atrium, Southern Gate, Chichester, West Sussex, PO19 8SQ, United Kingdom

Editorial Offices
350 Main Street, Malden, MA 02148-5020, USA
9600 Garsington Road, Oxford, OX4 2DQ, UK
The Atrium, Southern Gate, Chichester, West Sussex, PO19 8SQ, UK

For details of our global editorial offices, for customer services, and for information about how to apply for permission to reuse the copyright material in this book please see our website at www.wiley.com/wiley-blackwell.

Library of Congress Cataloging-in-Publication Data

African American voices : a documentary reader, 1619–1877 / edited by Steven Mintz. – 4th ed.
    p. cm. – (Uncovering the past : documentary readers in American history)
  Includes bibliographical references and index.
  ISBN 978-1-4051-8268-3 (hardcover : alk. paper) – ISBN 978-1-4051-8267-6 (pbk. : alk. paper)
  1. Slaves–United States–History–Sources. 2. Slaves–United States–Social conditions–Sources.
3. Slavery–Southern States–History–Sources. 4. African Americans–History–Sources. 5. African Americans–Social conditions–Sources. I. Mintz, Steven, 1953– II. Series: Uncovering the past (Malden, Mass.)

  E443.A37 2009
  306.3′620973–dc22

                                              2008044684

A catalogue record for this book is available from the British Library.

Set in 10/12.5pt Sabon
by SPi Publisher Services, Podicherry, India
Printed in Singapore by Utopia Press Pte Ltd

1 2009

Contents

Figures

Series Editors' Preface

Primary sources have become an essential component in the teaching of history to undergraduates. They engage students in the process of historical interpretation and analysis, helping them understand that facts do not speak for themselves. Rather, students see how historians construct narratives that recreate the past. Most students assume that the pursuit of knowledge is a solitary endeavor; yet historians constantly interact with their peers, building upon previous research and arguing among themselves over the interpretation of documents and their larger meaning. The documentary readers in this series highlight the value of this collaborative creative process. Documentary readers can be used in a variety of ways. The introduction to each reader will discuss the kinds of sources available for the study of the subject under investigation and suggest how the documents can be adapted to various classroom situations.

The books in this series introduce students in American history courses to two important dimensions of historical analysis. They enable students to engage actively in historical interpretation, and they further students' understanding of the interplay between social and political forces in historical developments. Consisting of primary sources and an introductory essay, these readers are aimed at the major courses in the American history curriculum. The documents in these texts include such items as illustrations of material artifacts, letters and diaries, sermons, maps, photographs, song lyrics, selections from fiction and memoirs, legal statutes, court decisions, presidential orders, speeches, and political cartoons.

Each volume in the series is edited by a specialist in the field who is concerned with undergraduate teaching. The goal of each volume is not to provide a comprehensive selection of material but to choose items that reflect major themes and debates and that illustrate significant social, cultural, political, and economic dimensions of an era or subject. The editor of each volume discusses the central questions that have occupied historians in this field and the ways historians have used primary sources to answer them. In addition, each introductory essay will contain an explanation of the kinds of materials available to investigate a particular subject, the methods by which historians analyze them, and the considerations that go into interpreting them. Each source selection will then be introduced by a short head note that gives students the necessary information and a context for understanding the document. Also, each section of the volume contains questions to guide student reading and stimulate classroom discussion.

Steven Mintz's *African American Voices: A Documentary Reader, 1619–1877* provides an array of documents dealing with the history of African Americans from the Colonial Era through emancipation and Reconstruction. Divided into 10 chapters, this volume covers the period of African enslavement and the horrific Middle Passage. It discusses the impact of the American Revolution on slavery and the development of the plantation economy in the South. The sources Mintz presents show the reader the conditions that slaves endured as well as the effect of bondage on women, children, and families. The sources also attest to the various forms of resistance and cultural expressions that slaves developed to keep alive hopes of gaining freedom. Mintz presents the voices of slaves and masters, men and women, abolitionists and runaways, politicians and reformers, and soldiers and generals in demonstrating the inner workings of the slave system from its earliest days and the war it finally took to destroy it. The author draws on travel accounts, advertisements, memoirs, visual displays, and much more to show the operation of slavery and emancipation in all its forms. In addition, Mintz provides a comprehensive bibliographic essay on sources, which explains and contextualizes the most significant issues of African American history during this period. He also includes a valuable list of sources to guide students in pursuing their own research projects.

Steven F. Lawson and Nancy A. Hewitt, Series Editors

Preface to the New Edition

Even though the subject evokes intense feelings of anger, frustration, guilt, and shame, it is absolutely essential that Americans study the history of slavery and the slave trade, for slavery occupies a central, if insufficiently recognized, place in America's past. A majority of the 650 workers who built the White House and the US Capitol were enslaved African Americans. The entire nation, not just the South, was complicit in slavery. Prior to the Revolution, every colony permitted slavery, and even after the institution was abolished north of the Mason–Dixon line and the Ohio River, northerners continued to benefit from slavery. Northern textile factories relied on slave-grown cotton, northern shipping interests transported the crop, midwestern meatpackers and farmers sold pork and corn to slave plantations, and northern banks and insurance companies financed and insured the production of cotton by slave labor. No major aspect of American history during the nation's formative era can be divorced from slavery. Slavery was central to the meaning and outcome of the American Revolution, the drafting of the US Constitution, American economic development, the growth of competing political parties, and the escalating sectional conflicts that resulted in civil war.

The history of the United States, and indeed of the entire western hemisphere, was inextricably bound up with slavery. African slaves and their descendants furnished the basic labor power that created dynamic New World economies and produced the first mass consumer goods such as sugar, rice, tobacco, and cotton. Even though it was abolished over a century ago, slavery has left a lasting legacy – a legacy evident in racism, economic inequality, and the social and economic underdevelopment of large parts of the Third World.

In recent years, slavery has become a divisive political battleground. Americans have bitterly debated whether to issue a national apology for slavery and to pay reparations to the descendants of slaves. To participate intelligently in this debate, it is essential to correct certain myths and misconceptions that many Americans hold about slavery: that slavery was a marginal and insignificant institution; that it was unprofitable and inefficient; and that freedom was a gift granted to African Americans solely by whites.

The history of slavery is profoundly unsettling. In the pages that follow you will discover that many of the most progressive societies in history were slave societies, including ancient Greece and Rome, the centers of Islamic civilization, Renaissance Italy, and, of course, the United States. You will learn that Europe's rise to global power was inextricably linked to slavery; that it is inconceivable that the New World could have been settled and developed by Europeans without slave labor; and that some Africans as well as many Europeans were complicit in the slave trade and exercised considerable control over it.

You will also discover that while politicians sought to suppress this fact, slavery was the supreme issue in American politics. The Constitution's three-fifths clause not only increased the South's representation in the House of Representatives and the Electoral College, it played a critical role in the two most important presidential elections before 1860: the election of Thomas Jefferson in 1800 and of Andrew Jackson in 1828. Even though the South had a free population just half that of the North as early as 1812, it held equal power in the US Senate for most of the pre-Civil War era. The South was also over-represented on the US Supreme Court, where slaveholders comprised 18 of the first 31 justices.

This book will tell several very different stories about slavery. One story is profoundly depressing. It describes the origins, development, and significance of the most extreme form of dehumanization and exploitation in history. But there are other stories that are more inspiring. Slavery is a story of human resilience and cultural survival under the most exploitative conditions imaginable. It is also a story of resistance that took cultural and physical forms. As we shall see, slavery involved a process of constant negotiation and testing of boundaries.

Above all, there is the remarkable story of how enslaved Africans and their descendants helped shape everything that we think of as American: our language, music, food, religion, and even our ideals of freedom. Today, African Americans constitute about 12 percent of the American population – about one in eight. But the influence that African Americans exert on American culture is far greater – an influence that began during this country's crucial formative period.

Preface

The experience of slavery defies simple generalizations. Novelists like Harriet Beecher Stowe might neatly divide slaves into docile and deferential Uncle Toms and militant and rebellious George Harrises, and masters into brutal and sadistic Simon Legrees and gentle, guilt-ridden Augustine St. Clares, but the realities of slavery were far more complex. A more holistic view of slavery requires us to look at slavery from the inside, from the perspective of the enslaved. This book tells the story of life under slavery from the inside, from the perspective of those who experienced it first hand. In this volume, readers will encounter such famous figures as Frederick Douglass and Nat Turner, as well as many less well known individuals who will help answer the question: what was it like to be a slave?

This volume is not simply another collection of documents. It begins with a thorough, up-to-date introduction that summarizes what we now know about the history of slavery, the African slave trade, the conditions of slave life, the impact of slavery on the southern economy, and the process of emancipation.

The introduction is followed by substantial excerpts from the published slave narratives, interviews with former slaves, and letters written by enslaved African Americans. Together, these documents draw a comprehensive portrait of slavery. These selections are organized around the concept of the cycle of life under slavery: from memories of growing up in Africa to the trials of the Middle Passage, the horrors of the auction block, the sustaining forces of family and religion, acts of resistance, and the meaning of the Civil War and emancipation. No single person experienced all of these phases of slave life. But all of the enslaved underwent many of these critical experiences.

Introduction

A woman listed in the census simply as Celia was just 14 years old in 1850, when a 60-year-old Missouri farmer named Robert Newsome purchased her. A widower with two grown daughters, the 60-year-old Newsome raped Celia before he had even brought her to his farm. For five years, he kept her as his sexual slave, forcing her to bear two illegitimate children. In 1855, pregnant a third time and ill, she struck back, knocking her abuser unconscious by hitting him on the head with a club and burning his body in her fireplace. During her murder trial, Celia's attorneys argued that a woman had a right to use deadly force to prevent rape. But the court ruled that in Missouri, as in other slave states, it was not a crime to rape a slave woman. Celia was found guilty and hanged.

A Virginia-born slave named Benjamin Montgomery was 17 when he was purchased by a Mississippi planter named Joseph Davis in 1850. Davis, Confederate president Jefferson Davis's elder brother, had met the British utopian reformer Robert Owen, and wanted to apply Owen's ideas to his own plantation. Davis instituted a system of self-government on his plantation, including a court system in which slaves ruled on any cases of misconduct. He also gave slaves like Benjamin Montgomery access to his personal library. Montgomery educated himself and became a skilled mechanic. He managed the plantation's steam-powered cotton gin and ran a retail store, eventually earning enough money to purchase his family's freedom. Nevertheless, he and his family decided to remain on the plantation. After the Civil War, Montgomery actually purchased the property from Davis, and ran it until his death in 1877.

The experience of slavery varied widely, depending primarily on a slaveholder's character and whims. Some masters, like Joseph Davis, attempted to treat their slaves in a kindly if paternalistic manner. Yet as Celia's example reveals, the institution of slavery could also bring out the very worst characteristics of human nature, for it allowed masters to treat a human being as a piece of property, to be exploited however they wished.

Slavery in Historical Perspective

During the nineteenth century, slavery was often described as "the peculiar institution." But throughout much of human history, free wage labor, not forced labor, was the truly peculiar institution. Most people worked not out of a desire to better their condition in life but because they were forced to: as slaves, serfs, peons, or indentured servants.

Slavery in the United States was not unique in treating human beings like animals. The institution of slavery could be found in societies as diverse as ancient Assyria, Babylonia, China, Egypt, India, Persia, and Mesopotamia; in classical Greece and Rome; in Africa, in the Islamic world, and among the New World Indians. At the time of Christ, there were probably between two and three million slaves in Italy, making up 35–40 percent of the population. England's Domesday book of 1086 indicated that 10 percent of the population was enslaved. Among some Indian tribes of the Pacific Northwest, nearly a quarter of the population consisted of slaves. In 1644, just before the Dutch ceded Manhattan to the British, enslaved Africans made up 40 percent of the population.

It is notable that the modern word for slaves comes from "Slav." During the Middle Ages, most slaves in Europe and the Islamic world were people from Slavic Eastern Europe. It was only in the fifteenth century that slavery became linked with people from sub-Saharan Africa.

Defining Slavery

How does slavery differ from other forms of exploitation such as serfdom, indentured servitude, or the subordination of women in patriarchal societies? The traditional definition of slavery was legal. Slaves were people's property and could be bought, sold, traded, leased, or mortgaged like livestock.

Recent research, however, has revealed a great deal of diversity among slavery's forms and functions. In the ancient and non-Western world some slaves served as field laborers. But others served as sex objects in harems; as eunuchs; and as bureaucrats, doctors, and soldiers. In the South, slavery's primary functions were economic. But in many ancient and non-Western societies, slavery served psychological, religious, sexual, and honorific functions.

To encompass slavery's diversity, scholars today tend to define the institution culturally. Slaves, according to this view, are people totally subject to their owners' will. They belong only to their owner, who can subject them to sexual exploitation and cruel punishment, and hold over them the power of life and death. In addition, slaves are people who are cut off from their traditional culture and dishonored in a variety of ways (for example, by being branded, tattooed, or required to wear distinctive collars, clothing, or hair styles). The most common form of dishonor is to disparage slaves' character and intellectual capacities. Regardless of place, time, or the slaves' ethnicity, all societies have imposed certain common stereotypes on slaves – that they were licentious, childlike, lazy, irresponsible, and incapable of freedom.

Slavery in the Ancient, Medieval, and Early Modern Worlds

Slavery dates to prehistoric times and was apparently modeled on the domestication of animals. From the earliest periods of recorded history, slavery was found in the world's most advanced regions. The first civilizations – along the Tigris and Euphrates rivers in Mesopotamia, the Nile in Egypt, the Indus Valley of India, and China's Yangtze River Valley – all practiced slavery. The earliest known system of laws, the Hammurabi Code, recognized slavery and declared that slaves could be sold or inherited. But the percentage of slaves in these early civilizations was small, in part because these societies kept relatively few male slaves. In the tales of Homer and in the Old Testament, male war captives were typically killed, while women were enslaved as field laborers or taken as concubines.

Although slavery was a universal institution in the ancient world, only a handful of societies made slavery the dominant labor force. The first true slave society in history emerged in ancient Greece between the sixth and fourth centuries BC. In Athens during the classical period, a third to a half of the population consisted of slaves. Ancient Rome would be even more dependent on slavery. It is not an accident that our modern ideas of freedom and democracy emerged in these slave societies. Most early societies lacked a word for freedom; but large-scale slavery in classical Greece and Rome made these people more aware of the distinctive nature of freedom.

Slavery never disappeared from medieval Europe. While slavery declined in northwestern Europe, where it was replaced by serfdom, it persisted in Sicily, southern Italy, Russia, southern France, Spain, and North Africa. Continuing warfare between Christians and Muslims generated large numbers of slaves to work in agriculture. Most of these slaves were "white," coming from areas in Eastern Europe or near the Black Sea.

When Western Europeans began to colonize the New World at the end of the fifteenth century, they were well aware of the institution of slavery. As early as 1300, Europeans were using black and Russian slaves to raise sugar on Italian plantations. During the 1400s, decades before Columbus's "discovery" of the New World, Europeans exploited African labor on slave plantations on sugar-producing islands off the coast of West Africa. European colonization of the New World led to a dramatic expansion in slavery. During the sixteenth century, Portugal and Spain extended racial slavery into the New World, opening sugar, coffee, and cotton plantations in Brazil and the West Indies and forcing black slaves in Mexico to work in mines. During the seventeenth century, England, France, Denmark, and Holland established slavery in their New World colonies.

The Newness of New World Slavery

Was the slavery that developed in the New World fundamentally different from the kinds of servitude found in classical antiquity or in other societies? In one respect, New World slavery was not unique. Slavery everywhere permitted cruelty and abuse. In Homer's Greece, it was not a crime for a master to beat or kill a slave, and the testimony of unskilled slaves was not allowed in court unless it was obtained through torture. Nor does the Bible prohibit the beating of slaves. In the Roman Republic, a master might kill a slave. Vedius Pollio, a citizen of Rome, reportedly fed the bodies of his slaves to his pet fish. Flavius Gratianus, a fourth-century Roman emperor, ruled that any slave who dared accuse his master of a crime should be immediately burned alive. Roman slaves who participated in revolts were crucified. In ancient India, Saxon England, and ancient China, a master might mistreat or even kill a slave with impunity. Aztec Mexico publicly staged the ritual torture and killing of slaves.

Yet in certain fundamental respects New World slavery differed from slavery in classical antiquity and in Africa, eastern and central Asia, or the Middle East. For one thing, slavery in the classical and the early medieval worlds was not based on racial distinctions. In ancient times, slavery had nothing to do with the color of a person's skin. In ancient Rome, for example, the slave population included Ethiopians, Gauls, Jews, Persians, and Scandinavians. Unlike seventeenth-, eighteenth-, or nineteenth-century Europeans, the people of the ancient world placed no premium on racial purity and attached no stigma to racial mixture. Ancient societies, however, did tattoo, brand, or mutilate their slaves as a symbol of their debased status.

Racial slavery originated during the Middle Ages, when Christians and Muslims increasingly began to recruit slaves from east, north-central, and west Africa. As late as the fifteenth century, however, slavery did not automatically mean black slavery. Many slaves – both in southern Europe and in the Islamic world – came from the Crimea, the Balkans, and the steppes of western Asia. But after 1453, when the Ottoman Turks captured Constantinople, the capital of eastern Christendom, and began to monopolize the supply of "white" slaves, Christian slave traders drew increasingly upon captive black Muslims, known as Moors, and upon slaves purchased on the west African coast or transported across the Sahara Desert. By the eighteenth century, Islamic societies also became dependent almost exclusively on sub-Saharan African slaves. For the first time, the most menial, arduous, and degrading forms of labor were associated with black slaves.

Apart from its racial basis, another distinction between modern and ancient slavery was that the ancient world did not necessarily regard slavery as a permanent condition. In many societies, slaves were allowed to marry free spouses and become members of their owners' families. In ancient Babylonia, for instance, freeborn women and male slaves frequently married, and their children were considered to be free. Access to freedom tended to be far easier under ancient slavery than it was under American slavery. In Greece and Rome, manumission of slaves was not uncommon, and former slaves carried little stigma from their previous status.

A third key difference between ancient and modern slavery was that slaves did not necessarily hold the lowest status in pre-modern societies. While we today draw a sharp distinction between slavery and wage labor, such a distinction was largely non-existent in the world of classical antiquity and slaves could be among the wealthiest or most influential people in a city. The Bible, for example, tells the story of Joseph, sold into slavery by his brothers, who became a trusted governor, counselor, and administrator in Egypt. In classical Greece, many educators, scholars, poets, and physicians were in fact slaves. And in ancient Rome, slaves ranged from those who labored in mines to many merchants and urban craftsmen. In the ancient Near East, slaves could conduct trade and business on their own. In certain Muslim societies, rulers were customarily recruited among the sons of female slaves.

Finally, it was only in the New World that slavery provided the labor force for a high-pressure, profit-making capitalist system of plantation agriculture producing cotton, sugar, coffee, and cocoa for distant markets. While many slaves in the ancient world toiled in mines and agricultural fields, or on construction and irrigation projects, and suffered extremely high death rates, it appears that ancient slavery was primarily a household institution. In general, ancient peoples did not breed slaves or subject them to the kind of regimented efficiency found on slave plantations in the West Indies or the American South. It appears that most slaves in Africa, in the Islamic world, and in the New World prior to European colonization worked as farmers or household servants, or served as concubines or eunuchs. They were symbols of prestige, luxury, and power rather than a source of labor. Under modern New World slavery, slaves became the dominant labor force in plantation agriculture.

Justifications of Slavery

Over time, justifications for slavery have changed profoundly. Many ancient societies considered slavery a matter of bad luck or accident. Slaves in these societies were often war captives or victims of piracy or children who had been abandoned by their parents.

The Greek philosopher Aristotle developed a justification for slavery that would have profound consequences for the future. This was the notion of the "natural slave." Slaves, in Aristotle's view, lacked the higher qualities of the soul necessary for freedom. Slavery was not only good for the master, according to Aristotle, it was also good for slaves, who received the guidance and discipline they were incapable of providing themselves.

In the Christian world, the most important rationalization for slavery was the so-called "Curse of Ham." According to this doctrine, the Biblical figure Noah had cursed his son Ham with blackness and the condition of perpetual slavery. In fact, this story rested on a misunderstanding of Biblical texts. In the Bible, Noah curses Canaan, the ancestor of the Canaanites, and not Ham. But the "Curse of Ham" was important in that it was the first justification of slavery based on ethnicity.

It was not until the late eighteenth century that pseudo-scientific racism provided the basic rationale for slavery. Yet even before this era, there can be no doubt that racism inclined many Europeans to see sub-Saharan Africans as fit for little more than slavery. In the fifteenth and sixteenth centuries, many European Christians associated Africans with their Islamic enemies. At the same time, many Europeans devised a clear color symbolism. They associated whiteness with purity, while blackness had sinister and even satanic connotations, since black was the color of the Devil.

Slavery in Africa

Slavery existed in Africa before the arrival of Europeans – as did a slave trade that exported a small number of sub-Saharan Africans to North Africa, the Middle East, and the Persian Gulf. It would be a grave mistake, however, to assume that the kinds of slavery found in Africa were identical to the system of plantation slavery that developed in the New World.

For one thing, hereditary slavery, extending over several generations, was rare. Many African slaves were eventually freed and absorbed into their owner's kin group. Another difference was that in African societies most slaves were female. Women were preferred because they bore children and performed most field labor. They were responsible not only for agricultural production, but for spinning and weaving and other productive tasks.

Slavery in early sub-Saharan Africa took a variety of forms. Before the fifteenth century, there was some chattel slavery there, under which slaves could be bought and sold like livestock. But most slavery in Africa took a different form. The gap in status between masters and slaves was not as wide as it would be in the New World. While most slaves were field workers, some served in royal courts as officials, soldiers, servants, and artisans. Under a system known as "pawnship," youths (usually girls) served as collateral for their family's debts. If their parents or kin defaulted on these debts, then these young girls were forced to labor to repay these debts. In many instances, these young women eventually married into their owner's lineage, and their family's debt was canceled.

Under a system known as "clientage," slaves owed a share of their crop or their labor to an owner or a lineage. Yet these slave "clients" owned the bulk of their crop and were even allowed to participate in the society's political activities. These slaves were often treated no differently than other peasant or tenant farmers.

The transatlantic trade profoundly changed the nature and scale of slavery in Africa itself – and imposed a heavy economic, political, and psychological cost on the continent. The development of the Atlantic slave trade led to the enslavement of far greater numbers of Africans and to more intense exploitation of slave labor within Africa. Over time, the Atlantic trade encouraged traders to seek slaves deeper in the interior.

The slave trade had an enormous impact on African society. One of its most profound consequences was demographic. While the trade probably did not reduce the overall population, it did produce a radically skewed sex ratio. During the slave trade era, in most parts of west and central Africa there were only 80 men in the age bracket 15–60 for every 100 women. In Angola, there were just 40 to 50 men per 100 women. As a result of the slave trade, there were fewer adult men to hunt, fish, rear livestock, and clear fields.

The slave trade had momentous social consequences. It generated violence, spread disease, and resulted in massive imports of European goods, undermining local industries. It also slowed population growth. According to one estimate, in the absence of the slave trade, there would have been 100 million Africans in 1850 instead of 50 million.

Why Africa?

Why was Africa so vulnerable to the slave trade? The answer lies first and foremost in west and central Africa's political fragmentation. By the era of the slave trade, many of the region's larger political units – such as the empires of Ghana and Mali – had declined. The absence of strong, stable political units made it more difficult for smaller states to resist the slave trade.

In retrospect, it seems clear that the Atlantic slave trade depended upon a highly complex set of variables. Trade winds and ocean currents made it easy to sail from the western African coast to Brazil and the Caribbean. The importation of new food crops from the Americas – such as cassava, squash, and peanuts – stimulated population growth in Africa. Rapid population growth, in turn, made the slave trade possible.

Enslavement

Many Americans, influenced by images in the 1977 television mini-series *Roots*, mistakenly believe that most slaves were captured by Europeans who landed on the African coast and captured or ambushed people. While Europeans did engage in some slave raiding, the majority of people who were transported to the Americas were enslaved by other Africans. It is important to understand that Europeans were incapable, on their own, of kidnapping 20 million Africans. Indeed, the system became so institutionalized that Europeans had little contact with the actual process of enslavement.

How were people enslaved? Most slaves in Africa were captured in wars or in surprise raids on villages. Adults were bound and gagged and infants were sometimes thrown into sacks. One of the earliest first-hand accounts of the African slave trade comes from a seaman named Gomes Eannes de Azurara, who witnessed a Portuguese raid on an African village. He said that some captives "drowned themselves in the water; others thought to escape by hiding under their huts; others shoved their children among the sea-weed."

The overwhelming majority of slaves sold to Europeans had not been slaves in Africa. They were free people who were captured in war or were victims of banditry or were enslaved as punishment for certain crimes. In Senegambia, the Guinea Coast, and the Slave Coasts of west Africa, war was the most important source of slaves. In Angola, kidnapping and condemnation for debt were very important. In most cases, rulers or merchants were not selling their own subjects, but people they regarded as alien. We must remember that Africans did not think of themselves as Africans, but as members of separate nations.

Apologists for the African slave trade long argued that European traders did not enslave anyone: they simply purchased Africans who had already been enslaved and who otherwise would have been put to death. Thus, apologists claimed, the slave trade actually saved lives. Such claims represent a gross distortion of the facts. Some independent slave merchants did in fact stage raids on unprotected African villages and kidnap and enslave Africans. Most professional slave traders, however, set up bases along the west African coast where they purchased slaves from Africans in exchange for firearms and other goods. Before the end of the seventeenth century, England, France, Denmark, Holland, and Portugal had all established slave trading posts on the west African coast.

Yet to simply say that Europeans purchased people who had already been enslaved seriously distorts historical reality. While there had been a slave trade within Africa prior to the arrival of Europeans, the massive European demand for slaves and the introduction of firearms radically transformed west and central African society. A growing number of Africans were enslaved for petty debts or minor criminal or religious offenses or following unprovoked raids on unprotected villages. An increasing number of religious wars broke out with the goal of capturing slaves. European weapons made it easier to capture slaves.

Some African societies – like Benin in southern Nigeria – refused to sell slaves. Others, like Dahomey, appear to have specialized in enslavement. Still other societies, like Asante, in present-day Ghana, and the Yoruba in western Nigeria, engaged in wars that produced as many as half of all eighteenth- and early nineteenth-century slaves.

In western and central Africa, many new commercial states, merchants, and traders, chronically short of capital, thrived by enslaving some people and selling others abroad. Birth rates often exceeded agriculture's capacity to feed the population. Drought, famine, or periods of violent conflict might lead a ruler or a merchant to sell slaves. In addition, many rulers sold slaves in order to acquire the trade goods – textiles, alcohol, and other rare imports – that were necessary to secure the loyalty of their subjects.

In the earliest years, most slaves came from coastal areas. Over time, the source moved further into the African interior. Many Africans retained females and sold off males. About two-thirds of the slaves sent to the New World were male.

After capture, the captives were bound together at the neck and marched barefoot hundreds of miles to the Atlantic coast. African captives typically suffered death rates of 20 percent or more while being marched overland. Observers reported seeing hundreds of skeletons along the slave caravan routes. At the coast, the captives were held in pens (known as barracoons) guarded by dogs. Our best guess is that another 15 to 30 percent of Africans died during capture, the march from the interior, or the wait for slave ships along the coast.

The captives who survived the forced march to the sea were then examined by European slave traders: "The Countenance and Stature, a good Set of Teeth, Pliancy in the Limbs and Joints, and being free of Venereal Taint, are the things inspected and governs our choice in buying," wrote John Atkins, an early eighteenth-century British slave trader. Those who were bought were branded with hot irons, assigned numbers, and forced aboard ships; the others were simply abandoned. (Representatives of the church sometimes branded enslaved Africans with the cross as a sign that they had been baptized.)

The Middle Passage

The transatlantic slave trade was the largest movement of people in history. Between 10 and 15 million Africans were forcibly removed from the continent between 1500 and 1900. But this figure grossly understates the actual number of Africans enslaved, killed, or displaced as a result of the slave trade. At least 2 million Africans died during the infamous "Middle Passage" across the Atlantic. Altogether, for every 100 slaves who reached the New World, another 40 had died in Africa or during the Middle Passage.

The Atlantic slave trade, however, was not the only slave trade within Africa. Nearly as many Africans were exported across the Sahara Desert, the Red Sea, and the Indian Ocean from AD 650 to 1900 as were shipped across the Atlantic. Islamic traders probably exported 10 million slaves into north Africa, Arabia, Yemen, Iraq, Iran, and India. In addition, it now seems clear that during the era of the Atlantic slave trade, many and perhaps most of the enslaved were kept in Africa. It is imaginable that as many as 60 million Africans died or were enslaved as a result of these various slave trades.

The level of slave exports to the New World grew from about 36,000 a year in the early eighteenth century to almost 80,000 a year during the 1780s. By 1750, slavers usually contained at least 400 slaves, with some carrying more than 700.

Once on shipboard, slaves were chained together and crammed into spaces sometimes less than five feet high. John Newton, a former slave ship captain, said that slaves were packed together "like books upon a shelf ... so close that the shelf would not easily contain one more." Conditions within the slave ships were unspeakably awful. Inside the hold, slaves had only half the space provided for indentured servants or convicts. Urine, vomit, mucus, and horrific odors filled the hold.

The Middle Passage usually took more than seven weeks. Men and women were separated, with men usually placed toward the vessel's bow and women toward the stern. The men were chained together and forced to lie shoulder to shoulder, while women were usually left unchained. During the voyage, the enslaved Africans were typically fed only once or twice a day and brought on deck for limited times.

The death rate on these slave ships was very high – reaching 25 percent in the seventeenth and early eighteenth centuries and remaining around 10 percent in the nineteenth century – as a result of malnutrition and such diseases as dysentery, measles, scurvy, and smallpox. This was a much higher death rate than that found among white immigrants, and it appears to have been due largely to dehydration, resulting from inadequate water rations. Diarrhea was widespread and many Africans arrived in the New World covered with sores or suffering fevers.

Many Africans resisted enslavement. On shipboard, many slaves mutinied, attempted suicide, jumped overboard, or refused to eat. The most recent estimate suggests that there was a revolt on one in every ten voyages across the Atlantic. To prevent their captives from starving themselves, slavers sometimes smashed out their teeth and fed them by force. Some captains actually cut off the arms and legs of a few kidnapped Africans.

Upon arrival in the New World, enslaved Africans underwent the final stage in the process of enslavement, a rigorous process known as "seasoning," during which Africans were forced to adapt to the harsh discipline of slavery. Many slaves died of disease or suicide, but many other African captives conspired to escape slavery by running away and forming "maroon" colonies in remote parts of South Carolina, Florida, Brazil, Guyana, Jamaica, and Suriname.

The Slave Trade's Significance

Slavery played a crucial role in the development of the modern world economy. Slaves provided the labor power necessary to settle and develop Europe's New World colonies. Slaves also produced the products for the first mass consumer markets: sugar, tobacco, coffee, cocoa, and later cotton. Slavery was an integral part of the earliest multinational systems of credit and trade that arose in the fifteenth and sixteenth centuries. The African slave trade also stimulated European shipping, manufacturing, and gun-making.

During the earliest phases of capitalist development, planters, master craftsmen, and other early capitalists could not afford to pay wages. Chronically in debt, New World planters could exploit slave labor without expending scarce currency. Slavery provided the cheapest and most expedient way to meet the demand for labor in mining and agriculture.

The slave trade had profound consequences for Europe. Between the early 1500s and the early 1800s, the slave trade became one of Europe's largest and most profitable industries. Profits from the slave trade were said to run as high as 300 percent. In the mid-eighteenth century, a third of the British merchant fleet was engaged in transporting 50,000 Africans a year to the New World.

But it wasn't just slave traders or New World planters who benefited from the slave trade. American shipowners, farmers, and fisherman also profited from slavery. Slavery played a pivotal role in the growth of commercial capitalism in the colonies. The slave plantations of the West Indies became the largest market for American fish, oats, corn, flour, lumber, peas, beans, hogs, and horses. New Englanders distilled molasses produced by slaves in the French and Dutch West Indies into rum.

While slavery did not create a major share of the capital that financed Europe's industrial revolution (profits from the slave trade and New World plantations added up to less than 5 percent of Britain's national income at the beginning of the industrial revolution), slave labor did produce the major consumer goods that were the basis of world trade during the seventeenth, eighteenth, and early nineteenth centuries: coffee, cotton, rum, sugar, and tobacco. In addition, the slave trade provided stimulus to shipbuilding, banking, and insurance, and Africa became a major market for iron, textiles, firearms, and rum.

The Atlantic Slave Trade

Before the nineteenth century, most immigrants to the New World were African. According to one recent estimate, about 80 percent of women immigrants and 90 percent of child immigrants came from Africa. By 1820, about 8.4 million Africans had been forcibly imported into the Americas, compared to just 2.4 million European immigrants. Even in the area that would become the United States, about half of all immigrants to the 13 colonies from 1700 to 1775 came from Africa.

Enslaved Africans arrived in the New World at least as early as 1502. During the peak years of the slave trade, between 1740 and 1810, Africa supplied 60,000 captives a year – outnumbering Europeans migrants by a ratio of 4 or 5 to 1.

By the beginning of the eighteenth century, black slaves could be found in every New World area colonized by Europeans, from Nova Scotia to Buenos Aires. While the concentrations of slave labor were greatest in England's southern colonies, the Caribbean, and Latin America, where slaves were employed in mines or on sugar, rice, tobacco, and cotton plantations, slaves were also put to work in northern seaports and on commercial farms. In 1690, one out of every nine families in Boston owned a slave. In New York City in 1703, the proportion was even higher. There, two out of every five families owned a slave.

The Origins of New World Slavery

Why did Spanish, Portuguese, French, Dutch, Danish, and English colonists all bring slaves to their New World colonies? Here, it is essential to recognize that it was not inevitable that Europeans in the New World would rely on African slaves to raise crops, clear forests, and mine precious metals. In every New World colony, Europeans experimented with Indian slavery, convict labor, and white indentured servants. For example, as late as the early 1700s, a third of South Carolina's labor force consisted of Indian slaves.

Why, then, did every European power eventually turn to African labor? Was this, as some have argued, the product of deep-seated racial prejudice? Or was it the product of a haphazard and random process that took place gradually with little real sense of the ultimate outcome? Or were other forces at work?

Certainly there is a great deal of evidence showing that sixteenth-century Europeans held deeply racist sentiments well before the establishment of slavery. We know, for example, that the Elizabethan English associated blackness with evil, death, and danger. They portrayed the Devil as having black skin and associated beauty with fair skin. Through their religion, the English denigrated people of color, claiming that Negroes were the descendants of Noah's son Ham who was cursed by having black offspring for daring to look upon his drunken and naked father. Long before the English had contact with Africa, racist stereotypes were widespread. One sixteenth-century author and traveler, Leo Africanus, claimed that Negroes were naturally "addicted unto Treason, Treacherie, Murther, Theft and Robberie." Without a doubt, it was easy for the English to accept slavery because they regarded Negroes as an alien people. But it also seems clear that racism was as much a consequence of racial slavery as it was a cause.

In colony after colony, Europeans shifted from Indian to African slaves partly for demographic reasons. As a result of epidemic diseases, which reduced the native population by 50 to 90 percent, the labor supply was insufficient to meet demand. But Africans also possessed many skills that were valuable in settling the New World. They were experienced in intensive agriculture and raising livestock and knew how to raise crops like rice that Europeans were unfamiliar with.

Initially, colonists in every English colony relied on indentured white servants rather than on black slaves. During the late fifteenth and early sixteenth centuries, England's population grew by over a third – much faster than its economy. To address a sudden explosion of crime and poverty, England's rulers forced the poor to toil in workhouses, and beginning in 1547, enslaved persistent vagabonds and branded them with the letter "S."

In the early 1600s, England viewed New World colonization as a providential solution to their country's problem of overpopulation. Thousands of England's unemployed and underemployed farmers, urban labors, debtors, and criminals were sent as "indentured servants" to the New World, where they contributed to England's wealth by raising tobacco and produced other goods. Over half of all white immigrants to the English colonies during the seventeenth century consisted of convicts or indentured servants.

Indentured servants agreed to work for a four- or five-year term of service in return for their transportation to the New World as well as food, clothing, and shelter. In certain respects, the status of white servants differed little from that of slaves. Like slaves, servants could be bought, sold, or leased. They could also be punished by whipping. Unlike slaves, however, servants were allowed to own property, and, if they survived their term of service, received their freedom along with a small sum of money known as "freedom dues." During the seventeenth century, indentured servants suffered an appalling death rate. Half of all white servants in the Chesapeake colonies of Virginia and Maryland died within five years of their arrival. Since servants cost half as much as slaves, they were a more economical investment.

Black slavery took root in the American colonies slowly. As early as 1619, a Dutch ship carried what were probably the first Africans to Virginia, but it was not until the 1680s that black slavery became the dominant labor system on plantations. As late as 1640, there were probably only 150 blacks in Virginia (the colony with the highest black population), and in 1650, 300. But by 1680, the number had risen to 3,000, and by 1704, to 10,000. Faced with a shortage of white indentured servants and fearful of servant revolt, English settlers increasingly resorted to enslaved Africans.

As the supply of English servants diminished, colonists in the Chesapeake imported increasing numbers of slaves directly from Africa. Many were sent to inland plantations, where planters believed that it would be easier to control the slave population.

To meet planters' growing demand for slaves, the English government established the Royal African Company in 1672. After 1698, when Britain ended the Royal African Company's monopoly of the slave trade, the number of enslaved Africans brought into the colonies soared. Between 1700 and 1775, more than 350,000 African slaves entered the American colonies. By the mid-eighteenth century, blacks made up almost 70 percent of the population of South Carolina, 40 percent in Virginia, 8 percent in Pennsylvania, and 4 percent in New England.

Slavery in Colonial North America

Slavery was a legal institution in all of the 13 American colonies. A majority of the founding fathers owned slaves, including the author of the Declaration of Independence, the Father of the Constitution, and the commander of the Continental Army.

Slavery during the colonial era was not static or unchanging. It was a dynamic, evolving institution that varied radically across time and space. During the early seventeenth century, slavery was far different from what it would later become. Anthony Johnson was one of Virginia's first slaves. Arriving in 1621, he was put to work on a plantation along the James River, where he took a wife, Mary, and raised at least four children. During the 1630s, Johnson and his family gained their freedom, probably by purchasing it themselves. Johnson subsequently acquired an estate of 250 acres, which he farmed with the help of white indentured servants and at least one slave. Just as remarkably, Johnson successfully sued in court for the return of a slave, who he claimed had been stolen by two white neighbors.

As Johnson's life suggests, the black experience in seventeenth-century America was extremely complex. Some blacks were permanently unfree; others, however, were treated like white indentured servants. They were allowed to own property and to marry and were freed after a term of service. A few slaves, like Francis Payne who lived in eastern Virginia, were assigned plots of land remote from their masters' homes, and were allowed to raise tobacco and other crops and purchase their own freedom. In several cases, black slaves who could prove that they had been baptized successfully sued for their freedom. In one eastern Virginia county in 1668, 29 percent of all blacks were free.

The first generation of Africans in the New World tended to be remarkably cosmopolitan. Few of the first generation came directly from Africa. Instead, they arrived from the West Indies and other areas of European settlement. These "Atlantic Creoles" were often multilingual and had Spanish or Portuguese names. Sometimes they had mixtures of African and non-African ancestry.

During the early and mid-seventeenth century, blacks experienced a period of relative racial tolerance and flexibility that lasted until the 1660s. A surprising number of Africans were allowed to own land or even purchase their freedom. Racial lines had not assumed the rigidity that they would subsequently acquire. White and black servants worked together, received the same punishments, and plotted escapes together. Blacks fathered about one-third of all the illegitimate children born to white servant women. In 1677, at the end of Bacon's Rebellion (a revolt against Virginia's royal government), the last holdouts were 20 white indentured servants and 80 black slaves.

Beginning in the late 1660s, colonists in the Chesapeake colonies of Maryland and Virginia imposed new laws that deprived blacks, free and slave, of many rights and privileges. At the same time, they began to import thousands of slaves directly from Africa. Yet slavery remained dispersed and decentralized. Even the wealthiest Chesapeake planters tended to divide their estates into many separate quarters where small groups of slaves lived and worked.

In the South Carolina and Georgia Low Country, slavery was also remarkably fluid during the pioneering period. Black soldiers played an indispensable role in protecting the colonies against the Indians and the Spanish. White planters were heavily dependent on the knowledge and skills of African-born slaves in growing rice, raising cattle, and building irrigation dikes.

Toward Slavery

As early as the late 1630s, English colonists began to make a sharper distinction between the status of white servants and that of black slaves. In 1639, Maryland became the first colony to specifically state that baptism as a Christian did not make a slave a free person. Discrimination against black servants began to increase. In 1640, when two white indentured servants and a black servant named John Punch fled from Virginia to Maryland, all three received 30 lashes. The whites also had their terms of service extended by four years, but Punch, the black servant, was condemned to lifelong servitude. In 1669, Virginia became the first colony to declare that it was not a crime to kill an unruly slave in the ordinary course of punishment.

As the slave population grew in size, racial lines grew increasingly rigid. By the end of the seventeenth century, Virginia and Maryland had forbidden interracial marriages and sexual relations. Laws adopted in several colonies in the early eighteenth century confiscated slaves' property, forbade masters from freeing their slaves, permitted masters to mutilate and dismember disobedient slaves, and declared that slave status was inherited through the mother. The law now defined Africans as chattel property, under the complete legal control of their masters.

The Diversity of Colonial Slavery

During the late seventeenth and eighteenth centuries, three distinctive systems of slavery emerged in the American colonies. In the Chesapeake colonies of Maryland and Virginia, slavery was widely used in raising tobacco and corn and other grains. Yet while raising tobacco or corn was less debilitating and taxing than growing sugar cane in the West Indies or rice in the South Carolina and Georgia Low Country, slavery in the Chesapeake may have been more difficult psychologically. Even in the eighteenth century, slaveholders in the Chesapeake supervised their slaves much more closely than in the Low Country or the Caribbean and intervened more frequently in their lives. Also, in the Chesapeake, unlike in the West Indies or the Low Country, virtually all people with any African ancestry were defined as slaves. Beginning in the 1720s, slaves in the Chesapeake region became the first slave population in the New World able to naturally reproduce their numbers. Eager to encourage a rapid population increase, slave owners in the Chesapeake consciously imported many female slaves.

In the South Carolina and Georgia Low Country, slaves raised rice and indigo and were able to reconstitute African social patterns and maintain a separate Gullah dialect. Although slaves were subjected to a harsh labor regime, the task system became the norm. Each day, slaves were required to achieve a precise work objective. This allowed them to leave the fields early in the afternoon to tend their own gardens and raise their own livestock. Slaves often passed their property down for generations. The kind of slavery that emerged in the Low Country was similar to some west and central African forms of slavery and was very different from the kinds of slavery found in the Chesapeake. Far more than in the Chesapeake, planters in the Low Country openly acknowledged sexual unions with black women. An elite of free, light-skinned people of color emerged that served as intermediaries between whites and blacks.

In the North, slavery was concentrated in productive agriculture on Long Island and in southern Rhode Island and New Jersey. Most slaves were engaged in farming and stock raising for the West Indies or as household servants for the urban elite. A massive influx of slaves from Africa in the mid-eighteenth century inspired the creation of many churches and benevolent societies prefaced with the word "African." Northern slaves developed a vibrant African American culture. They celebrated a number of popular festivals like Election Day, during which roles between whites and blacks were temporarily reversed.

Slavery's Evolution

At the time that Thomas Jefferson was born, in 1743, most slaves were born in Africa, few were Christian, and very few were engaged in raising cotton. Slavery was largely confined to eastern areas near the Atlantic Ocean, and in the Carolinas and Georgia, the slave population was not yet able to reproduce its numbers naturally.

By the time of Jefferson's death in 1826, slavery had changed dramatically. A series of momentous revolutions had transformed the institution. First, as a result of a demographic revolution, a majority of slaves had been born in the New World and were capable of increasing the slave population by natural reproduction. During the seventeenth century, slaves had had few opportunities to establish stable family relationships. In the Chesapeake colonies and the Carolinas, two-thirds of all slaves were male, and most lived on plantations with fewer than 10 slaves. These units were so small and widely dispersed, and the sex ratio was so skewed, that it was difficult for slaves to find spouses. A high death rate meant that many slaves did not live long enough to marry or, if they did, their marriages did not last very long. But by the 1720s in the Chesapeake and the 1750s and 1760s in the South Carolina and Georgia Low Country, the slave population was naturally reproducing its numbers.

Second, the so-called "plantation revolution" not only increased the size of plantations, but made them more productive and efficient economic units. Planters expanded their operations and imposed more supervision on their slaves.

A third revolution was religious. During the colonial period, many planters resisted the idea of converting slaves to Christianity out of a fear that baptism would change a slave's legal status. The black population was virtually untouched by Christianity until the religious revivals of the 1730s and 1740s. By the early nineteenth century, slaveholders increasingly adopted the view that Christianity would make slaves more submissive, orderly, and conscientious, and encouraged missionary activities among slaves.

Slaves themselves found in Christianity a faith that could give them hope in an oppressive world. While Christianity has sometimes been called a "religion of passivity," it proved impossible to purge it of its antislavery overtones with its promise of deliverance from bondage. Beginning in the 1740s and greatly accelerating in the early 1800s, many slaves converted to Christianity. In general, slaves did not join their masters' churches. Most became Baptists or Methodists.

A fourth revolution altered the areas in which slaves lived and worked. Between 1790 and 1860, 835,000 slaves were moved from Maryland, Virginia, and the Carolinas to Alabama, Mississippi, Louisiana, and Texas. We know that slaves were frequently sold apart from their families or separated from family members when they were moved to the Old Southwest.

Finally, there was a revolution in moral values and sensibility. For the first time in history, religious and secular groups denounced slavery as sinful and as a violation of natural rights. During the 1760s, the first movements in history began to denounce slavery. The earliest groups to oppose slavery were "perfectionist" religious sects like the Quakers who challenged all traditional authorities and wanted to live free from sin.

The American Revolution and Slavery

The meaning and outcome of the American Revolution was intimately tied to slavery. Leaders of the patriot cause repeatedly argued that British policies would make the colonists slaves of the British. The colonists' emphasis on the danger of mass enslavement derived in part from the highly visible example of racial slavery. In 1774, George Washington explained that if the colonists failed to aggressively assert their rights, then the British ministry "shall make us as tame and abject slaves, as the blacks we rule over with such arbitrary sway."

Both the British and the colonists believed that slaves could serve an important role during the Revolution. In April 1775, Lord Dunmore, the royal governor of Virginia, threatened that he would free the colony's slaves if the colonists resorted to force against his authority. In November, he promised freedom to all slaves belonging to rebels who would join "His Majesty's Troops." Some 800 slaves joined British forces, some wearing the emblem "Liberty to the Slaves."

Meanwhile an American diplomat, Silas Deane, hatched a secret plan to incite slave insurrections in Jamaica. Two South Carolinians, John Laurens and his father Henry, persuaded Congress to unanimously approve a plan to recruit an army of 3,000 slave troops to stop a British invasion of South Carolina and Georgia. The federal government would compensate the slaves' owners and each black would, at the end of the war, be emancipated and receive $50. The South Carolina legislature rejected the plan, scuttling the proposal. In the end, and in contrast to the later Latin American wars of independence and the US Civil War, neither the British nor the Americans proved willing to risk a full-scale social revolution by issuing an emancipation proclamation.

As a result of the Revolution, a surprising number of slaves were manumitted, while thousands of others freed themselves by running away. Georgia lost about a third of its slaves and South Carolina lost 25,000. Yet despite these losses, slavery quickly recovered in the South. By 1810, South Carolina and Georgia had three times as many slaves as in 1770.

The Revolution had contradictory consequences for slavery. In the South, slavery became more firmly entrenched. In the North, every state freed slaves as a result of court decisions or the enactment of gradual emancipation schemes. Yet even in the North, there was strong resistance to emancipation, and freeing of slaves was accompanied by the emergence of a virulent form of racial prejudice.

Antebellum Slavery

During the last years of the eighteenth century, New World slavery seemed to be declining. As a result of the American and French revolutions, thousands of black slaves escaped slavery through revolt or simply by running away. Revolutionary ideals of liberty and equality encouraged many slave owners in the United States, the Caribbean, and Spanish America to emancipate their slaves. In the 10 years after Virginia enacted a law allowing private manumissions, masters freed 10,000 slaves. A French traveler, the Marquis de Chastellux, reported that people throughout the South "are constantly talking of abolishing slavery, of contriving some other means of cultivating their estates."

But slavery was not, in fact, on the road to extinction. During the early nineteenth century, slavery underwent a new boom, rapidly expanding in Brazil, Cuba, Trinidad, Guiana, the Windward Islands, and new territories southwest of the Appalachian mountains in the United States: into Georgia, Alabama, Mississippi, Louisiana, Arkansas, Missouri, and Texas.

Eli Whitney's invention of the cotton gin gave slavery a new lease on life. Between 1792, when Whitney invented the gin, and 1794, the price of slaves doubled. By 1825, field hands, who had brought $500 apiece in 1794, were worth $1,500. As the price of slaves grew, so, too, did their numbers. During the first decade of the nineteenth century, the number of slaves in the United States rose by 33 percent; during the following decade, the slave population grew another 29 percent.

What Was Life Like Under Slavery?

Under southern law, slaves were considered chattel property. Like a domestic animal, they could be bought, sold, leased, and physically punished. Slaves were prohibited from owning property, testifying against whites in court, or traveling without a pass. Their marriages lacked legal sanction. During the nineteenth century, in response to abolitionist attacks on slavery, southern legislatures enacted laws setting set down minimal standards for housing, food, and clothing–but these statutes were largely unenforced.

Prior to the Civil War, abolitionists charged that slaves were overworked, poorly clad, inadequately housed, and cruelly punished; that slavery was a highly profitable investment; and that far from being content, slaves longed for freedom. Apologists for slavery, in turn, accused abolitionists of exaggerating slavery's evils, asserting that slaves were rarely whipped, that marriages were seldom broken by sale, and that most slaves were able to maintain stable family lives. They maintained that paternalism and public opinion protected slaves from cruelty; that slave insurrections were rare because most slaves were contented with bondage; that slavery was an economic burden that planters bore out of a sense of responsibility; and that slaves enjoyed a higher standard of living, a better diet, superior housing, and a greater life expectancy than many free urban workers in the North and in Europe.

Recent historical research has largely confirmed the abolitionist indictment of slavery. We now know that slaves suffered extremely high mortality. Half of all slave infants died during their first year of life, twice the rate of white babies. And while the death rate declined for those who survived their first year, it remained twice the white rate through age 14. As a result of this high infant and childhood death rate, the average life expectancy of a slave at birth was just 21 or 22 years, compared to 40 to 43 years for antebellum whites. Compared to whites, relatively few slaves lived into old age. Between 1830 and 1860, only 10 percent of US slaves were over 50 years old.

A major contributor to the high infant and child death rate was chronic undernourishment. Slave owners showed surprisingly little concern for slave mothers' health or diet during pregnancy, providing pregnant women with no extra rations and employing them in intensive field work even in the last week before they gave birth. Not surprisingly, slave mothers suffered high rates of spontaneous abortions, stillbirths, and deaths shortly after birth. Half of all slave infants weighed less than 5.5 pounds at birth, or what we would today consider to be severely underweight.

Infants and children were badly malnourished. Most infants were weaned early, within three or four months of birth, and then fed gruel or porridge made of cornmeal. Around the age of three, they began to eat vegetables soups, potatoes, molasses, grits, hominy, and cornbread. This diet lacked protein, thiamine, niacin, calcium, magnesium, and vitamin D, and as a result, slave children often suffered from night blindness, abdominal swellings, swollen muscles, bowed legs, skin lesions, and convulsions. These apparently stemmed from beriberi, pellagra, tetany, rickets, and kwashiorkor, diseases that are caused by protein and nutritional deficiencies.

Squalid living conditions aggravated health problems. Chickens, dogs, and pigs lived next to the slave quarters, and in consequence animal feces contaminated the area. Lacking privies, slaves had to urinate and defecate in the cover of nearby bushes. Such squalor contributed to high rates of diarrhea, dysentery, whooping cough, respiratory diseases, hepatitis, typhoid fever, and intestinal worms.

Deprived of an adequate diet, slave children were very small by modern standards. Their average height at age three was shorter than 99 percent of present-day American three-year-olds. At age 17, slave men were shorter than 96 percent of present-day 17-year-old men and slave women were shorter than 80 percent of contemporary women.

Slave Labor

It is a mistake to think that slave labor was simply unskilled, brutish work. Cultivation of cotton, tobacco, rice, and sugar requires careful, painstaking effort. On larger plantations, masters relied on slave carpenters, bricklayers, blacksmiths, wheelwrights, tanners, tailors, butchers, masons, coopers, cabinet makers, metal workers, and silversmiths. Large numbers also worked as boatmen, waiters, cooks, drivers, housemaids, spinners, and weavers. At Monticello, Thomas Jefferson worked slave women in a small textile mill and a nail-making factory.

For the vast majority of slaves, however, slavery meant back-breaking field work, planting, cultivating, and harvesting cotton, hemp, rice, tobacco, or sugar cane. On a typical plantation, slaves worked 10 or more hours a day, "from day clean to first dark," six days a week, with only the Sabbath off. At planting or harvesting time, planters required slaves to stay in the fields 15 or 16 hours a day. When they were not raising a cash crop, slaves grew other crops, such as corn or potatoes; cared for livestock; and cleared fields, cut wood, and repaired buildings and fences.

On cotton, sugar, and tobacco plantations, slaves worked together in gangs under the supervision of a supervisor or a driver. On many rice and hemp plantations and the coastal areas of South Carolina and Georgia, slave owners adopted the task system. Slaves had specific daily work assignments, and after they completed their tasks, their time was their own.

There is a tendency to think of slavery as an economically backward and inefficient institution. But far from being an economic anachronism, recent research has shown that slavery was highly productive precisely because slaves could be forced to work far longer hours than free workers. During the peak cotton-picking or sugar-harvesting seasons, 18-hour days were common.

Sugar plantations were the most innovative economic units of their time in terms of labor management and organization. They were the first true factories in the world and anticipated the assembly line and the factory system in their reliance on close supervision and division of tasks.

Slave masters extracted labor from virtually the entire slave community, young, old, healthy, and physically impaired. Children as young as three or four were put to work, usually in special "trash gangs" weeding fields, carrying drinking water, picking up trash, and helping in the kitchen. Young children also fed chickens and livestock, gathered wood chips for fuel, and drove cows to pasture. Around the age of 11, boys began to perform adult field jobs. Between the ages of seven and twelve, boys and girls were put to work in intensive field work. Children made up about a third of the slave labor force.

Older or physically handicapped slaves were put to work in cloth houses, spinning cotton, weaving cloth, and making clothes. Altogether, masters forced two-thirds of all slaves to work–twice the labor force participation rate among the free population, reflecting the high proportion of children, women, and the elderly toiling in cotton or rice fields.

Because slaves had no direct incentive to work hard, slave owners combined harsh penalties with positive incentives. Some masters denied passes to disobedient slaves. Other confined recalcitrant slaves to private jails. Chains and shackles were widely used to control runaways. Whipping was a key part of plantation discipline. On one Louisiana plantation, a slave was lashed every four-and-a-half days.

But physical pain was not enough to elicit hard work. To stimulate productivity, some masters gave slaves small garden plots and permitted them to sell their produce. Others distributed gifts of food or money at the end of the year. Still other planters awarded prizes, holidays, and year-end bonuses to particularly productive slaves.

Not all slaves were field hands. During the 1850s, half a million slaves lived in southern towns and cities, where they worked in textile mills, iron works, tobacco factories, laundries, and shipyards. Others slaves labored as lumberjacks, as deckhands on riverboats, and in sawmills, gristmills, and quarries. Many slaves were engaged in construction of roads and railroads. Even on plantations not all slaves were menial laborers. About 250,000 were craftsmen such as blacksmiths, shoemakers, or carpenters or held domestic posts such as coachmen or house servants.

Slave Family Life

Slaves marriages and family ties were not recognized by American law. Any owner was free to sell husbands from wives, parents from children, and brothers from sisters. In many cases, slave spouses lived apart. Many large slaveholders had numerous plantations and frequently shifted slaves, splitting families in the process.

Although some masters, like George Washington, were reluctant to buy or sell slaves, economic need or an owner's death often led to the separation of husbands from wives and parents from children. The most conservative estimates indicate that at least 10 to 20 percent of slave marriages were destroyed by sale. The sale of children from parents was even more common. Over the course of a 35-year lifetime, a slave had a fifty-fifty chance of being sold at least once and was likely to witness the sale of several members of his or her immediate family.

Slave families were extremely vulnerable to separation. As a result of the sale or death of a father or mother, over a third of all slave children grew up in households from which one or both parents were absent. About a quarter of all slave children grew up in a single-parent household (nearly always with their mother) and another tenth grew up apart from both parents.

Even in instances in which marriages were not broken by sale, slave spouses often resided on separate plantations, owned by different individuals. On large plantations, one slave father in three had a different owner than his wife, and could visit his family only at his master's discretion. On smaller holdings, divided ownership and mother-headed households occurred even more frequently. Just one-third of the children on farms or plantations with 15 or fewer slaves lived in a two-parent family, compared to two-thirds of the children on larger plantations.

Because many planters prohibited marriages across plantations (and because slaves, like west Africans but unlike white southerners, did not marry first cousins), many slaves were unable to find a spouse. On the largest plantations, nearly 20 percent of the slaves who reached adulthood remained single throughout their lives.

Other obstacles stood in the way of an independent family life. Many slaves had to share their single-room cabins with relatives or other unrelated slaves. Even on model plantations, children between the ages of seven and ten were taken from their parents and sent to live in separate cabins.

Slavery severely circumscribed the authority of slave parents. When a slave child named Jacob Stroyer was regularly beaten, his father told him: "Go back to your work and be a good boy, for I cannot do anything for you."

Of all the threats to slave family life, one of the most terrible was the sexual abuse of slave women. Some masters, like James H. Hammond, a congressman, governor, and US senator from South Carolina, took slave mistresses and concubines. Hammond, whose wife bore him eight children, purchased an 18-year-old slave named Sally and her infant daughter, Louisa, in 1839. He made Sally his mistress, and fathered several children on her, and then when the daughter reached the age of 12, fathered several children on her. Nor was Hammond alone. Governor Francis Pickens of South Carolina and Confederate General Jubal Early each took slave mistresses. One ex-slave remembered that his master "would ship ... husbands out of bed and get in with their wives." Interviews with former slaves conducted in the 1930s revealed that 4.5 percent of their fathers had been white.

Despite the frequent breakup of families by sale, African Americans managed to forge strong and durable family and kin ties within the institution of slavery. In spite of the refusal of southern law to recognize the legality of slave marriages, most slaves married and lived with the same spouse until death, and most slave children grew up in two-parent households.

To sustain a sense of family identity, slaves often named their children after parents, grandparents, recently deceased relatives, and other kin. It used to be believed that masters assigned names to slaves or that slaves simply imitated their masters' system of naming. We now know that slaves were usually not named for owners. To be sure, some slaves were given classical names (like George Washington's slave Hercules). But many names reflected African practices. Many children received "day names" (after the day they were born) and "name-saking" (such as naming children after grandparents).

Slaves passed down family names to their children, usually the name of an ancestor's owner rather than their current owner. The strength of slave families is nowhere more evident than in the advertisements slave owners posted for runaway slaves. Over a third of the advertisements indicate that fugitives left an owner to visit a spouse, a child, or other relatives.

Ties to an immediate family stretched outward to an involved network of extended kin. Family destruction and dispersal created extended kinship networks stretching across whole counties. Whenever children were sold to neighboring plantations, grandparents, aunts, uncles, and cousins often took on the functions of parents. When blood relatives were not present, strangers cared for and protected children. Slave parents taught their children to call all adult slaves "aunt" or "uncle" and younger slaves "sister" or "brother." In this way, slave culture taught the young that they were members of a broader community in which all slaves had mutual obligations and responsibilities.

Slave Culture

As brutal and destructive as the institution of slavery was, slaves were not defenseless victims. Through their families, religion, folklore, and music, as well as more direct forms of resistance, African Americans resisted the debilitating effects of slavery and created a vital culture supportive of human dignity. As recently as 1964, the sociologist E. Franklin Frazier claimed that "the Negroes were practically stripped of their social heritage." This view is completely wrong. Slaves were able to maintain a great deal of their African traditions and created a new African American culture that they successfully transmitted to their children. In addition, slaves exerted a profound influence on white culture: on speech, religion, music, and cuisine.

The American language is filled with Africanisms. Such words as *bogus*, *bug*, *phony*, *yam*, *tote*, *gumbo*, *jazz*, and *funky* all have African roots. Our cuisine, too, is heavily influenced by African practices. Deep-fat frying, gumbos, and fricasees stem from west and central Africa. Our music is heavily dependent on African traditions. Sea chanties and yodeling, as well as spirituals and the use of falsetto, were heavily influenced by African traditions. The frame construction of houses; the "call and response" pattern in sermons; the stress on the holy spirit and an emotional conversion experience – these too appear to derive at least partly from African customs.

Finally, Africans played a critical role in the production of such crops as rice or sweet potatoes that the English had not previously encountered.

Their religious and cultural traditions played a particularly important role in helping slaves survive the harshness and misery of life under slavery. Many slaves drew on African customs when they buried their dead. Conjurors adapted and blended African religious rites that made use of herbs and supernatural powers. Slaves also perpetuated a rich tradition of west and central African parables, proverbs, verbal games, and legends. They also retained in their folklore certain central figures. Cunning tricksters, often represented as tortoises, spiders, or rabbits, outwitted their more powerful enemies. Through folklore, slaves also sustained a sense of separate identity and conveyed valuable lessons to their children. Animal trickster stories, like the Brer Rabbit tales, derived from similar African stories, told of powerless creatures who achieved their will through wit and guile, not power and authority.

In the realms of art, dance, folklore, language, music, and religion, slaves created a distinctive culture which blended African and European elements into a new synthesis. During the late eighteenth and early nineteenth centuries, slaves embraced Christianity, but transformed it to meet their own needs. Slave religious beliefs, a mixture of Christianity and African traditions, provided slaves with the patience and hope necessary to endure slavery. Slave religion also upheld a vision of the spiritual equality of all human beings that strengthened their hopes of eventual deliverance from bondage. Spirituals like "Go Down, Moses," with its refrain "let my people go," indicate slaves identified with the Hebrew people who had overcome oppression and enslavement.

American Slavery in Comparative Perspective

Only about 6 percent of the slaves exported from Africa ended up in what is now the United States. The overwhelming majority went to Brazil or the West Indies, where they labored on plantations producing sugar, tobacco, coffee, and other subtropical products. Of the 10 to 15 million Africans who survived the voyage to the New World, over one-third landed in Brazil and between 60 and 70 percent ended up in Brazil or the sugar colonies of the Caribbean. Yet by 1860, approximately two-thirds of all New World slaves lived in the American South.

How did American slavery compare and contrast with slavery in Latin America and the Caribbean? Was it more repressive or more benign? For a long time it was widely assumed that southern slavery was harsher and crueler than slavery in Latin America, where the Catholic church insisted that slaves had a right to marry, to seek relief from a cruel master, and to purchase their freedom. In contrast to the American South, it was pointed out, there were no legal bars in Latin America to educating or freeing slaves; moreover, Spanish and Portuguese colonists were thought to be less tainted by racial prejudice than North Americans, and Latin American slavery was believed to be less subject to the pressures of a competitive capitalist economy.

This contrast between a supposedly kinder, gentler system of Latin American slavery and a harsher system of North American slavery appears to be grossly overdrawn. In practice, neither the Catholic church nor the courts offered much protection to Latin American slaves. Cruel punishments were not unknown, such as tying slaves down and flogging them for nine to thirteen consecutive days. Slave owners in Latin America, like those in the American South, frequently sold slaves apart. Access to freedom was greater in Latin America, but in many cases masters freed sick, elderly, crippled, or simply unneeded slaves in order to relieve themselves of financial responsibilities.

In certain respects, Latin American slavery may have been even harsher than North American slavery. Death rates among slaves in the Caribbean were one-third higher than in the South and suicide appears to have been much more common. Sometimes Latin American slaves were forced to wear iron masks to keep them from eating dirt or drinking liquor. Unlike slaves in the South, West Indian slaves were expected to produce their own food in their "free time," and care for the elderly and the infirm.

For all the similarities between slavery in the American South and in Latin America, there were a number of crucial differences. Perhaps the most obvious were demographic. The slave population in Brazil and the West Indies had a low proportion of female slaves, a tiny slave birth rate, and a high proportion of recent arrivals from Africa. In striking contrast, southern slaves had an equal sex ratio, a high birth rate, and a predominantly American-born population.

By the mid-nineteenth century, US slaves were much further removed from Africa than those in the Caribbean. While a majority of early nineteenth-century slaves in the British Caribbean and Brazil were born in Africa, in 1850 most US slaves were third-, fourth-, or fifth-generation Americans. In addition, by the nineteenth century there were relatively few African-born slaves, which made it more difficult to maintain African practices in an unmodified form.

Slavery in the United States was especially distinctive in the ability of the slave population to increase its numbers by natural reproduction. In the

Caribbean, Suriname, and Brazil, the slave death rate was so high and the birth rate so low that slaves could not sustain their population without imports from Africa. Rates of natural decrease ran as high as 5 percent a year. While the death rate of US slaves was as high as that in Jamaica, the birth rate was 80 percent higher. The average number of children born to an early nineteenth-century southern slave woman was 9.2 – twice as many as in the West Indies.

Slaves in the United States and the West Indies made up sharply differing proportions of the total population. In the West Indies, slaves constituted 80 to 90 percent of the population, while in the South only about a third of the population was slaves. Plantation size also differed widely. In the Caribbean, slaves were held on much larger units, with many plantations holding as many as 500 slaves. In the American South, in contrast, only one slave owner held as many as a thousand slaves, and just 125 had over 250 slaves. Half of all slaves in the United States worked on units of 20 or fewer slaves; three-quarters had fewer than 50. These demographic differences had important social implications. Slaves in the American South had much more contact with whites than did West Indian slaves.

In the American South, slave owners lived on their plantations and slaves dealt with their owners regularly. Most planters placed plantation management, supply purchasing, and supervision in the hands of black drivers and foremen, and at least two-thirds of all slaves worked under the supervision of black drivers. In contrast, absentee ownership was far more common in the West Indies, where planters relied heavily on paid managers and relied on a distinct class of free blacks and mulattoes to serve as intermediaries with the slave population.

Standards of diet, housing, and medicine in the South may have exceeded those in the Caribbean, but southern masters also interfered more frequently in their personal lives. In the South, masters provided slaves with food, housing, and clothing; in the Caribbean, in contrast, slaves had to raise their own food in their spare time.

Another important difference between Latin America and the United States involved the concept of race. In Spanish and Portuguese America, an intricate system of racial classification emerged. The Spanish and Portuguese were much more tolerant of racial mixing than were the British and French, an attitude encouraged by a shortage of European women, and recognized a wide range of racial gradations, including black, mestizo, quadroon, and octoroon.

The American South, in contrast, adopted a two-category system in which any person with a black mother was automatically considered to be black. It has been said, half-facetiously, that southerners are color blind, in the sense that individuals, despite their racial composition, are considered to be either white or black, while Latin Americans recognized degrees of blackness and whiteness.

A final difference between slavery in the United States and elsewhere in the Americas was that only in the South did it depend on the loyalty of non-slaveholding whites. In the South, three-quarters of white families owned no slaves. The key to maintaining their loyalty ultimately depended on appeals to racism.

Slave Revolts and Resistance

Slave resistance is a difficult subject to discuss. It is hard for us today to imagine how slavery could function as an efficient economic system in the face of slave resistance. On larger plantations, there were only about two adult white males to oversee 50 or more slaves. We like to think that if we were enslaved, we would actively resist the institution. As a popular anthem of the Civil Rights era put it: "Before I'd be a slave, I'd be buried in my grave."

Although slave masters described their slave population as faithful, docile, and contented, slave owners in the South, Brazil, and the West Indies always feared slave revolt. In fact no enslaved people in history revolted as frequently as the New World slaves. One historian, Herbert Aptheker, has identified over 200 examples of open rebellion or fears of slave conspiracies in America between the early seventeenth and the mid-nineteenth centuries.

Southern slaveholders cited the rarity of large-scale slave revolts as proof that slaves were contented under slavery. Yet African Americans resisted slavery in a variety of active and passive ways. For the most part, they sought realistic incremental gains, though in a number of instances, slaves did organize major revolts against slavery. Even when slaves did not resist their condition directly and openly, they sought autonomy in less dramatic ways.

"Day-to-day resistance" was the most common form of opposition to slavery. Breaking tools, feigning illness, staging slowdowns, and committing acts of arson and sabotage – all were forms of resistance and expressions of slaves' alienation from their masters. One North Carolina cook named Delia later recalled: "How many times I spit in the biscuits and peed in the coffee just to get back at them mean white folks."

Running away was another form of resistance. Most slaves ran away relatively short distances and were not trying to permanently escape from slavery. Instead, they were temporarily withholding their labor as a form of economic bargaining and negotiation. Slavery involved a constant process of negotiation as slaves bargained over the pace of work, the amount of free time they would enjoy, monetary rewards, access to garden plots, and the freedom to practice burials, marriages, and religious ceremonies without white oversight.

Some fugitives, however, did try to permanently escape slavery. While the idea of this quickly brings to mind the Underground Railroad to the free states, in fact more than half of these long-distance runaways headed southward or to cities or to natural refuges like swamps. Often, runaways were relatively privileged slaves who had served as river boatmen or coachmen and were familiar with the outside world.

Especially in the colonial period, fugitive slaves tried to form runaway communities known as "maroon colonies." Located in swamps, mountains, or frontier regions, some of these communities resisted capture for several decades. Many revolts were in fact collective efforts to run away from slavery. In a famous revolt in colonial South Carolina known as the Stono Rebellion, the slaves were headed for refuge in Spanish Florida.

Probably the first slave revolt erupted in Hispaniola in 1522. During the early eighteenth century there were slave uprisings in Long Island in 1708 and in New York City in 1712. Slaves in South Carolina staged several insurrections, culminating in the Stono Rebellion in 1739, when they seized arms, killed whites, and burned houses. In 1740 and 1741, conspiracies were uncovered in Charleston and New York. During the late eighteenth century, slave revolts erupted in Guadeloupe, Jamaica, Suriname, Saint-Domingue (Haiti), Venezuela, and the Windward Islands, and many fugitive slaves, known as maroons, fled to remote regions and carried on guerrilla warfare (during the 1820s, a fugitive slave named Bob Ferebee led a band of fugitive slaves in guerrilla warfare in Virginia). During the early nineteenth century, major conspiracies or revolts against slavery took place in Richmond, Virginia, in 1800; in Louisiana in 1811; in Barbados in 1816; in Charleston, South Carolina, in 1822; in Demerara in 1823; and in Jamaica and in Southampton County, Virginia, in 1831.

Slave revolts were most likely when slaves outnumbered whites, when masters were absent, and during periods of economic distress. They were also most common in areas with the largest plantations, at times when the white elite was divided, and when large numbers of native-born Africans had been brought into an area at one time.

Black religion made a major contribution to resistance to slavery. When Denmark Vesey sought to gain recruits for his plot to overthrow slavery in Charleston in 1822, one slave, a prosecution witnessed named William, said, "he tries to prove ... that slavery and bondage is against the Bible." Nat Turner's 1831 insurrection was inspired by his religious vision.

The main result of slave insurrections, throughout the Americas, was the mass executions of blacks. After a slave conspiracy was uncovered in New York City in 1740, 18 slaves were hanged and 13 were burned alive. After Denmark Vesey's conspiracy was uncovered, the authorities in Charleston hanged 37 blacks. Following Nat Turner's insurrection, the local militia killed about 100 blacks, and 20 more slaves, including Turner, were later executed. In the South, the preconditions for successful rebellion did not exist, and attempts tended to bring increased suffering and repression to the slave community.

Violent rebellion was rarer and smaller in scale in the American South than in Brazil or the Caribbean, reflecting the relatively small proportion of blacks in the southern population, the low proportion of recent migrants from Africa, and the relatively small size of southern plantations. In Jamaica, slaves outnumbered whites by ten or eleven to one; in the South, a much larger white population was committed to suppressing rebellion. In general, Africans were more likely than New World-born slaves to participate in outright revolts. Not only did many Africans have combat experience prior to enslavement, but they also had fewer family and community ties that might inhibit violent insurrection.

The Economics of Slavery

During the years before the Civil War many northerners charged that slavery was incompatible with rapid economic growth. Despite clear evidence that slavery was profitable for individual planters, a growing number of people felt that slavery was inherently wasteful and inefficient, that it degraded labor, inhibited urbanization and mechanization, thwarted industrialization, and stifled progress. They associated slavery with economic backwardness, soil exhaustion, low labor productivity, indebtedness, and economic and social stagnation. In his "Address Delivered in Concord on the Anniversary of the Emancipation of the Negroes in the British West Indies," the poet and philosopher Ralph Waldo Emerson said that "slavery is no scholar, no improver ... it does not increase the white population; it does not improve the soil; everything goes to decay."

Like other slave societies, the South did not produce urban centers on a scale equal to those in the North. Virginia's largest city, Richmond, had a population of just 15,274 in 1850. That same year, Wilmington, North Carolina's largest city, had only 7,264 inhabitants. Southern cities were small because they failed to develop diversified economies. Unlike the cities of the North, southern cities rarely became centers of commerce, finance, or processing and manufacturing, and southern ports rarely engaged in international trade.

By northern standards, the South's transportation network was primitive. Traveling the 1,460 miles from Baltimore to New Orleans in 1850 meant riding five different railroads, two stage coaches, and two steamboats. Its educational system also lagged far behind the North's. In 1850, 20 percent of adult white southerners could not read or write, compared to a national figure of 8 percent.

Does this mean that slavery was a declining institution? Was it doomed to extinction, even in the absence of Civil War? The answer appears to be "no." In 1860, the South was more prosperous than any European nation except England, and had a higher per capita income than Italy on the eve of World War II.

Slave labor was efficient, productive, and adaptable to a variety of occupations, ranging from agriculture and mining to factory work. Slavery was the basis of the nation's most profitable industry. During the decades before the Civil War, slave-grown cotton accounted for over half the value of all United States exports, and provided virtually all the cotton used in the northern textile industry and 70 percent of the cotton used in British mills. Furthermore, a disproportionate share of the richest Americans made their fortunes from slavery. In 1860, two out of every three Americans worth $100,000 or more lived in the South. Slave prices soared during the 1850s, an indication of slave owners' confidence in the future.

Nevertheless, the South's political leaders had good reason for concern. Within the South, slave ownership was becoming concentrated in a smaller number of hands. The proportion of southern families owning slaves declined from 36 percent in 1830 to 25 percent in 1860. At the same time, slavery was sharply declining in the upper South. Between 1830 and 1860, the proportion of slaves in Missouri's population fell from 18 to 10 percent; in Kentucky, from 24 to 19 percent; in Maryland, from 23 to 13 percent. By the middle of the nineteenth century, slavery was becoming an exception in the New World, confined to Brazil, Cuba, Puerto Rico, a number of small Dutch colonies, and the American South. But the most important threat to slavery came from abolitionists, who denounced slavery as immoral.

Abolition

The growth of public opposition to slavery represents one of the most momentous moral transformations in history. As late as 1750, no church condemned slave ownership or slave trading. Britain, Denmark, France,

Holland, Portugal, and Spain all openly participated in the slave trade. Beginning with the Quakers in the late 1750s, however, organized opposition to slavery quickly grew. In 1787, the Northwest Ordinance barred slavery from the territories north of the Ohio River; by 1804, the nine states north of Delaware had freed slaves or adopted gradual emancipation plans. In Haiti in 1791, nearly a half million slaves emancipated themselves by insurrection and revolutionary struggle. In 1807, Britain and the United States outlawed the African slave trade.

The wars of national liberation in Spanish America ended slavery in Spain's mainland New World empire. In 1821, the region that now includes Ecuador, Colombia, and Venezuela adopted a gradual emancipation plan. Two years later, Chile agreed to emancipate its slave. In 1829, Mexico abolished slavery.

In 1833, Britain emancipated 780,000 slaves, paying 20 million pounds sterling compensation to their owners. In 1848, Denmark and France freed slaves in their colonial empires. Slavery survived in Suriname and other Dutch New World colonies until 1863 and in the United States until 1865. The last New World slaves were emancipated in Cuba in 1886 and in Brazil in 1888.

Within the span of a century and a half, slavery, long regarded as an inevitable part of the social order, came to be seen as a violation of Christian morality and the natural, inalienable rights of man. The main impetus behind antislavery came from religion. New religious and humanitarian values contributed to a view of slavery as "the sum of all villainies," a satanic institution which gave rise to every imaginable sin: violence, despotism, racial prejudice, and sexual corruption.

Initially, many opponents of slavery supported "colonization" – the deportation of black Americans to Africa, the Caribbean, or Central America. But by the late 1820s, it was obvious that colonization was a wholly impractical solution to the problem of slavery. Each year the nation's slave population rose by 50,000, but in 1830, the American Colonization Society persuaded only 259 free blacks to migrate to Liberia, bringing the total number of blacks colonized in Africa to just 1,400.

In 1829, a 25-year-old white Bostonian named William Lloyd Garrison denounced colonization as a cruel hoax designed to promote the racial purity of the North while doing nothing to end slavery in the South. He demanded "immediate emancipation" of slaves without compensation to their owners. Within six years, 200 antislavery societies had sprouted up in the North, and had mounted a massive propaganda campaign against slavery.

The growth of militant abolitionism provoked a harsh public reaction. Mobs led by "gentlemen of property and standing" attacked the homes and businesses of abolitionist merchants, destroyed abolitionist printing presses, attacked black neighborhoods, and murdered the Reverend Elijah P. Lovejoy, the editor of an abolitionist newspaper. In the face of vicious attacks, the antislavery movement divided over questions of strategy and tactics. Radicals, led by Garrison, began to attack all forms of inequality and violence in American society, withdrew from churches that condoned slavery, demanded equal rights for women, and called for voluntary dissolution of the Union. Other abolitionists turned to politics as the most promising way to end slavery, helping to form the Liberty party in 1840, the Free Soil party in 1848, and the Republican party in 1854.

By the late 1850s, a growing number of northerners were convinced that slavery posed an intolerable threat to free labor and civil liberties. Many believed that an aggressive Slave Power had seized control of the federal government, had incited revolution in Texas and war with Mexico, and was engaged in a systematic plan to extend slavery into the western territories. At the same time, an increasing number of southerners believed that antislavery radicals dominated northern politics and sought to bar slavery from the western territories and to undermine the institution in the states where it already existed. John Brown's raid on the federal arsenal at Harpers Ferry in October 1859 produced shock waves throughout the South, producing fears of slave revolt and race war. When Abraham Lincoln was elected in 1860, many white southerners were convinced that this represented the triumph of abolitionism in the North and thought they had no choice but to secede from the Union. The new president, however, was passionately committed to the preservation of the Union, and peaceful secession proved to be impossible.

The Experience of Liberation

Slaves played a pivotal role in their own liberation. During the first two years of the Civil War, federal officials refused to enlist black soldiers in the Union army. But by early 1863, voluntary enlistments had fallen so sharply that the federal government instituted an unpopular military draft and decided to enroll black troops. Indeed, it was the availability of black troops that allowed President Lincoln to resist demands for a negotiated peace that might have retained slavery in the United States. Altogether, 186,000 black soldiers served in the Union army and another 29,000 served in the navy, accounting for nearly 10 percent of all Union forces and 68,178 of the Union dead or missing. Three-fifths of all black troops were former slaves. The active participation of black troops made it inconceivable that African Americans would remain in slavery after the Civil War.

In 1863, at Fort Wagner in South Carolina and Port Hudson and Milliken's Bend in Louisiana, black troops proved their mettle in battle. But black troops also faced another battle: against discrimination in pay, promotions, and medical care. Despite promises of equal treatment, blacks were relegated to separate regiments commanded by white officers. Black soldiers received less pay than a white private, inferior benefits, and poorer food and equipment. While a white private was paid $13 a month plus a $3.50 clothing allowance, blacks received just $10 a month, out of which $3 was deducted for clothing. Until the end of the war, the government refused to commission black officers. Within the ranks, black troops faced repeated humiliations; most were employed in menial assignments and kept in rear-echelon, fatigue assignments. Within the Union army, they were punished by whipping, others were tied up by their thumbs, and, if captured by the Confederates, they faced execution. But despite these trials, black soldiers won the opportunity to fight and the battle for equal pay (in 1864). Drawing upon the education and training they received in the military, many black troops became community leaders during Reconstruction.

During the war, many southern slaves contributed to their own emancipation by deserting plantations and fleeing to Union lines. While slaves staged few insurrections during the war, the slave system began to unravel. Planters were stunned to see trusted house slaves and drivers lead field hands in deserting to the Union army.

For ex-slaves, emancipation was a moment of exhilaration, fear, and uncertainty. While some greeted the announcement of freedom with jubilation, others reacted with stunned silence. "You could hear a pin drop, everything was so quiet," Mary Anderson, a former slave, recalled. Thousands of freedmen wandered the South, struggling desperately, but largely unsuccessfully, to reunite families forcibly separated by sale. A northern journalist met an ex-slave in North Carolina who had walked 600 miles searching for his wife and children who had been sold four years before. Many couples, forbidden to marry during slavery, took the opportunity to formalize their unions, while others, who had lived apart from their families on separate plantations, were finally free to reside with their spouses. To display their emancipation, many freedmen changed their slave names, adopted new surnames, and insisted on being address as "mister" and "missus."

Shocked at seeing former slaves transformed into free women and men, southern whites complained of "betrayal" and "ingratitude" when the freedmen left their plantations. Revealing slave owners' capacity for self-deception, one former master complained that "those we loved best, and who loved us best – as we thought – were the first to leave us." In many parts of the South, the end of the war was followed by an outburst of white rage: whites whipped, clubbed, and murdered freed slaves. In contrast, the vast majority of former slaves refrained from vengeance against former masters. Instead, they struggled to achieve economic and political independence by forming separate black churches and schools, mutual aid societies, lodges, newspapers, and political organizations.

The Aftermath of Slavery

Except for Haiti, the American South was the only region in the western hemisphere in which slavery was overthrown by force of arms. It was the only region, except for Brazil, in which slave owners received no compensation for the loss of their slave property; and the only region, except for Guadeloupe and Martinique, in which former slaves received civil and political rights. And it was the only post-emancipation society in which large slave owners were deprived of the right to hold public office and in which former slaves formed successful political alliances with whites.

Nevertheless, the abolition of slavery did not mean that former slaves had achieved full freedom. Throughout the western hemisphere, the end of slavery was followed by a period of reconstruction in which race relations were redefined and new systems of labor emerged. In former slave societies throughout the Americas, ex-slaves sought to free themselves from the gang system of labor on plantation and establish small-scale, self-sufficient farms, while planters or local governments sought to restore the plantation system. The outcome, in many former slave societies, was the emergence of a caste system of race relations and a system of involuntary or forced labor, such as peonage, debt bondage, apprenticeship, contract laborers, indentured laborers, tenant farming, and sharecropping.

In every post-emancipation society, the abolition of slavery resulted in acute labor problems and declining productivity, spurring efforts to restore plantation discipline. Even in Haiti, where black revolution had overthrown slavery, repeated attempts were made to restore the plantation system. On Caribbean islands – like Antigua, Barbados, and St Kitts – where land was totally controlled by white planters, the plantation system was reimposed. In other areas – like British Guiana, Jamaica, or Trinidad – where former slaves were able to squat on unsettled land and set up subsistence farms, staple production fell sharply. To counteract the precipitous decline in sugar production, the British government imported tens of thousands of "coolie" laborers from China, India, Java, and west Africa into British Guiana, Jamaica, Mauritius, Suriname, and Trinidad. In many plantation societies, governments sought to force former slaves back to work on plantations with strict vagrancy laws, coercive labor contracts, and regressive taxes.

The story of Reconstruction in the American South echoes that broader concern with labor control. Immediately following the war, all-white state legislatures passed "black codes" designed to force freed blacks to work on plantations, where they would be put to work in gangs. These codes denied blacks the right to purchase or even rent land. Vagrancy laws allowed authorities to arrest blacks "in idleness" and assign them to a chain gang or auction them off to a planter for as long as a year. Other statutes required blacks to have written proof of employment and barred them from leaving plantations. The Freedmen's Bureau, ostensibly designed to aid former slaves, helped to enforce laws against vagrancy and loitering and refused to allow ex-slaves to keep land that they had occupied during the war. One black army veteran, Elijah Marrs, asked rhetorically: "If you call this Freedom, what did you call Slavery?"

Such efforts to virtually re-enslave the freedmen led Congressional Republicans to seize control of Reconstruction from President Andrew Johnson, deny representatives from the former Confederate states their Congressional seats, pass the Civil Rights Act of 1866, and write the Fourteenth Amendment to the Constitution to extend citizenship rights to African Americans and guarantee them the equal protection of the laws. In 1870, the country went even further by ratifying the Fifteenth Amendment, which extended voting rights to black men. But the most radical proposal advanced during Reconstruction – to confiscate plantations and redistribute portions of the land to the freedmen – was defeated.

The freedmen, in alliance with carpetbaggers (northerners who had migrated to the South following the Civil War) and southern white Republicans known as scalawags, temporarily gained power in every former Confederate state except Virginia. Altogether, over 600 blacks served as legislators in Reconstruction governments (though blacks comprised a majority only in the lower house of South Carolina's legislature). The Reconstruction governments drew up democratic state constitutions, expanded women's rights, provided debt relief, and established the South's first state-funded schools. During the 1870s, however, internal divisions within the southern Republican party, white terror, and northern apathy allowed white Democrats, known as Redeemers, to return to power in the South's state governments. The North's failure to enforce the Fourteenth and Fifteenth Amendments permitted racial segregation and disfranchisement in the South.

During Reconstruction, former slaves – and many small white farmers – became trapped in a new system of economic exploitation: sharecropping.

Lacking capital and land of their own, former slaves were forced to work for large landowners. Initially, planters, with the support of the Freedmen's Bureau, sought to restore gang labor under the supervision of white overseers. The freedmen, who wanted autonomy and independence, refused to sign contracts that required gang labor. Ultimately, sharecropping emerged as a sort of compromise.

Instead of cultivating land in gangs supervised by overseers, landowners divided plantations into 20- to 50-acre plots suitable for farming by a single family. In exchange for land, a cabin, and supplies, sharecroppers agreed to raise a cash crop (usually cotton) and to give half the crop to their landlord. The high interest rates landlords and merchants charged for goods bought on credit transformed sharecropping into a system of economic dependency and poverty. The freedmen found, in the words of Felix Haywood, a former Texas slave, that "freedom could make folks proud but it didn't make 'em rich."

Nevertheless, the sharecropping system did allow freedmen a degree of freedom and autonomy greater than that experienced under slavery. As a symbol of their newly won independence, freedmen had teams of mules drag their former slave cabins away from the slave quarters into their own fields. Black wives and daughters sharply reduced their labor in the fields and instead devoted more time to childcare and housework. For the first time, black families could divide their time between field work and housework in accordance with their own family priorities.

Chattel slavery had been defeated. The gang system of labor, enforced by the whip, was dead. Real gains had been won. But full freedom remained an unfulfilled promise.

In 1970, the countries of the Arabian peninsula became the last in the world to abolish legal slavery. Nevertheless, the buying and selling of human beings continues to flourish in many parts of the world. Each year, an estimated one million Asian women and children, in Bangladesh, Burma, India, Pakistan, Sri Lanka, Thailand, and elsewhere, are sold or auctioned into slavery to serve as prostitutes or child laborers. Methods of procurement have changed since the eighteenth century; instead of being kidnapped, slaves are bought in impoverished villages for a few hundred dollars. But the cruelties of slavery remain, with contemporary slaves chained to beds in brothels or at workbenches in sweatshops. The final chapter in the history of slavery remains unfinished.

Chapter 1   "Death's Gwineter Lay His Cold Icy Hands on Me": Enslavement

In 1441, a Portuguese sailor named Antam Concalvez sailed south to what is now Morocco, carrying a cargo of sea-lion skins and oil. During the voyage, Concalvez reportedly expressed a desire to please Prince Henry of Portugal by bringing him African captives. While ashore, his crew wounded an African with a javelin and took him prisoner; and subsequently they captured an African woman. Then the crew staged a raid, in which four Africans were killed and ten others were captured. The capture of these 12 African prisoners marked the beginning of the European slave trade with sub-Saharan Africa.

The exact number of Africans caught up in the Atlantic slave trade over the next four centuries remains unknown. The best estimates suggest that over nine and a half million Africans survived the transatlantic crossing and another two million died during the Middle Passage. But no one knows how many people died in Africa during wars in which slaves were seized, in the forced march to the coast, or in the coastal dungeons, pens, or barracoons where slaves were herded. The figure may well have been more than seven million, bringing the total number of Africans entrapped in the slave trade to more than 18 million people.

As early as the mid-1450s, Europeans began to acquire west African slaves through trade rather than raids. By the seventeenth century, the English, French, Dutch, Danes, and Swedes had joined the Portuguese and Spanish in the African slave trade. Along the west African coast, European merchants established forts and trading posts – known as "factories" or "castles" – to serve as centers for collecting slaves.

Within west Africa, war, crop failure, drought, famine, political instability, small-scale raiding, taxation, and judicial or religious punishment produced large numbers of slaves. War captives, condemned criminals, debtors, aliens, famine victims, and political dissidents – all might find themselves sold into slavery.

The slave trade was greatly encouraged by the low cost of slaves. Even though the price of slaves rose three- or four-fold during the eighteenth century, many Europeans were convinced that it was "cheaper to buy than to breed." Between the sixteenth and mid-eighteenth centuries, it was cheaper to import a slave from Africa than to raise a child to the age of 14. During the late seventeenth century, merchants in the Senegambia region of west Africa paid as little as one pound sterling each for young males, whom they sold to European traders for the equivalent of three pounds ten shillings sterling, or 11 muskets, 31 gallons of brandy, or 93 pounds of wrought iron. Initially, many slaves were acquired from regions within 50 or 100 miles of the west African coast. During the eighteenth century, however, rising prices led slavers to search for captives in interior regions, 500 to 1,000 miles inland.

The impact of the slave trade on west African society is almost impossible to calculate. The demographic consequences are the most obvious. While the slave trade probably did not drastically depopulate west Africa, it may well have caused sharp population declines in particular regions and it certainly kept the overall population growth rate low.

But the slave trade had other high social costs. Throughout west Africa, the slave trade fostered warfare, skewed local economies, expanded servitude within the region, and distorted class and political structures. While the slave trade enhanced the power, prestige, and wealth of particular west African rulers, merchants, and states, it contributed to economic stagnation and long-term political instability. The introduction of European guns and gunpowder reinforced political fragmentation, allowing particular states to grow at the expense of others. Meanwhile, the influx of European textiles and manufactured goods undermined local west African industries.

Of course, the greatest cost of the slave trade was its human toll. The selections that follow document the African side of the Atlantic slave trade: capture, transit to the coast, and sale to Europeans. They disclose the human meaning of enslavement – as told by its victims.

1 A European Slave Trader, John Barbot, Describes the African Slave Trade (1682)

"prepossessed with the opinion ... that Europeans are fond of their flesh"

John Barbot, an agent for the French Royal African Company, made at least two voyages to the West Coast of Africa, in 1678 and 1682. In the following document, he describes how people came to be enslaved; how they were treated after enslavement; and how the captives responded to enslavement. He also reveals how apologists for slavery defended their involvement in the slave trade.

Those sold by the Blacks are for the most part prisoners of war, taken either in fight, or pursuit, or in the incursions they make into their enemies territories; others stolen away by their own countrymen; and some there are, who will sell their own children, kindred, or neighbours. This has been often seen, and to compass it, they desire the person they intend to sell, to help them in carrying something to the factory by way of trade, and when there, the person so deluded, not understanding the language, is sold and deliver'd up as a slave, notwithstanding all his resistance, and exclaiming against the treachery....

The kings are so absolute, that upon any slight pretense of offences committed by their subjects, they order them to be sold for slaves, without regard to rank, or possession. ...

Abundance of little Blacks of both sexes are also stolen away by their neighbours, when found abroad on the roads, or in the woods; or else in the Cougans, or corn-fields, at the time of the year, when their parents keep them there all day, to scare away the devouring small birds, that come to feed on the millet, in swarms, as has been said above.

In times of dearth and famine, abundance of those people will sell themselves, for a maintenance, and to prevent starving. When I first arriv'd at Goerree, in December, 1681, I could have bought a great number, at very easy rates, if I could have found provisions to subsist them; so great was the dearth then, in that part of Nigritia.

To conclude, some slaves are also brought to these Blacks, from very remote inland countries, by way of trade, and sold for things of very inconsiderable value; but these slaves are generally poor and weak, by reason of the barbarous usage they have had in traveling so far, being continually beaten, and almost famish'd; so inhuman are the Blacks to one another. ...

The trade of slaves is in a more peculiar manner the business of kings, rich men, and prime merchants, exclusive of the inferior sort of Blacks.

These slaves are severely and barbarously treated by their masters, who subsist them poorly, and beat them inhumanly, as may be seen by the scabs and wounds on the bodies of many of them when sold to us. They scarce allow them the least rag to cover their nakedness, which they also take off from them when sold to Europeans; and they always go bare-headed. The wives and children of slaves, are also slaves to the master under whom they are married; and when dead, they never bury them, but cast out the bodies into some by place, to be devoured by birds, or beasts of prey.

This barbarous usage of those unfortunate wretches, makes it appear, that the fate of such as are bought and transported from the coast to America, or other parts of the world, by Europeans, is less deplorable, than that of those who end their days in their native country; for aboard ships all possible care is taken to preserve and subsist them for the interest of the owners, and when sold in America, the same motive ought to prevail with their masters to use them well, that they may live the longer, and do them more service. Not to mention the inestimable advantage they may reap, of becoming christians, and saving their souls, if they make a true use of their condition. ...

Many of those slaves we transport from Guinea to America are prepos-sessed with the opinion, that they are carried like sheep to the slaughter, and that the Europeans are fond of their flesh; which notion so far prevails with some, as to make them fall into a deep melancholy and despair, and to refuse all sustenance, tho' never so much compelled and even beaten to oblige them to take some nourishment: notwithstanding all which, they will starve to death; whereof I have had several instances in my own slaves both aboard and at Guadalupe. And tho' I must say I am naturally compassionate, yet have I been necessitated sometimes to cause the teeth of those wretches to be broken, because they would not open their mouths, or be prevailed upon by any entreaties to feed themselves; and thus have forced some sustenance into their throats. ...

As the slaves come down to Fida from the inland country, they are put into a booth, or prison, built for that purpose, near the beach, all of them together; and when the Europeans are to receive them, every part of every one of them, to the smallest member, men and women being all stark naked. Such as are allowed good and sound, are set on one side, and the others by themselves; which slaves so rejected are there called Mackrons, being above thirty five years of age, or defective in their limbs, eyes or teeth; or grown grey, or that have the venereal disease, or any other imperfection. These being set aside, each of the others, which have passed as good, is marked on the breast, with a red-hot iron, imprinting the mark of the French, English, or Dutch companies, that so each nation may distinguish their own, and to prevent their being chang'd by the natives for worse, as they are apt enough to do. In this particular, care is taken that the women, as tenderest, be not burnt too hard.

The branded slaves, after this, are returned to their former booth, where the factor is to subsist them at his own charge, which amounts to about two-pence a day for each of them, with bread and water, which is all their allowance. There they continue sometimes ten or fifteen days, till the sea is still enough to send them aboard; for very often it continues too boister-ous for so long a time, unless in January, February and March, which is commonly the calmest season: and when it is so, the slaves are carried off by parcels, in bar-canoes, and put aboard the ships in the road. Before they enter the canoes, or come out of the booth, their former Black masters strip them of every rag they have, without distinction of men or women; to supply which, in orderly ships, each of them as they come aboard is allowed a piece of canvas, to wrap around their waist, which is very acceptable to those poor wretches. ...

If there happens to be no stock of slaves at Fida, the factor must trust the Blacks with his goods, to the value of a hundred and fifty, or two hundred slaves; which goods they carry up into the inland, to buy slaves, at all the markets, for above two hundred leagues up the country, where they are kept like cattle in Europe; the slaves sold there being generally prisoners of war, taken from their enemies, like other booty, and perhaps some few sold by their own countrymen, in extreme want, or upon a famine; as also some as a punishment of heinous crimes: tho' many Europeans believe that parents sell their own children, men their wives and relations, which, if it ever happens, is so seldom, that it cannot justly be charged upon a whole nation, as a custom and common practice. ...

One thing is to be taken notice of by sea-faring men, that this Fida and Ardra slaves are of all the others, the most apt to revolt aboard ships, by a conspiracy carried on amongst themselves; especially such as are brought down to Fida, from very remote inland countries, who easily draw others into their plot: for being used to see mens flesh eaten in their own country, and publick markets held for the purpose, they are very full of the notion, that we buy and transport them to the same purpose; and will therefore watch all opportunities to deliver themselves, by assaulting a ship's crew, and murdering them all, if possible: whereof, we have almost every year some instances, in one European ship or other, that is filled with slaves.

Source: John Barbot, "A Description of the Coasts of North and South Guinea," in Thomas Astley and John Churchill, eds., *Collection of Voyages and Travels* (London, 1732).

2 A Muslim Merchant, Ayubah Suleiman Diallo, Recalls His Capture and Enslavement (1733)

"he was no common slave"

> *Any west African, regardless of status, might be enslaved. Ayuba Suleiman Diallo, who was born around 1701 to a family of Muslim clerics, was a well-educated merchant in the Senegambian region of west Africa, which had supplied Europe with beeswax, gold, gum, ivory, and small numbers of slaves since the fifteenth century. In 1730, he was kidnapped and transported to Maryland. In Maryland, he wrote a letter to his father, which came to the attention of James Oglethorpe, the founder of Georgia, who helped purchase his freedom and bring him to England, where he was known as Job ben Solomon.*

In February, 1730, Job's father hearing of an English ship at Gambia River, sent him, with two servants to attend him, to sell two Negroes, and to buy paper, and other necessities; but desired him not to venture over the river, because the country of the Mandingoes, who are enemies ... lies on the other side. Job not agreeing with Captain Pike ... sent back the two servants to acquaint his father with it, and to let him know that he intended to go farther. Accordingly having agreed with another man, named Loumein Yoas, who understood the Mandingoe language, to go with him as his interpreter, he crossed the River Gambia, and disposed of his Negroes for some cows. As he was returning home, he stopped for some refreshment at the house of an old acquaintance; and the weather being hot, he hung up his arms in the house, while he refreshed himself. Those arms were very valuable; consisting of a gold-hilted sword, a gold knife, which they wear by their side, and a rich quiver of arrows, which King Sambo had made him a present of. It happened that a company of the Mandingoes, who live upon plunder, passing by at that time, and observing him unarmed, rushed in, to the number of seven or eight at once, at a back door, and pinioned Job, before he could get to his arms, together with his interpreter, who is a slave in Maryland still. They then shaved their heads and beards, which Job and his man resented as the highest indignity; tho' the Mandingoes meant no more by it, than to make them appear like Slaves taken in war. On the 27th of February, 1730, they carried them to Captain Pike at Gambia, who purchased them; and on the first of March they were put on board. Soon after Job found means to acquaint Captain Pike that he was the same person that came to trade with him a few days before, and after what manner he had been taken. Upon this Captain Pike gave him leave to redeem himself and his man; and Job sent to an acquaintance of his father's, near Gambia, who promised to send to Job's father, to inform him of what had happened, that he might take some course to have him set at liberty. But it being a fortnight's journey between that friend's house and his father's, and the ship sailing in about a week after, Job was brought with the rest of the slaves to Annapolis and Maryland, and delivered to Mr. Vachell Denton, factor to Mr. Hunt, before mentioned. Job heard since, by vessels that came from Gambia, that his father sent down several slaves, a little after Captain Pike sailed, in order to procure his redemption; and that Sambo, King of Futa, had made war upon the Mandingoes, and cut off great numbers of them, upon of the account of the injury they had done to his schoolfellow.

Mr. Vachell Denton sold Job to one Mr. Tolsey in Kent Island in Maryland, who put him to work in making tobacco; but he was soon convinced that Job had never been used to such labour. He every day showed more and more uneasiness under this exercise, and at last grew sick, being no way able to bear it; so that his master was obliged to find easier work for him, and therefore put him to tend the cattle. Job would often leave the cattle, and withdraw into the woods to pray; but a white boy frequently watched him, and whilst he was at his devotion would mock him, and throw dirt in his face. This very much disturbed Job, and added considerably to his other misfortunes; all which were increased by his ignorance of the English language, which prevented him from complaining, or telling his case to any person about him. Grown in some measure desperate, by reason of his present hardship, he resolved to travel at a venture; thinking he might possibly be taken up by some master, who would use him better or otherwise meet with some lucky accident, to divert or abate his grief. Accordingly, he travelled thro' the woods, till he came to the County of Kent, upon Delaware Bay, now esteemed part of Pensilvania; altho' it is properly a part of Maryland, and belongs to my Lord Baltimore. There is a law in force, throughout the colonies of Virginia, Maryland, Pensilvania, etc. as far as Boston in New England, viz. that any Negroe, or white servant who is not known in the county, or has no pass, may be secured by any person, and kept in the common gaol, till the master of such servant shall fetch him. Therefore Job being able to give no account of himself, was put in prison there.

This happened about the beginning of June, 1731 when I, who was attending the courts there, and had heard of Job, went with several gentlemen to the gaoler's house, being a tavern, and desired to see him. He was brought into the tavern to us, but could not speak one word of English. Upon our taking and making signs to him, he wrote a line or two before us, and when he read it, pronounced the words Allah and Mahommed; by which, and his refusing a glass of wine we offered him, we perceived he was a Mahomedtan, but could not imagine of what country he was, or how he got thither; for by his affable carriage, and the easy composure of his countenance, we could perceive he was no common slave.

When Job had been some time confined, an old Negroe man, who lived in that neighbourhood, and could speak the Jalloff language, which Job also understood, went to him, and conversed with him. By this Negroe the keeper was informed to whom Job belonged, and what was the cause of his leaving his master. The keeper thereupon wrote to his master, who soon after fetched him home, and was much kinder to him than before; allowing him a place to pray in, and some other conveniences, in order to make his slavery as easy as possible. Yet slavery and confinement was by no means agreeable to Job, who had never been used to it; he therefore wrote a letter in Arabick to his father, acquainting him with his misfortunes, hoping he might yet find means to redeem him. This letter he sent to Mr. Vachell Denton, desiring it might be sent to Africa by Captain Pike; but he being gone to England, Mr. Denton sent the letter inclosed to Mr. Hunt, in order to be sent to Africa by Captain Pike from England; but Captain Pike had sailed for Africa before the letter came to Mr. Hunt, who therefore kept it in his own hands, till he should have a proper opportunity of sending it. It happened that this letter was seen by James Oglethorpe, Esq. [an English philanthropist who founded the colony of Georgia as a haven for debtors], who, according to his usual goodness and generosity, took compassion on Job, and gave his bond to Mr. Hunt for the payment of a certain sum, upon the delivery of Job here in England. Mr. Hunt upon this sent to Mr. Denton, who purchased him again of his master for the same money which Mr. Denton had formerly received for him; his master being very willing to part with him, as finding him no ways fit for his business.

Source: Thomas Bluett, *Some Memoirs of the Life of Job, the Son of Solomon* (London, 1734).

3 An Employee of Britain's Royal African Company Describes the Workings of the Slave Trade (1738)

"they strain hard for crimes, in order to obtain the benefit of selling the criminal"

Writing in the 1730s, Francis Moore, an employee at a Royal African Company trading post along the Gambia River, describes the workings of the slave trade. He offers vivid descriptions of how people came to be enslaved, and of the individuals who, he believes, lay behind the trade.

The trade of the natives consists in gold, slaves, elephants teeth, and bees-wax ...

The same merchants bring down elephants teeth, and in some years slaves to the amount of 2000, most of whom they say are prisoners of war; and bought of the different princes by whom they are taken. The way of bringing them is, by tying them by the neck with leather thongs, at about a yard distance from each other, 30 or 40 in a string, having generally a bundle of corn, or an elephant's tooth upon each of their heads. In their way from the mountains they travel through extensive woods, where they cannot for some days get water; they therefore carry in skin bags enough to support them for that time. I cannot be certain of the number of merchants who carry on this trade; but there may perhaps be about 100 who go up into the inland country with the goods, which they buy from the white men, and with them purchase, in various countries, gold, slaves, and elephants teeth. They use asses, as well as slaves, in carrying their goods, but no camels or horses.

Beside the slaves brought down by the negro merchants, there are many bought along the river, who are either taken in war like the former, or condemned for crimes, or stolen by the people: but the company's servants never buy any which they suspect to be of the last sort, till they have sent for the alcalde, and consulted with him. Since this slave trade has been used, all punishments are changed into slavery; and the natives reaping advantage from such condemnations, they strain hard for crimes, in order to obtain the benefit of selling the criminal: hence not only murder, adultery, and theft, are here punished by selling the malefactor; but every trifling crime is also punished in the same manner. Thus at Cantore, a man seeing a tyger eating a deer, which he himself had killed and hung up near his house, fired at the tyger, but unhappily shot a man: when the king had not only the cruelty to condemn him for this accident; but had the injustice and inhumanity to order also his mother, his three brothers, and his three sisters, to be sold. They were brought down to me at Yamyamacunda, when it made my heart ache to see them; but on my refusing to make this cruel purchase, they were sent farther down the river, and sold to some separate traders at Joar, and the vile avaricious king had the benefit of the goods for which they were sold.

Indeed the cruelty and villainy of some of these princes can scarcely be conceived. Thus, whenever the king of Barsally, some of whose villainies I have already mentioned, wants goods or brandy, he sends to the governor of James's Fort, to desire him to send a sloop there with a proper cargo; which is readily complied with. Mean while, the king goes and ransacks some of his enemies towns, and seizing the innocent people, sells them to the factors in the sloop for such commodities as he wants, as brandy, rum, guns, gunpowder, ball, pistols, and cutlasses, for his attendants and soldiers with coral and silver for his wives and concubines: but in case he is not at war with any neighbouring king, he then falls upon one of his own towns, which are very numerous, and uses them in the same manner, selling those for slaves, whom he is bound by every obligation to protect.

Source: Francis Moore, *Travels into the Inland Parts of Africa* (London, 1738).

4 Olaudah Equiano, an 11-Year-Old Ibo from Nigeria, Remembers His Kidnapping into Slavery (1789)

"they ... carry off as many as they could seize"

A former slave, Gustavus Vassa or Olaudah Equiano traveled across the Atlantic and the Mediterranean on British merchant ships, served in the British navy, and became a leading figure in the eighteenth-century British antislavery movement. His autobiography, which went through nine editions between 1789 and 1797 and was translated into Dutch, German, and Russian, awakened thousands of readers to the horrors of the Atlantic slave trade. In this excerpt, Equiano describes his kidnapping into slavery at the age of 11. Held captive in West Africa for seven months, he was subsequently sold to British slavers, who shipped him to Barbados and then took him to Virginia. After serving a British naval officer, he was sold to a Quaker merchant from Philadelphia, who allowed him to purchase his freedom in 1766.

Recently, a debate has erupted over whether Equiano was actually born in Africa. Two surviving documents – Equiano's baptismal records and the Royal

Navy's muster rolls – indicate that he was born in "Carolina," leading Equiano's leading biographer, Vincent Carretta, to conclude that his "account of Africa may be based on oral history and reading, rather than personal experience."

My father, besides many slaves, had a numerous family, of which seven lived to grow up, including myself and a sister, who was the only daughter. As I was the youngest of the sons, I became, of course, the greatest favourite of my mother, and was always with her; and she used to take particular pains to form my mind. I was trained up from my earliest years in the arts of agriculture and war; and my mother adorned me with emblems, after the manner of our greatest warriors. In this way I grew up till I was turned the age of eleven, when an end was put to my happiness in the following manner: – Generally, when the grown people in the neighbourhood were gone far in the fields to labour, the children assembled together in some of the neighbourhood's premises to play; and commonly some of us used to get up a tree to look out for any assailant, or kidnapper, that might come upon us; for they sometimes took those opportunities of our parents' absence, to attack and carry off as many as they could seize. One day, as I was watching at the top of a tree in our yard, I saw one of those people come into the yard of our next neighbour but one, to kidnap, there being many stout young people in it. Immediately, on this, I gave the alarm of the rogue, and he was surrounded by the stoutest of them, who entangled him with cords, so that he could not escape till some of the grown people came and secured him. But alas! ere long, it was my fate to be thus attacked, and to be carried off, when none of the grown people were nigh. One day, when all our people were gone out to their works as usual, and only I and my dear sister were left to mind the house, two men and a woman got over our walls, and in a moment seized us both; and, without giving us time to cry out, or make resistance, they stopped our mouths, and ran off with us into the nearest wood. Here they tied our hands, and continued to carry us as far as they could, till night came on, when we reached a small house, where the robbers halted for refreshment, and spent the night. We were then unbound; but were unable to take any food; and, being quite overpowered by fatigue and grief, our only relief was some sleep, which allayed our misfortune for a short time.

Source: Olaudah Equiano, *The Interesting Narrative of the Life of Olaudah Equiano or Gustavus Vassa the African* (London, 1789).

5 A Scottish Explorer, Mungo Park, Offers a Graphic Account of the African Slave Trade (1797)

"the poor wretches are kept constantly fettered"

A Scottish-born surgeon and explorer, Mungo Park, between 1795 and 1797 led an expedition find the source of the Niger River. His account of his travels, which became a best-seller, includes a description of the workings of the slave trade in that region, including the price paid by European traders to acquire slaves.

The commodities exported to the Gambia from Europe consist chiefly of firearms and ammunition, iron-ware, spirituous liquors, tobacco, cotton caps, a small quantity of broadcloth, and a few articles of the manufacture of Manchester; a small assortment of India goods, with some glass beads, amber, and other trifles, for which are taken in exchange slaves, gold dust, ivory, beeswax, and hides. Slaves are the chief article, but the whole number which at this time are annually exported from the Gambia by all nations is supposed to be under one thousand.

Most of these unfortunate victims are brought to the coast in periodical caravans; many of them from very remote inland countries, for the language which they speak is not understood by the inhabitants of the maritime districts. ...

On their arrival at the coast, if no immediate opportunity offers of selling them to advantage, they are distributed among the neighbouring villages, until a slave ship arrives, or until they can be sold to black traders, who sometimes purchase on speculation. In the meanwhile, the poor wretches are kept constantly fettered, two and two of them being chained together, and employed in the labours of the field, and, I am sorry to add, are very scantily fed, as well as harshly treated. The price of a slave varies according to the number of purchasers from Europe, and the arrival of caravans from the interior; but in general I reckon that a young and healthy male, from sixteen to twenty-five years of age, may be estimated on the spot from 18 pounds to 20 pounds sterling.

Source: Mungo Park, *Travels in the Interior Districts of Africa*, vol. 1 (London, 1799).

6 Venture Smith Relates the Story of His Kidnapping at the Age of Six (1798)

"I then had a rope put about my neck"

Kidnapped at the age of six, Venture Smith was sold to the steward on a slave ship and brought to Connecticut. At the age of 31, after several changes of ownership, he purchased his freedom with money that he earned by hiring out his labor and "cleaning musk-rats and minks, raising potatoes and carrots, and by fishing in the night, and at odd spells." In order to purchase his wife and sons, he fished, sailed on a whaler, ferried wood from Long Island to Rhode Island, and raised watermelons. Later, he actually became a slaveholder, purchasing at least three slaves. At his death at the age of 77 in 1805 in East Haddam, Connecticut, he left a 100-acre farm and three houses.

In this excerpt from his autobiography, Smith describes his childhood and his family in Africa as well as his capture and enslavement.

I was born in Dukandarra, in Guinea, about the year 1729. My father's name was Saungm Furro, Prince of the tribe of Dukandara. My father had three wives. Polygamy was not uncommon in that country, especially among the rich, as every man was allowed to keep as many wives as he could maintain. ...

The first thing worthy of notice which I remember was, a contention between my father and mother, on account of my father marrying his third wife without the consent of his first and eldest, which was contrary to the custom generally observed among my countrymen. In consequence of this rupture, my mother left her husband and country, and travelled away with her three children to the eastward. I was then five years old. ... After five days travel ... my mother was pleased to stop and seek a refuge for me. She left me at the house of a very rich farmer. I was then, as I should judge, not less than one hundred and forty miles from my native place, separated from all my relations and acquaintance. ...

My father sent a man and horse after me. After settling with my guardian for keeping me, he took me away and went for home. It was then about one year since my mother brought me here. Nothing remarkable occurred to us on our journey until we arrived safe home.

I found then that the difference between my parents had been made up previous to their sending for me. On my return, I was received both by my father and mother with great joy and affection, and was once more restored to my paternal dwelling in peace and happiness. I was then about six years old.

Not more than six weeks had passed after my return before a message was brought by an inhabitant of the place where I lived the preceding year to my father, that that place had been invaded by a numerous army from a nation not far distant, furnished with musical instruments, and all kinds of arms then in use; that they were instigated by some white nation who equipped and sent them to subdue and possess the country; that his nation had made no preparation for war, having been for a long time in profound peace; that they could not defend themselves against such a formidable train of invaders, and must therefore necessarily evacuate their lands to the fierce enemy, and fly to the protection of some chief; and that if he would permit them they would come under his rule and protection when they had to retreat from their own possessions. He was a kind and merciful prince, and therefore consented to these proposals. . . .

He gave them every privilege and all the protection his government could afford. But they had not been there longer than four days before news came to them that the invaders had laid waste their country, and were coming speedily to destroy them in my father's territories. This affrighted them, and therefore they immediately pushed off to the southward, into the unknown countries there, and were never more heard of.

Two days after their retreat, the report turned out to be but too true. A detachment from the enemy came to my father and informed him, that the whole army was encamped not far out of his dominions, and would invade the territory and deprive his people of their liberties and rights, if he did not comply with the following terms. These were to pay them a large sum of money, three hundred fat cattle, and a great number of goats, sheep, asses, etc.

My father told the messenger he would comply rather than that his subjects should be deprived of their rights and privileges, which he was not then in circumstances to defend from so sudden an invasion. Upon turning out those articles, the enemy pledged their faith and honor that they would not attack him. On these he relied and therefore thought it unnecessary to be on his guard against the enemy. But their pledges of faith and honor proved no better than those of other unprincipled hostile nations; for a few days after a certain relation of the king came and informed him, that the enemy who sent terms of accommodation to him and received tribute to their satisfaction, yet meditated an attack upon his subjects by surprise and that probably they would commence their attack in less than one day, and concluded with advising him, as he was not prepared for war, to order a speedy retreat of his family and subjects. He complied with this advice.

The same night which was fixed upon to retreat, my father and his family set off about the break of day. The king and his two younger wives went in one company, and my mother and her children in another. We left our dwellings in succession, and my father's company went on first. We directed our course for a large shrub plain, some distance off, where we intended to conceal ourselves from the approaching enemy, until we could refresh ourselves a little. But we presently found that our retreat was not secure. For having struck up a little fire for the purpose of cooking victuals, the enemy who happened to be encamped a little distance off, had sent out a scouting party who discovered us by the smoke of the fire, just as we were extinguishing it, and about to eat. As soon as we had finished eating, my father discovered the party, and immediately began to discharge arrows at them. This was what I first saw, and it alarmed both me and the women, who being unable to make any resistance, immediately betook ourselves to the tall thick reeds not far off, and left the old king to fight alone. For some time I beheld him from the reeds defending himself with great courage and firmness, till at last he was obliged to surrender himself into their hands.

They then came to us in the reeds, and the very first salute I had from them was a violent blow on the back part of the head with the fore part of a gun, and at the same time a grasp round the neck. I then had a rope put about my neck, as had all the women in the thicket with me, and were immediately led to my father, who was likewise pinioned and haltered for leading. In this condition we were all led to the camp. The women and myself being pretty submissive, had tolerable treatment from the enemy, while my father was closely interrogated respecting his money which they knew he must have. But as he gave them no account of it, he was instantly cut and pounded on his body with great inhumanity, that he might be induced by the torture he suffered to make the discovery. All this availed not in the least to make him give up his money, but he despised all the tortures which they inflicted, until the continued exercise and increase of torment, obliged him to sink and expire. He thus died without informing his enemies where his money lay. I saw him while he was thus tortured to death. The shocking scene is to this day fresh in my mind, and I have often been overcome while thinking on it. . . .

The army of the enemy was large, I should suppose consisting of about six thousand men. Their leader was called Baukurre. After destroying the old prince, they decamped and immediately marched toward the sea, lying to the west, taking with them myself and the women prisoners. In the march a scouting party was detached from the main army. To the leader of this party I was made waiter, having to carry his gun, etc. As we were a scouting we came across a herd of fat cattle, consisting of about thirty in number. These we set upon, and immediately wrested from their keepers, and afterwards converted them into food for the army. The enemy had remarkable success in destroying the country wherever they went. For as far as they had penetrated, they laid the habitations waste and captured the people. The distance they had now brought me was about four hundred miles. All the march I had very hard tasks imposed on me, which I must perform on pain of punishment. I was obliged to carry on my head a large glat stone used for grinding our corn, weighing as I should suppose, as much as twenty-five pounds; besides victuals, mat and cooking utensils. Though I was pretty large and stout at my age, yet these burdens were very grievous to me, being only six years and a half old.

We were then come to a place called Malagasco. When we entered the place we could not see the least appearance of either houses or inhabitants, but upon stricter search found, that instead of houses above ground they had dens in the sides of hillocks, contiguous to ponds and streams of water. In these we perceived they had all hid themselves, as I supposed they usually did on such occasions. In order to compel them to surrender, the enemy contrived to smoke them out with faggots. These they put to the entrance of the caves and set them on fire. While they were engaged in this business, to their great surprise some of them were desperately wounded with arrows which fell from above on them. This mystery they soon found out. They perceived that the enemy discharged these arrows through holes on top of the dens, directly into the air. Their weight brought them back, point downwards on their enemies heads, whilst they were smoking the inhabitants out. The points of their arrows were poisoned, but their enemy had an antidote for it, which they instantly applied to the wounded part. The smoke at last obliged the people to give themselves up. They came out of their caves, first putting the palms of their hands together, and immediately after extended their arms, crossed at their wrists, ready to be bound and pinioned. ...

The invaders then pinioned the prisoners of all ages and sexes indiscriminately, took their flocks and all their effects, and moved on their way towards the sea. On the march the prisoners were treated with clemency, on account of their being submissive and humble. Having come to the next tribe, the enemy laid siege and immediately took men, women, children, flocks, and all their valuable effects. They then went on to the next district which was contiguous to the sea, called in Africa, Anamaboo. The enemies provisions were then almost spent, as well as their strength. The inhabitants knowing what conduct they had pursued, and what were their present intentions, improved the favorable opportunity, attacked them, and took enemy, prisoners, flocks and all their effects. I was then taken a second time. All of us were then put into the castle [a European slave trading post], and kept for market. On a certain time I and other prisoners were put on board a canoe, under our master, and rowed away to a vessel belonging to Rhode Island, commanded by Captain Collingwood, and the mate Thomas Mumford. While we were going to the vessel, our master told us all to appear to the best possible advantage for sale. I was bought on board by one Robert Mumford, steward of said vessel, for four gallons of rum, and a piece of calico, and called Venture, on account of his having purchased me with his own private venture. Thus I came by my name. All the slaves that were bought for that vessel's cargo, were two hundred and sixty.

Source: Venture Smith, *A Narrative of the Life and Adventures of Venture, A Native of Africa* (New London, Conn., 1798; expanded edn, Hamden, Conn., 1896).

Discussion Questions

1. How were slaves acquired?
2. Why did Europeans rely on sub-Saharan Africans rather than other Europeans to provide labor for their New World colonies?
3. What was the impact of the slave trade on African societies?

Chapter 2   "God's A-Gwineter Trouble de Water": The Middle Passage and Arrival

When the British frigate *North Star* stopped and boarded a slave ship in the south Atlantic in 1829 – two decades after the United States and Britain outlawed the Atlantic slave trade – the crew found conditions aboard the slaver almost unspeakably horrible. Its cargo consisted of 505 African men and women. Another 55 had been tossed overboard during 17 days at sea. The slaves "were all enclosed under grated hatchways, between decks. The space was so low that they sat between each other's legs, and stowed so close together, that there was no possibility of lying down, or at all changing their position, by night or by day.... They were all branded like sheep ... burnt with a red hot iron." Each captive, chained by the neck and legs, had just one square foot of sitting space.

No aspect of the Atlantic slave trade aroused more passionate denunciation than the Middle Passage – the transoceanic voyage to the New World. On many ships, slaves were crowded almost beyond belief. Typically, slaves had less than half the space provided for convicts aboard prison ships. A parliamentary inquiry concluded that conditions aboard the British slaver *Brooks* were fairly typical. To carry its cargo of 451 slaves, every man was allowed a space just 6' long, 16" wide, and 2' 7" high; every woman, a space 5' 10" long and 16" wide; every boy, 5' by 14"; every girl, 4' by 12". But on at least one voyage, the ship carried as many as 609 slaves.

Average death rates were extraordinary, running as high as 168 deaths for every 1,000 slaves leaving the African coast. Average child mortality was even higher. Some voyages were particularly deadly. The British slaver *Hero* lost 360 slaves – over half – mainly from smallpox; the *Briton* lost half its 375 slaves.

The major cause of death was amebic dysentery – "the bloody flux" – caused by contaminated food and water supplies, reflecting the low level of sanitation aboard the ships. Other killers included smallpox, measles, and other communicable diseases. In addition, many slaves died in shipboard revolts, attacks by pirates, and shipwrecks, or by suicide. In one gruesome incident in 1781, the captain of the slave ship *Zong* decided that many of the 440 slaves on the ship were so ill that they could not be sold. He ordered 122 infected slaves thrown overboard. Another 10 committed suicide by jumping overboard. Under English law, the captain believed, correctly, that the ship's insurers would pay if the cargo was lost, but not if it was damaged.

Shipboard slave revolts were not uncommon. Nearly 500 have been documented. In one revolt, in 1773, captives aboard the slave ship *New Britannia* succeeded in unlocking their chains and shackles and broke into the ship's gunroom. When, after an hour-long battle with the ship's crew, the revolt was about to be suppressed, the captives set fire to the ship's gunpowder magazine, killing nearly everyone on board.

The terrors of the Middle Passage were followed by another series of shocks. The "unpitied sable beings" were put on public auction. In 1806, a year before the United States and Britain outlawed the African slave trade, George Pinckard, an English physician, witnessed the sale of a newly arrived boatload of enslaved Africans in the West Indies. To the white settlers, he wrote, "it seemed a day of feasting and hilarity, but to the poor Africans it was a period of heavy grief and affliction; for they were to be sold as beasts of burden – torn from each other – and widely dispersed." The purchasers, observed Pinckard, "handled and inspected them, with as little concern as if they had been examining cattle." "They turned them about, felt them, viewed their shapes and limbs, and looked into their mouths, made them jump and throw out their arms, and subjected them to all the means of trial as if dealing for a horse or other brute animal."

Family ties were often disregarded by the purchasers. One slave, Pinckard wrote, told to stand up, refused, and "sunk his chin upon his breast and hung his head." He pointed to an African woman, "held up two fingers to the auctioneer, and implored the multitude in anxious suppliant gestures … which seemed to say – 'Let us be sold together.'"

1 A European Slave Trader, James Barbot, Jr., Describes a Shipboard Revolt by Enslaved Africans (1700)

"premeditated a revolt"

> *James Barbot, Jr., a sailor aboard the English slaver* Don Carlos, *describes a slave uprising that took place aboard the vessel. He also describes the great length to which the ship's crew goes to prevent such revolts from taking place. Especially unsettling is his remark that the crew should treat the captives as they themselves would wish to be treated.*

About one in the afternoon, after dinner, we, according to custom caused them, one by one, to go down between decks, to have each his pint of water; most of them were yet above deck, many of them provided with knives, which we had indiscreetly given them two or three days before, as not suspecting the least attempt of this nature from them; others had pieces of iron they had torn off our forecastle door, as having premeditated a revolt, and seeing all the ship's company, at best but weak and many quite sick, they had also broken off the shackles from several of their companions feet, which served them, as well as billets they had provided themselves with, and all other things they could lay hands on, which they imagin'd might be of use for this enterprize. Thus arm'd, they fell in crouds and parcels on our men, upon the deck unawares, and stabb'd one of the stoutest of us all, who receiv'd fourteen or fifteen wounds of their knives, and so expir'd. Next they assaulted our boatswain, and cut one of his legs so round the bone, that he could not move, the nerves being cut through; others cut our cook's throat to the pipe, and others wounded three of the sailors, and threw one of them over-board in that condition, from the fore-castle into the sea; who, however, by good providence, got hold of the bowline of the fore-sail, and sav'd himself . . . we stood in arms, firing on the revolted slaves, of whom we kill'd some, and wounded many: which so terrif'd the rest, that they gave way, dispersing themselves some one way and some another between decks, and under the fore-castle; and many of the most mutinous, leapt over board, and drown'd themselves in the ocean with much resolution, shewing no manner of concern for life. Thus we lost twenty seven or twenty eight slaves, either kill'd by us, or drown'd; and having master'd them, caused all to go betwixt decks, giving them good words. The next day we had them all again upon deck, where they unanimously declar'd, the Menbombe slaves had been the contrivers of the mutiny, and for an example we caused about thirty of the ringleaders to be very severely whipt by all our men that were capable of doing that office....

I have observ'd, that the great mortality, which so often happens in slave-ships, proceeds as well from taking in too many, as from want of knowing how to manage them aboard....

As to the management of our slaves aboard, we lodge the two sexes apart, by means of a strong partition at the main mast; the forepart is for men, the other behind the mast for the women. If it be in large ships carrying five or six hundred slaves, the deck in such ships ought to be at least five and a half or six foot high, which is very requisite for driving a continual trade of slaves: for the greater height it has, the more airy and convenient it is for such a considerable number of human creatures; and consequently far the more healthy for them, and fitter to look after them. We build a sort of half-decks along the sides with deals and spars provided for that purpose in Europe, that half-deck extending no father than the sides of our scuttles and so the slaves lie in two rows, one above the other, and as close together as they can be crouded....

The planks, or deals, contract some dampness more or less, either from the deck being so often wash'd to keep it clean and sweet, or from the rain that gets in now and then through the scuttles or other openings, and even from the very sweat of the slaves; which being so crouded in a low place, is perpetual, and occasions many distempers, or at best great inconveniences dangerous to their health....

It has been observ'd before, that some slaves fancy they are carry'd to be eaten, which make them desperate; and others are so on account of their captivity: so that if care be not taken, they will mutiny and destroy the ship's crue in hopes to get away.

To prevent such misfortunes, we use to visit them daily, narrowly search-ing every corner between decks, to see whether they have not found means, to gather any pieces of iron, or wood, or knives, about the ship, notwith-standing the great care we take not to leave any tools or nails, or other things in the way: which, however, cannot be always so exactly observ'd, where so many people are in the narrow compass of a ship.

We cause as many of our men as is convenient to lie in the quarter-deck and gun-room, and our principal officers in the great cabin, where we keep all our small arms in a readiness, with sentinels constantly at the doors and avenues to it; being thus ready to disappoint any attempts our slave might make on a sudden.

These precautions contribute very much to keep them in awe; and if all those who carry slaves duly observ'd them, we should not hear of so many revolts as have happen'd. Where I was concern'd, we always kept our slaves in such order, that we did not perceive the least inclination in any of them to revolt, or mutiny, and lost very few of our number in the voyage.

It is true, we allow'd them much more liberty, and us'd them with more tenderness than most other Europeans would think prudent to do; as, to have them all upon deck every day in good weather; to take their meals twice a-day, at fix'd hours, that is, at ten in the morning, and at five at night; which being ended, we made the men go down again between the decks; for the women were almost entirely at their own discretion, to be upon deck as long as they pleas'd, nay even many of the males had the same liberty by turns, successively; few or none being fetter'd or kept in shackles, and that only on account of some disturbances, or injuries, offer'd to their fellow captives, as will unavoidably happen among a numerous croud of such savage people. Besides, we allow'd each of them betwixt their meals a handful of Indian wheat and Mandioca, and now and then short pipes and tobacco to smoak upon deck by turns, and some coconuts; and to the women a piece of coarse cloth to cover them, and the same to many of the men, which we took care they did wash from time to time, to prevent vermin, which they are very subject to; and because it look'd sweeter and more agreeable. Toward the evening they diverted themselves on the deck, as they thought fit, some conversing together, others dancing, singing, and sporting after their manner, which pleased them highly, and often made us pastime; especially the female sex, who being apart from the males, on the quarterdeck, and many of them young sprightly maidens, full of jollity and good-humour, afforded us abundance of recreation; as did several little fine boys, which we mostly kept to attend on us about the ship.

We mess'd the slaves twice a day, as I have observed; the first meal was of our large beans boil'd, with a certain quantity of Muscovy lard.... The other meal was of pease, or of Indian wheat, and sometimes meal of Mandioca ... boiled with either lard, or suet, or grease by turns: and sometimes with palm-oil and malaguette or Guinea pepper. I found they had much better stomachs for beans, and it is a proper fattening food for captives....

At each meal we allow'd every slave a full coconut shell of water, and from time to time a dram of brandy, to strengthen their stomachs....

Much more might be said relating to the preservation and maintenance of slaves in such voyages, which I leave to the prudence of the officers that govern aboard, if they value their own reputation and their owners advantage; and shall only add these few particulars, that tho' we ought to be circumspect in watching the slaves narrowly, to prevent or disappoint their ill designs for our own conservation, yet must we not be too severe and haughty with them, but on the contrary, caress and humor them in every reasonable thing. Some commanders, of a morose peevish temper are perpetually beating and curbing them, even without the least offence, and will not suffer any upon deck but when unavoidable to ease themselves does require; under pretence it hinders the work of the ship and sailors and that they are troublesome by their nasty nauseous stench, or their noise; which makes those poor wretches desperate, and besides their falling into distempers thro' melancholy, often is the occasion of their destroying themselves.

Such officers should consider, those unfortunate creatures are men as well as themselves, tho' of a different colour, and pagans; and that they ought to do to others as they would be done by in like circumstances.

Source: James Barbot, Jr., "A Supplement to the Description of the Coasts of North and South Guinea," in Awnsham Churchill and John Churchill, *Collection of Voyages and Travels* (London, 1732).

2 Olaudah Equiano, Who Was Born in Eastern Nigeria, Describes the Horrors of the Middle Passage (1789)

"a multitude of black people ... chained together"

> *Olaudah Equiano vividly recounts the shock and isolation that he felt during the Middle Passage to Barbados. Note his fear that the European slavers would eat him.*

Their complexions, differing so much from ours, their long hair and the language they spoke, which was different from any I had ever heard, united to confirm me in this belief [that his European captors would eat him]. Indeed, such were the horrors of my views and fears at the moment, that if ten thousand worlds had been my own, I would have freely parted with them all to have exchanged my condition with that of the meanest slave of my own country. When I looked around the ship and saw a large furnace of copper boiling, and a multitude of black people of every description chained together, every one of their countenances expressing dejection and sorrow, I no longer doubted my fate. Quite overpowered with horror and anguish, I fell motionless on the deck and fainted. When I recovered a little, I found some black people about me, and I believe some were those who had brought me on board and had been receiving their pay. They talked to me in order to cheer me up, but all in vain. I asked them if we were not to be eaten by those white men with horrible looks, red faces and long hair. They told me I was not.

I took a little down my palate, which, instead of reviving me as they thought it would, threw me into the greatest consternation at the strange feeling it produced, having never tasted such liquor before. Soon after this, the blacks who had brought me on board went off and left me abandoned to despair.

I now saw myself deprived of all chance of returning to my native country or even the least glimpse of hope of gaining the shore, which I now considered as friendly. I even wished for my former slavery in preference to my present situation, which was filled with horrors of every kind.

There I received such a salutation in my nostrils as I had never experienced in my life. With the loathesomeness of the stench and the crying together, I became so sick and low that I was not able to eat, nor had I the least desire to taste anything. I now wished for the last friend, Death, to relieve me.

Soon, to my grief, two of the white men offered me eatables and on my refusing to eat, one of them held me fast by the hands and laid me across the windlass and tied my feet while the other flogged me severely. I had never experienced anything of this kind before. If I could have gotten over the nettings, I would have jumped over the side, but I could not. The crew used to watch very closely those of us who were not chained down to the decks, lest we should leap into the water. I have seen some of these poor African prisoners most severely cut for attempting to do so, and hourly whipped for not eating. This indeed was often the case with myself.

I inquired of these what was to be done with us. They gave me to understand we were to be carried to these white people's country to work for them. I then was a little revived, and thought if it were no worse than working, my situation was not so desperate. But still I feared that I should be put to death, the white people looked and acted in so savage a manner. I have never seen among my people such instances of brutal cruelty, and this not only shown towards us blacks, but also to some of the whites themselves.

One white man in particular I saw, when we were permitted to be on deck, flogged so unmercifully with a large rope near the foremast that he died in consequence of it, and they tossed him over the side as they would have done a brute. This made me fear these people the more, and I expected nothing less than to be treated in the same manner.

I asked them if these people had no country, but lived in this hollow place? They told me they did not but came from a distant land. "Then," said I, "how comes it that in all our country we never heard of them?"

They told me because they lived so far off. I then asked where were their women? Had they any like themselves? I was told they had.

"And why do we not see them" I asked. They answered, "Because they were left behind."

I asked how the vessel would go? They told me they could not tell, but there was cloth put upon the masts by the help of the ropes I saw, and then vessels went on, and the white men had some spell or magic they put in the water when they liked in order to stop the vessel when they liked.

I was exceedingly amazed at this account, and really thought they were spirits. I therefore wished much to be from amongst them, for I expected they would sacrifice me. But my wishes were in vain – for we were so quartered that it was impossible for us to make our escape.

At last, when the ship we were in had got in all her cargo, they made ready with many fearful noises, and we were all put under deck, so that we could not see how they managed the vessel.

The stench of the hold while we were on the coast was so intolerably loathsome, that it was dangerous to remain there for any time … some of us had been permitted to stay on the deck for the fresh air. But now that the whole ship's cargo were confined together, it became absolutely pestilential. The closeness of the place and the heat of the climate, added to the number of the ship, which was so crowded that each had scarcely room to turn himself, almost suffocated us.

This produced copious perspirations so that the air became unfit for respiration from a variety of loathsome smells, and brought on a sickness among the slaves, of which many died – thus falling victims of the improvident avarice, as I may call it, of their purchasers. This wretched situation was again aggravated by the galling of the chains, which now became insupportable, and the filth of the necessary tubs [toilets] into which the children often fell and were almost suffocated. The shrieks of the women and the groans of the dying rendered the whole a scene of horror almost inconceivable.

Happily perhaps for myself, I was soon reduced so low that it was necessary to keep me almost always on deck and from my extreme youth I was not put into fetters. In this situation I expected every hour to share the fate of my companions, some of whom were almost daily brought upon the deck at the point of death, which I began to hope would soon put an end to my miseries. Often did I think many of the inhabitants of the deep much more happy than myself. I envied them the freedom they enjoyed, and as often wished I could change my condition for theirs. Every circumstance I met with, served only to render my state more painful and heightened my apprehensions and my opinion of the cruelty of the whites.

One day, when we had a smooth sea and moderate wind, two of my wearied countrymen who were chained together (I was near them at the time), preferring death to such a life of misery, somehow made through the nettings and jumped into the sea. Immediately another quite dejected fellow, who on account of his illness was suffered to be out of irons, followed their example. I believe many more would very soon have done the same if they had not been prevented by the ship's crew, who were instantly alarmed. Those of us that were the most active were in a moment put down under the deck, and there was such a noise and confusion among the people of the ship as I never heard before to stop her and get the boat out to go after the slaves. However, two of the wretches were drowned, but they got the other and afterwards flogged him unmercifully for thus attempting to prefer death to slavery.

I can now relate hardships which are inseparable from this accursed trade. Many a time we were near suffocation from the want of fresh air, which we were often without for whole days together. This, and the stench of the necessary tubs, carried off many.

Source: Olaudah Equiano, *The Interesting Narrative of the Life of Olaudah Equiano or Gustavus Vassa the African* (London, 1789).

3 A Doctor, Alexander Falconbridge, Describes Conditions on an English Slaver (1788)

"The men Negroes ... are ... fastened together ... by handcuffs"

Alexander Falconbridge, a surgeon aboard slave ships and later the governor of a British colony for freed slaves in Sierra Leone, offers a vivid account of the Middle Passage. He provides a graphic description of how the captives are treated on shipboard, including their diet and health.

From the time of the arrival of the ships to their departure, which is usually about three months, scarce a day passes without some Negroes being purchased and carried on board; sometimes in small and sometimes in large numbers. The whole number taken on board depends on circumstances. In a voyage I once made, our stock of merchandise was exhausted in the purchase of about 380 Negroes, which was expected to have procured 500 ...

The unhappy wretches thus disposed of are bought by the black traders at fairs, which are held for that purpose, at the distance of upwards of two hundred miles from the sea coast; and these fairs are said to be supplied from an interior part of the country. Many Negroes, upon being questioned relative to the places of their nativity, have asserted that they have travelled during the revolution of several moons (their usual method of calculating time) before they have reached the places where they were purchased by the black traders.

At these fairs, which are held at uncertain periods, but generally every six weeks, several thousands are frequently exposed to sale who had been collected from all parts of the country for a very considerable distance around.... During one of my voyages, the black traders brought down, in different canoes, from twelve to fifteen hundred Negroes who had been purchased at one fair. They consisted chiefly of men and boys, the women seldom exceeding a third of the whole number. From forty to two hundred Negroes are generally purchased at a time by the black traders, according to the opulence of the buyer, and consist of all ages, from a month to sixty years and upwards. Scarcely any age or situation is deemed an exception, the price being proportionable. Women sometimes form a part of them, who happen to be so far advanced in their pregnancy as to be delivered during their journey from the fairs to the coast; and I have frequently seen instances of deliveries on board ship....

When the Negroes, whom the black traders have to dispose of, are shown to the European purchasers, they first examine them relative to their age. They then minutely inspect their persons and inquire into the state of their health; if they are inflicted with any disease or are deformed or have bad eyes or teeth; if they are lame or weak in the joints or distorted in the back or of a slender make or narrow in the chest; in short, if they have been ill or are afflicted in any manner so as to render them incapable of much labor. If any of the foregoing defects are discovered in them they are rejected. But if approved of, they are generally taken on board the ship the same evening. The purchaser has liberty to return on the following morning, but not afterwards, such as upon re-examination are found exceptionable....

Near the mainmast a partition is constructed of boards which reaches athwart the ship. This division is called a barricado. It is about eight feet in height and is made to project about two feet over the sides of the ship. In this barricado there is a door at which a sentinel is placed during the time the Negroes are permitted to come upon the deck. It serves to keep the different sexes apart; and as there are small holes in it, where blunderbusses are fixed and sometimes a cannon, it is found very convenient for quelling the insurrections that now and then happen....

The men Negroes, on being brought aboard the ship, are immediately fastened together, two and two, by handcuffs on their wrists and by irons riveted on their legs. They are then sent down between the decks and placed in an apartment partitioned off for that purpose. The women also are placed in a separate apartment between the decks, but without being ironed. An adjoining room on the same deck is appointed for the boys. Thus they are all placed in different apartments.

But at the same time, however, they are frequently stowed so close, as to admit of no other position than lying on their sides. Nor will the height between decks, unless directly under the grating, permit the indulgence of an erect posture; especially where there are platforms, which is generally the case. These platforms are a kind of shelf, about eight or nine feet in breadth, extending from the side of the ship toward the centre. They are placed nearly midway between the decks, at the distance of two or three feet from each deck. Upon these the Negroes are stowed in the same manner as they are on the deck underneath.

In each of the apartments are placed three or four large buckets, of a conical form, nearly two feet in diameter at the bottom and only one foot at the top and in depth of about twenty-eight inches, to which, when necessary, the Negroes have recourse. It often happens that those who are placed at a distance from the buckets, in endeavoring to get to them, tumble over their companions, in consequence of their being shackled. These accidents, although unavoidable, are productive of continual quarrels in which some of them are always bruised. In this distressed situation, unable to proceed and prevented from getting to the tubs, they desist from the attempt; and as the necessities of nature are not to be resisted, ease themselves as they lie. This becomes a fresh source of boils and disturbances and tends to render the condition of the poor captive wretches still more uncomfortable. The nuisance arising from these circumstances is not infrequently increased by the tubs being too small for the purpose intended and their being emptied but once every day. The rule for doing so, however, varies in different ships according to the attention paid to the health and convenience of the slaves by the captain.

About eight o'clock in the morning the Negroes are generally brought upon deck. Their irons being examined, a long chain, which is locked to a ring-bolt fixed in the deck, is run through the rings of the shackles of the men and then locked to another ring-bolt fixed also in the deck. By this means fifty or sixty and sometimes more are fastened to one chain in order to prevent them from rising or endeavoring to escape. If the weather proves favorable they are permitted to remain in that situation till four or five in the afternoon when they are disengaged from the chain and sent below.

The diet of the Negroes while on board, consists chiefly of horse beans boiled to the consistency of a pulp; of boiled yams and rice and sometimes a small quantity of beef or pork. The latter are frequently taken from the provisions laid in for the sailors. They sometimes make use of a sauce composed of palm-oil mixed with flour, water and pepper, which the sailors call slabber-sauce. Yams are the favorite food of the Eboe [Ibo] or Bight Negroes, and rice or corn of those from the Gold or Windward Coast; each preferring the produce of their native soil. . . .

They are commonly fed twice a day; about eight o'clock in the morning and four in the afternoon. In most ships they are only fed with their own food once a day. Their food is served up to them in tubs about the size of a small water bucket. They are placed round these tubs, in companies of ten to each tub, out of which they feed themselves with wooden spoons. These they soon lose and when they are not allowed others they feed themselves with their hands. In favorable weather they are fed upon deck but in bad weather their food is given them below. Numberless quarrels take place among them during their meals; more especially when they are put upon short allowance, which frequently happens if the passage form the coast of Guinea to the West Indies islands proves of unusual length. In that case, the weak are obliged to be content with a very scanty portion. Their allowance of water is about half a pint each at every meal. It is handed round in a bucket and given to each Negro in a pannekin, a small utensil with a straight handle, somewhat similar to a sauce-boat. However, when the ships approach the islands with a favourable breeze, the slaves are no longer restricted.

Upon the Negroes refusing to take sustenance, I have seen coals of fire, glowing hot, put on a shovel and placed so near their lips as to scorch and burn them. And this has been accompanied with threats of forcing them to swallow the coals if they any longer persisted in refusing to eat. These means have generally had the desired effect. I have also been credibly informed that a certain captain in the slave-trade, poured melted lead on such of his Negroes as obstinately refused their food.

Exercise being deemed necessary for the preservation of their health they are sometimes obliged to dance when the weather will permit their coming on deck. If they go about it reluctantly or do not move with agility, they are flogged; a person standing by them all the time with a cat-o'-nine-tails in his hands for the purpose. Their music, upon these occasions, consists of a drum, sometimes with only one head; and when that is worn out they make use of the bottom of one of the tubs before described. The poor wretches are frequently compelled to sing also; but when they do so, their songs are generally, as may naturally be expected, melancholy lamentations of their exile from their native country.

The women are furnished with beads for the purpose of affording them some diversion. But this end is generally defeated by the squabbles which are occasioned in consequence of their stealing from each other.

On board some ships the common sailors are allowed to have intercourse with such of the black women whose consent they can procure. And some of them have been known to take the inconstancy of their paramours so much to heart as to leap overboard and drown themselves. The officers are permitted to indulge their passions among them at pleasure and sometimes are guilty of such excesses as disgrace human nature. . . .

The hardships and inconveniences suffered by the Negroes during the passage are scarcely to be enumerated or conceived. They are far more violently affected by seasickness than Europeans. It frequently terminates in death, especially among the women. But the exclusion of fresh air is among the most intolerable. For the purpose of admitting this needful refreshment, most of the ships in the slave trade are provided, between the decks, with five or six air-ports on each side of the ship of about five inches in length and four in breadth. In addition, some ships, but not one in twenty, have what they denominate wind-sails. But whenever the sea is rough and the rain heavy it becomes necessary to shut these and every other conveyance by which the air is admitted. The fresh air being thus excluded, the Negroes' rooms soon grow intolerable hot. The confined air, rendered noxious by the effluvia exhaled from their bodies and being repeatedly breathed, soon produces fevers and fluxes, which generally carries of great numbers of them.

During the voyages I made, I was frequently witness to the fatal effects of this exclusion of fresh air. I will give one instance, as it serves to convey some idea, though a very faint one, of their terrible sufferings. . . . Some wet and blowing weather having occasioned the port-holes to be shut and the grating to be covered, fluxes and fevers among the Negroes ensued. While they were in this situation, I frequently went down among them till at length their room became so extremely hot as to be only bearable for a very short time. But the excessive heat was not the only thing that rendered their situation intolerable. The deck, that is the floor of their rooms, was so covered with the blood and mucus which had proceeded from them in consequence of the flux, that it resembled a slaughter-house. It is not in the power of the human imagination to picture a situation more dreadful or disgusting. Numbers of the slaves having fainted, they were carried upon deck where several of them died and the rest with great difficulty were restored. . . .

As very few of the Negroes can so far brook the loss of their liberty and the hardships they endure, they are ever on the watch to take advantage of the least negligence in their oppressors. Insurrections are frequently the consequence; which are seldom expressed without much bloodshed. Sometimes these are successful and the whole ship's company is cut off. They are likewise always ready to seize every opportunity for committing some acts of desperation to free themselves from their miserable state and notwith-standing the restraints which are laid, they often succeed.

Source: Alexander Falconbridge, *An Account of the Slave Trade on the Coast of Africa* (London, 1788).

4 Olaudah Equiano Describes His Arrival in the New World (1789)

"dread and trembling"

> *Olaudah Equiano offers a first-hand account of his arrival in the West Indies in 1756. He describes his initial impressions of the new environment and the procedures by which slaves were sold.*

As the vessel drew nearer, we plainly saw the harbor and other ships of different kinds and sizes and we soon anchored amongst them off Bridge-town. Many merchants and planters came on board ... They put us in separate parcels and examined us attentively. They also made us jump, and pointed to the land, signifying we were to go there. We thought by this we should be eaten by these ugly men, as they appeared to us. When soon after we were all put down under the deck again, there was much dread and trembling among us and nothing but bitter cries to be heard all the night from the apprehensions. At last the white people got some old slaves from the land to pacify us. They told us we were not to be eaten, but to work, and were soon to go on land, where we should see many of our country people. This report eased us much, and sure enough, soon after we landed, there came to us Africans of all languages.

We were conducted immediately to the merchant's yard, where we were all pent up together, like so many sheep in a fold, without regard to sex or age. As every object was new to me, everything I saw filled me with surprise. What struck me first was that the houses were built with bricks and stories, and in every respect different from those I had seen in Africa, but I was still more astonished to see people on horseback. I did not know what this could mean, and indeed I thought these people were full of nothing but magical arts. While I was in this astonishment, one of my fellow prisoners spoke to a countryman of his about the horses who said they were the same kind they had in their country. I understood them, though they were from a distant part of Africa and I thought it odd I had not seen any horses there; but afterwards when I came to converse with different Africans, I found they had many horses amongst them, and much larger than those I then saw.

We were not many days in the merchant's custody, before we were sold after their usual manner... On a signal given, (as the beat of a drum), buyers rush at once into the yard where the slaves are confined, and make a choice of that parcel they like best. The noise and clamor with which this is attended, and the eagerness visible in the countenances of the buyers, serve not a little to increase the apprehension of terrified Africans ... In this manner, without scruple, are relations and friends separated, most of them never to see each other again. I remember in the vessel in which I was brought over ... there were several brothers who, in the sale, were sold in different lots; and it was very moving on this occasion, to see and hear their cries in parting.

Source: Olaudah Equiano, *The Interesting Narrative of the Life of Olaudah Equiano or Gustavus Vassa the African* (London, 1789).

5 An English Physician, Alexander Falconbridge, Describes the Treatment of Newly Arrived Slaves in the West Indies (1788)

"Various deceptions are used in the disposal of sick slaves"

Alexander Falconbridge describes the reaction of enslaved Africans to their sale. He also offers an especially unsettling description of how traders dealt with slaves who were sick.

When the ships arrive in the West Indies (the chief mart for this inhuman merchandize), the slaves are disposed as I have before observed by different methods. Sometimes the mode of disposal is that of selling them by what is termed a scramble, and a day is soon fixed for that purpose. Previously the sick or refuse slaves, of which there are frequently many, are usually conveyed on shore and sold at a tavern, by vendue or public auction. These in general are purchased ... upon speculation, at so low a price as five or six dollars a head. I was informed by a mulatto woman that she purchased a sick slave at Grenada, upon speculation, for the small sum of one dollar, as the poor wretch was apparently dying of the flux. It seldom happens that any who are carried ashore in the emaciated state to which they are generally reduced by that disorder long survive after their landing. I once saw sixteen conveyed on shore and sold in the foregoing manner, the whole of whom died before I left the island. Sometimes the captains march their slaves through the town at which they intend to dispose of them, and then place them in rows where they are examined and purchased.

The mode of selling them by scramble having fallen under my observation the oftenest, I shall be more particular in describing it. Being some years ago, at one of the islands in the West Indies, I was witness to a sale by scramble, where about 250 Negroes were sold. Upon this occasion all the Negroes scrambled for bear an equal price; which is agreed upon between the captains and the purchasers before the sale begins. On a day appointed, the Negroes were landed and placed together in a large yard belonging to the merchants to whom the ship was consigned. As soon as the hour agreed on arrived, the doors of the yard were suddenly thrown open and in rushed a considerable number of purchasers, with all the ferocity of brutes. Some instantly seized such of the Negroes as they could conveniently lay hold of with their hands. Others being prepared with several handkerchiefs tied together, encircled as many as they were able. While others, by means of a rope, effected the same purpose. It is scarcely possible to describe the confusion of which this mode of selling is productive. It likewise causes much animosity among the purchasers who not infrequently fall out and quarrel with each other. The poor astonished Negroes were so terrified by these proceedings, that several of them, through fear climbed over the walls of the courtyard and ran wild about the town, but were soon hunted down and retaken. . . .

Various deceptions are used in the disposal of sick slaves and many of these must excite in every humane mind the liveliest sensations of horror. I have been well informed that a Liverpool captain boasted of his having cheated some Jews by the following stratagem. A lot of slaves afflicted with the flux, being about to be landed for sale, he directed the ship's surgeons to stop the anus of each of them with oakum. Thus prepared they were landed and taken to the accustomed place of sale, where, being unable to stand but for a very short time, they were usually permitted to sit. The buyers, when they examined them, oblige them to stand up in order to see if there be any discharge; and when they do not perceive this appearance they consider it as a symptom of recovery. In the present instance, such an appearance being prevented, the bargain was struck and the slaves were accordingly sold. But it was not long before discovery ensued. The excruciating pain which the prevention of a discharge of such an acrimonious nature occasioned, not being able to be borne by the poor wretches, the temporary obstruction was removed and the deluded purchasers were speedily convinced of the imposition.

Source: Alexander Falconbridge, *An Account of the Slave Trade on the Coast of Africa* (London, 1788).

Discussion Questions

1. How long did the Middle Passage take, how many Africans were forcibly transported to the Americas, and what proportion died along the way?
2. What were conditions like on shipboard?
3. How frequently did shipboard revolts take place and how did crew members seek to inhibit revolts?
4. The period after arrival in the New World was called "seasoning." What happened during this period?
5. How, according to the accounts, were captives treated after their arrival in the New World, and how did they respond?
6. What were the characteristics of a slave sale?

Chapter 3   "A Change is Gonna Come": Slavery in the Era of the American Revolution

When Thomas Jefferson was born in 1743, slavery was a radically different institution than it was when he died 83 years later. In the early eighteenth century, slaves grew tobacco or rice – not cotton. Slavery was concentrated along the Atlantic coast – not in the black belt of Alabama, Mississippi, Louisiana, and Texas. A significant proportion of the enslaved population consisted of native-born Africans, and few slaves had converted to Christianity. Equally striking, slavery was not yet a sectional institution. Before the American Revolution, slaves could be found in each of the 13 colonies. Perhaps the most glaring difference was that in the 1740s slavery was not yet a moral issue. Not a single religious denomination had yet denounced slavery and every major Western European country was involved in the African slave trade.

It was the American Revolution that transformed slavery into an explosive moral issue. The Revolution was justified by principles that undercut earlier rationalizations for slavery, and the first Continental Congress called for an end to the African slave trade. The American revolutionaries defended their cause on the grounds that all human beings shared certain inalienable rights, including the right to life, liberty, and equality. This revolutionary ideology was reinforced by an evangelical religion that was hostile to any compromises with sin.

Among the Revolution's most radical consequences was that it inspired every northern state to abolish slavery, either by legislative action or by court decision, or to adopt a gradual emancipation scheme. Many of these schemes worked extremely slowly. Slavery was not ended in Connecticut until 1848 and there were still slaves in New Jersey on the eve of the Civil War. Nevertheless, the northern states had made a crucial ideological commitment to emancipation.

The Revolution's very outcome depended on slavery. British threats to emancipate slaves who joined the British army had the unexpected consequence of encouraging many conservative southern planters to support the American Patriots. The Revolution profoundly disrupted the institution of slavery, freeing some 5,000 slaves in Georgia and 25,000 in South Carolina.

The Revolution had contradictory consequences for the institution of slavery. By the 1790s, slavery had grown more entrenched in the South and a virulent racial prejudice had grown in all parts of the new nation. At the same time, however, slavery came under attack like never before. Enslaved African Americans themselves began to speak the language of natural rights, and demanded liberty as a God-given right.

1 The Poet Phillis Wheatley Writes about Freedom and Equal Rights (1774)

"in every human breast God has implanted a principle ... impatient of oppression"

Born most likely in the Senegambia region of western Africa, Phillis Wheatley was the first enslaved African American and third woman to publish a book of poems in the American colonies. Kidnapped when she was around the age of seven, she was purchased by the wife of a wealthy Boston tailor. At the time she arrived in Boston, there were about 230,000 African Americans in the British colonies and about 16,000 slaves in New England.

Educated in English, Latin, literature, and philosophy, she published her first poem in a Newport, Rhode Island, newspaper in 1767, when she was only 14. In 1773, she published a collection entitled Poems on Various Subjects, Religious and Moral. *To dispel rumors that she was not the author of the poems, a committee examined her and testified that they believed she had written the poems herself.*

The Revolution enabled thousands of enslaved women and children to secure their freedom. In some cases, they were emancipated by their owners, like Wheatley, who was freed after her mistress's death in 1774. But in many instances, wartime disruptions allowed mothers and their children to flee from bondage. During the course of the Revolution, a third of the slaves in Georgia and a quarter in South Carolina freed themselves by running away.

This letter to the Rev. Samson Occom, a Presbyterian clergyman and a member of the Mohegan nation, written in 1774, illustrates how the colonial struggle against British imperial authority raised fundamental questions about freedom, equality, and natural rights.

Reverend and honoured Sir,

I have this day received your obliging kind epistle, and am greatly satisfied with your reasons respecting the negroes, and think highly reasonable what you offer in vindication of their natural rights: Those that invade them cannot be insensible that the divine light is chasing away the thick darkness which broods over the land of Africa; and the chaos which has reigned so long, is converting into beautiful order, and reveals more and more clearly the glorious dispensation of civil and religious liberty, which are so inseparably united, that there is little or no enjoyment of one without the other: Otherwise, perhaps, the Israelites had been less solicitous for their freedom from Egyptian slavery; I do not say they would have been contented without it, by no means; for in every human breast God has implanted a principle, which we call love of Freedom; it is impatient of oppression, and pants for deliverance; and by the leave of our modern Egyptians I will assert, that the same principle lives in us. God grant deliverance in his own way and time, and get him honour upon all those whose avarice impels them to countenance and help forward the calamities of their fellow creatures. This I desire not for their hurt, but to convince them of the strange absurdity of their conduct, whose words and actions are so diametrically opposite. How well the cry for liberty, and the reverse disposition for the exercise of oppressive power over others agree – I humbly think it does not require the penetration of a philosopher to determine.

Source: Phillis Wheatley, *Connecticut Gazette*, March 11, 1774.

2 Massachusetts Slaves Petition for Freedom (1774)

"we have in common with all other men a naturel right to our freedoms"

The ideology of the American Revolution, with its emphasis on freedom and equality, was seized upon by enslaved African Americans, who pointed out the inconsistency of slaveholders fighting for their own liberty even as they deprived blacks of theirs. In 1774, before the Revolution had begun, a group of Massachusetts slaves invoked the language of natural rights in a petition to the colony's governor and assembly.

The Petition of a Grate Number of Blackes of this Province who by divine permission are held in a state of Slavery within the bowels of a free and christian Country

Humbly Shewing

That your Petitioners apprehind we have in common with all other men a naturel right to our freedoms without Being depriv'd of them by our fellow men as we are a freeborn Pepel and have never forfeited this Blessing by aney compact or agreement whatever. But we were unjustly dragged by the cruel hand of power from our dearest frinds and sum of us stolen from the bosoms of our tender Parents and from a Populous Pleasant and plentiful country and Brought hither to be made slaves for Life in a Christian land. Thus are we deprived of every thing that hath a tendency to make life even tolerable, the endearing ties of husband and wife we are strangers to for we are no longer man and wife then our masters or mestreses thinkes proper marred or onmarred. Our children are also taken from us by force and sent maney miles from us wear we seldom or never see them again there to be made slaves of for Life which sumtimes is vere short by Reson of Being dragged from their mothers Breest Thus our Lives are imbittered to us on these accounts By our deplorable situation we are rendered incapable of shewing our obedience to Almighty God how can a slave perform the duties of a husband to a wife or parent to his child How can a husband leave master and work and cleave to his wife How can the wife submit themselves to there husbands in all things. How can the child obey thear parents in all things. There is a grat number of us sencear ... members of the Church of Christ how can the master and the slave be said to fulfil that command Live in love let Brotherly Love contuner and abound Beare yea onenothers Bordenes How can the master be said to Beare my Borden when he Beares me down whith the Have chanes of slavery and operson against my will and how can we fulfill our parte of duty to him whilst in this condition and as we cannot searve our God as we ought whilst in this situation Nither can we reap an equal benefet from the laws of the Land which doth not justifi but condemns Slavery or if there had bin aney Law to hold us in Bondege we are Humbely of the Opinon ther never was aney to inslave our children for life when Born in a free Countrey. We therefor Bage your Excellency and Honours will give this its deu weight and consideration and that you will accordingly cause an act of the legislative to be pessed that we may obtain our Natural right our freedoms and our children be set at lebety at the yeare

of Twenty one for whoues sekes more petequeley your Petitioners is in Duty
ever to Pray.

Source: May 25, 1774, Massachusetts Historical Society *Collections*, 5th ser.
(1871–87), 3.

3 Virginia's Royal Governor Promises Freedom to Slaves Who Join the British Army (1775)

"I do hereby further declare all indented Servants, Negroes, or others,
(appertaining to Rebels,) free that are able and willing to bear Arms"

> *The American Revolution made slavery into an inescapable moral problem.*
> *The American revolutionaries were convinced that the British Parliament was*
> *seeking to reduce them to political slavery, and it proved impossible to ignore*
> *the parallel between political slavery and chattel slavery.*
>   *African American soldiers served with valor at the battles of Lexington and*
> *Bunker Hill. In November 1775, however, Congress, fearful of the reaction of*
> *southern slaveholders, voted to bar blacks from enlisting. On November 17,*
> *1775, Virginia's royal governor, Lord Dunmore, whose forces had been*
> *reduced to just 300 men, offered to emancipate slaves who joined the Royal*
> *Army. More than 700 flocked to his lines. Fear that Lord Dunmore's*
> *proclamation would lead even more slaves to join the British army led*
> *Congress reluctantly to reverse its decision.*

As I have ever entertained Hopes, that an Accommodation might have taken
Place between GREAT-BRITAIN and this Colony, without being compelled
by my Duty to this most disagreeable but now absolutely necessary Step,
rendered so by a Body of armed Men unlawfully assembled, firing on His
MAJESTY'S Tenders, and the formation of an Army, and that Army now on
their March to attack his MAJESTY'S Troops and destroy the well disposed
subjects of the Colony. To defeat such treasonable Purposes, and that all
such Traitors, and their Abettors, may be brought to Justice, and that the
Peace, and good Order of this Colony may be again restored, which the
ordinary Course of the Civil Law is unable to effect; I have thought fit to
issue this my Proclamation, hereby declaring, that until the aforesaid good
Purpose can be obtained, I do in Virtue of the Power and Authority to ME
given, by His MAJESTY, determine to execute Martial Law, and cause the
same to be executed throughout this Colony: and to the end that Peace and

good Order may the sooner be restored, I do require every Person capable of bearing Arms, to resort to His MAJESTY'S STANDARD, or be looked upon as Traitors to His MAJESTY'S Crown and Government, and thereby become liable to the Penalty the Law inflicts upon such Offenses; such as forfeiture of Life, confiscation of Lands, &. &. And I do hereby further declare all indented Servants, Negroes, or others, (appertaining to Rebels,) free that are able and willing to bear Arms, they joining His MAJESTY'S Troops as soon as may be, soe the more speedily reducing this Colony to a proper Sense of their Duty, to His MAJESTY'S Crown and Dignity. I do further order, and require, all His MAJESTY'S Liege Subjects, to retain their Quitrents, or any other Taxes due or that may become due, in their own Custody, till such a Time as Peace may be again restored to this at present most unhappy Country, or demanded of them for their former salutary Purposes, by Officers properly to receive the same.

Source: Reuben Gold Thwaites and Louise Phelps Kellogg, eds., *Documentary History of Dunmore's War* (Madison, 1905).

4 Virginia's Assembly Denounces Lord Dunmore's Proclamation (1775)

"encouragement to a general insurrection"

Virginia's Assembly responded to Lord Dunmore's proclamation by branding it an incitement to slave insurrection and announced that slaves who deserted their masters and joined the British army would be subject to the most severe penalty.

Virginia, Dec. 14, 1775.

By the Representatives of the People of the Colony and Dominion of VIRGINIA, assembled in GENERAL CONVENTION

A DECLARATION

WHEREAS lord Dunmore, by his proclamation, dated on board the ship William, off Norfolk, the 7th day of November 1775, hath offered freedom to such able-bodied slaves as are willing to join him, and take up arms, against the good people of this colony, giving thereby encouragement to a general insurrection, which may induce a necessity of inflicting the severest punishments upon those unhappy people, already deluded by his base and insidious arts; and whereas, by an act of the General Assembly now in force in this colony, it is enacted, that all negro or other slaves, conspiring to rebel or make insurrection, shall suffer death, and be excluded all benefit of clergy: We think it proper to declare, that all slaves who have been, or shall be seduced, by his lordship's proclamation, or other arts, to desert their masters' service, and take up arms against the inhabitants of this colony, shall be liable to such punishment as shall hereafter be directed by the General Convention. And to that end all such, who have taken this unlawful and wicked step, may return in safety to their duty, and escape the punishment due to their crimes, we hereby promise pardon to them, they surrendering themselves to Col. William Woodford, or any other commander of our troops, and not appearing in arms after the publication hereof. And we do farther earnestly recommend it to all humane and benevolent persons in this colony to explain and make known this our offer of mercy to those unfortunate people.

EDMUND PENDLETON, president.

Source: Virginia. General Assembly. House of Burgesses. *The proceedings of the House of Burgesses of Virginia, : convened in General Assembly, on Thursday the first day of June, 1775 .... Williamsburg, Va., [1775].

5   Connecticut Slaves Petition for Freedom (1779)

"without any Crime, by them committed, doomed, and bound down, to perpetual Slavery"

> In 1779, slaves in Fairfield County, Connecticut, sent a petition to the state
> assembly denouncing slavery. Both houses of the assembly rejected the
> petition.

That many of your Petitioners, were (as they verily believe) most unjustly torn, from the Bosoms of their dear Parents, and Friends, and without any Crime, by them committed, doomed, and bound down, to perpetual Slavery; and as if the Perpetrators of this horrid Wickedness, were Conscious (that we poor Ignorant africans, upon the least Glimmering Light, derived from a Knowledge of the Sense and Practice of civilized Nations) should Convince them of their Sin, they have added another dreadful Evil of holding us in gross Ignorance, so as to render Our Subjection more easy and tolerable. may it please your Honours, we are most grievously affected, under the Consideration of the flagrant Injustice; Your Honours who are nobly contending, in the Cause of Liberty, whose Conduct excites the Admiration, and Reverence, of all the great Empires of the World, will not resent our thus freely animadverting, on this detestable Practice; altho our Skins are different in Colour, from those who we serve, yet Reason & Revelation join to declare, that we are the Creatures of that God who made of one Blood, and Kindred, all the Nations of the Earth; we perceive by our own Reflection, that we are endowed, with the same Faculties, with our Masters, and there is nothing, that leads us to a Belief, or Suspicion, that we are any more obliged to serve them, than they us, and the more we Consider of this Matter, the more we are Convinced, of our Right (by the Law's of Nature and by the whole Tenor, of the Christian Religion, so far as we have been taught) to be free; we have Endeavoured rightly to understand, what is our Right, and what is our Duty, and can never be convinced, that we were made to be Slaves Altho God almighty, may justly lay this, and more, upon us, yet we deserve it not, from the hands of Men. we are impatient under the grievous Yoke, but our Reason teaches us, that it is not best for us, to use violent measures, to cast it off; we are also Convinced, that we are unable to extricate ourselves, from our abject State; but we think we may with the greatest Propriety, look up to your Honours, (who are the fathers of the People) for Relief. And we not only groan under our own Burden, but with Concern & Horror, look forward & Contemplate, the miserable Condition, of our Children, who are training up, and kept in Preparation, for a like State of Bondage, and Servitude. We beg leave to submit to your Honours serious Consideration, whether it is Consistent with the Present Claims, of the united States to hold so many Thousands, of the Race of Adam, our Common Father, in perpetual Slavery. Can human Nature endure the Shocking Idea? can your Honours any longer Suffer, this great Evil to prevail, under your Government? we entreat your Honours, let no Considerations of Publick Inconvenience, deter your Honours, from interposing in Behalf of your Petitioners; who ask for nothing, but what we are fully persuaded, is ours to Claim. we beseech your Honours, to weigh this Matter, in the Scale of Justice, and in your great Wisdom and Goodness, apply such Remedy, as the Evil does require; and let your Petitioners. rejoice with your Honours, in the Participation, with your Honours, of that inestimable Blessing.

Source: Revolutionary War Papers, State Archives collection of the Connecticut State Library, ser. 1, vol. 37, document 232.

6 Boston King, a Black Loyalist, Seeks Freedom Behind British Lines (1798)

"the horrors and devastation of war"

Born near Charleston, South Carolina, around 1760, Boston King was one of thousands of slaves who fled to British lines during the Revolution. When the Revolutionary war was over, the British resettled King and hundreds of other black loyalists in Nova Scotia. But the harsh climate and inadequate food left many free blacks near starvation. In 1792, King was among nearly 1,200 blacks in Nova Scotia who were resettled in the British colony of Sierra Leone in West Africa.

My father was stolen away from Africa when he was young.... He was beloved by this master, and had the charge of the Plantation as a driver for many years. In his old age he was employed as a mill-cutter.... My mother was employed chiefly in attending upon those that were sick, having some knowledge of the virtue of herbs, which she learned from the Indians. She likewise had the care of making the people's clothes, and on these accounts was indulged with many privileges which the rest of the slaves were not.

When I was six years old I waited in the house upon my master. I my 9th year I was put to mind the cattle.... Being obliged to travel in different parts of America with racehorses, I suffered many hardships. Happening one time to lose a boot belonging to the Groom, he would not suffer me to have any shoes all that Winter, which was a great punishment to me. When 16 years old, I was bound apprentice to a trade. After being in the shop about two years, I had the charge of my master's tools, which being very good, were often used by the men, if I happened to be out of the way: When this was the case, or any of them were lost, or misplaced, my master beat me severely, striking me upon my head, or any other part without mercy....

Having obtained leave one day to see my parents, who had lived about 12 miles off, and it being late before I could go, I was obliged to borrow one of ... [a neighbor's] horses; but a servant of my master's, took the horse from me to go a little journey, and stayed two or three days longer than he ought. This involved me in the greatest perplexity, and I expected the severest punishment, because the gentleman to who the horse belonged was a very bad man, and knew not how to shew mercy. To escape his cruelty, I determined to go to Charles-Town, and throw myself into the hands of the English. They received me readily, and I began to feel the happiness, liberty, of which I knew nothing before, altho' I was grieved at first, to be obliged to leave my friends, and among strangers. In this situation I was seized with the smallpox and suffered great hardships; for all the Blacks affected with that disease, were ordered to be carried a mile from the camp, lest the soldiers should be infected, and disabled from marching. This was a grievous circumstance to me and many others. We lay sometimes a whole day without any thing to eat or drink....

[In 1783] the horrors and devastation of war happily terminated and peace was restored between America and Great Britain, which diffused universal joy among all parties; except us, who had escaped from slavery and taken refuge in the English army; for a report prevailed at New-York, that all the slaves, in number 2000, were to be delivered up to their masters altho' some of them had been three or four years among the English. This dreadful rumour filled us all with inexpressible anguish and terror, especially when we saw our old masters coming from Virginia, North Carolina, and other parts, and seizing upon their slaves in the streets of New York, or even dragging them out of their beds. Many of the slaves had very cruel masters, so that the thoughts of returning home with them embittered life to us. For some days we lost our appetite for food, and sleep departed from our eyes. The English had compassion upon us in the day of distress, and issued out a Proclamation, importing, That all slaves should be free, who had taken refuge in the British lines, and claimed the sanction and privileges of the Proclamations respecting the security and protection of Negroes. In consequence of this, each of us received a certificate from the commanding officer at New-York, which dispelled all our fears, and filled us with joy and gratitude. Soon after, ships were fitted out, and furnished with every necessary for conveying us to Nova Scotia. We arrived at Birch Town in the month of August, where we all safely landed. Every family had a lot of land, and we exerted all our strength in order to build comfortable huts before the cold weather set in.

[Nova Scotia] was visited with a dreadful famine.... Many of the poor people were compelled to sell their best gowns for five pounds of flour, in order to support life. When they had parted with all their clothes, even to their blankets, several of them fell down dead in the streets, thro' hunger. Some killed and eat their dogs and cats; and poverty and distress prevailed on every side; so that to my great grief I was obliged to leave Birchtown, because I could get no employment. I traveled from place to place, to procure the necessaries of life, but in vain....

Source: Boston King, "Memoirs of the Life of Boston King, A Black Preacher. Written by Himself, during his Residence at Kingswood School," *Methodist Magazine*, March–June 1798.

7 A Participant in Gabriel's Rebellion Explains Why He Took Part in the Attempted Insurrection (1812)

"I have adventured my life ... to obtain ... liberty"

> *In 1800 a group of slaves in Virginia plotted to seize the city of Richmond. Led by a man known as Gabriel, the insurrection was inspired in part by the slave revolt that began in the French colony of Saint-Domingue (Haiti) in 1791. It was also motivated by the ideals of liberty and natural rights that had led the American colonists to revolt against Britain. About 30 of the accused conspirators were executed and many others were sold as slaves to Spanish and Portuguese colonies. Here, a visitor to Virginia describes why one of the slaves had decided to participate in Gabriel's revolt.*

In the afternoon I passed by a field in which several poor slaves had lately been executed, on the charge of having an intention to rise against their masters. A lawyer who was present at their trials at Richmond, informed me that on one of them being asked, what he had to say to the court, in his defence, he replied, in a manly tone of voice: "I have nothing more to offer than what General Washington would have had to offer, had he been taken by the British and put to trial by them. I have adventured my life in endeavouring to obtain the liberty of my countrymen, and am a willing sacrifice in their cause: and I beg, as a favour, that I may be immediately led to execution. I know that you have pre-determined to shed my blood, why then all this mockery of a trial?"

Source: Robert Sutcliff, *Travels in some parts of North America in the years 1804, 1805, & 1806* (Philadelphia, 1812).

8 Gabriel's Brother Explains the Rebellion's Objectives (1800)

"we might conquer the white people"

> *Solomon describes his brother Gabriel's plan for overthrowing white rule in Virginia. He also explains why Gabriel thought the plan had a realistic chance of success.*

My brother Gabriel was the person who influenced me to join him and others in order that (as he said) we might conquer the white people and possess ourselves of their property. I enquired how we were to effect it. He said by falling upon them (the whites) in the dead of night, at which time they would be unguarded and unsuspicious.... He applied to me to make scythe-swords, which I did to the number of twelve. Every Sunday he came to Richmond to provide ammunition and to find where the military stores were deposited. Gabriel informed me, in case of success that they intended to subdue the whole of the country where slavery was permitted, but no further.

The first places Gabriel intended to attack in Richmond were, the Capitol, the Magazine, the Penitentiary, the Governor's house and his person. The inhabitants were to be massacred, save those who begged for quarter and agreed to serve as soldiers with them. The reason why the insurrection was to be made at this particular time was, the discharge of the number of soldiers, one or two months ago, which induced Gabriel to believe the plan would be more easily executed.

Source: H. W. Flournoy, ed., *Calender of Virginia State Papers and Other Manuscripts from January 1, 1799, to December 31, 1807; preserved in the Capitol at Richmond*, 11 vols (Richmond, 1890).

9 President Thomas Jefferson Tries to Arrange for the Deportation of Men Involved in Gabriel's Rebellion (1802)

"There is a strong sentiment that there has been hanging enough"

Thomas Jefferson recognized that the Virginian slaves had been motivated by the same ideals that had inspired white colonists to revolt against Britain. In a letter to the US Minister to Britain, Jefferson proposed that a group of the insurgent slaves be deported to Sierra Leone in West Africa, where an English abolitionist organization had established Freetown as a home for former slaves. Jefferson told the minister to assure the British that the rebel slaves were not criminals, but men aspiring to freedom.

The negotiations with the British were unsuccessful, and most of the accused conspirators were sold as slaves to Spain's and Portugal's New World colonies. For Jefferson, Gabriel's Rebellion reinforced his view that race war could be avoided only if emancipation were tied to expatriation–what came to be called colonization.

There is a strong sentiment that there has been hanging enough. The other states & the world at large will forever condemn us if we indulge in a principle of revenge, or go one step beyond absolute necessity.... Our situation is indeed a difficult one: for I doubt whether these people can ever be permitted to go at large among us with safety. To reprieve them and keep them in prison till the meeting of the legislature will encourage efforts for their release.... Surely the legislature would pass a law for their exportation, the proper measure on this & all similar occasions?

Source: Paul Leicester Ford, ed., *The Writings of Thomas Jefferson*, vol. VII, 1795–1801 (New York, 1896).

Discussion Questions

1. How were white American patriots able to reconcile their struggle for liberty with the reality of slavery?
2. Why did the Revolution weaken slavery in the North while failing to undermine it in the South?
3. How did African Americans respond to the revolutionary call for liberty and equality?

Chapter 4   "We Raise de Wheat, Dey Gib Us de Corn": Conditions of Life

In 1852, the *New York Times* commissioned Frederick Law Olmsted to travel through the Cotton Kingdom and conduct an objective investigation of slavery. His assignment: to assess slaves' working conditions, the type of food they ate, the use of the whip by masters and overseers, and the amount of free time available to slaves. For 14 months, Olmsted crisscrossed the South on horseback, stagecoach, and train; then, between 1856 and 1860, he published three volumes of his observations. He depicted slavery as a wasteful and inefficient system, which degraded labor, exhausted the soil, and deprived slaves of any incentives to work hard. He charged that planters, fearful of sabotage or carelessness, provided slaves with only simple, heavy implements, and depicted slave labor as crude, brutish work.

Historians now know that Olmsted's portrait of slavery was seriously distorted. Far from being inefficient, slave labor was highly productive. While cultivating cotton, rice, and tobacco was hard, back-breaking work, it also required a high degree of care and skill. Moreover, many slaves served as skilled craftsmen, working as blacksmiths, butchers, carpenters, coopers, bricklayers, metal workers, tanners, weavers, and wheelwrights.

1 A Free Black Kidnapped from New York, Solomon Northrup, Describes the Working Conditions of Slaves on a Louisiana Cotton Plantation (1853)

"there is no such thing as rest"

Solomon Northrup was a free black who was kidnapped in New York and sold into slavery for 12 years. He was finally returned to freedom through the efforts of New York's governor. In the following selection he describes how cotton was raised on his Louisiana plantation.

The hands are required to be in the cotton field as soon as it is light in the morning, and, with the exception of ten or fifteen minutes, which is given them at noon to swallow their allowance of cold bacon, they are not permitted to be a moment idle until it is too dark to see, and when the moon is full, they often times labor till the middle of the night. They do not dare to stop even at dinner time, nor return to the quarters, however late it be, until the order to halt is given by the driver.

The day's work over in the field, the baskets are "toted," or in other words, carried to the gin-house, where the cotton is weighed. No matter how fatigued and weary he may be – no matter how much he longs for sleep and rest – a slave never approaches the gin-house with his basket of cotton but with fear. If it falls short in weight – if he has not performed the full task appointed him, he knows that he must suffer. And if he has exceeded it by ten or twenty pounds, in all probability his master will measure the next day's task accordingly. So, whether he has too little or too much, his approach to the gin-house is always with fear and trembling. Most frequently they have too little, and therefore they are not anxious to leave the field. After weighing, follow the whippings; and then the baskets are carried to the cotton house, and their contents stored away like hay, all hands being sent in to tramp it down. If the cotton is not dry, instead of taking it to the gin-house at once, it is laid upon platforms, two feet high, and some three times as wide, covered with boards or plank, with narrow walks running between them.

This done, the labor of the day is not yet ended, by any means. Each one must then attend to his respective chores. One feeds the mules, another the swine – another cuts the wood, and so forth; besides, the packing is all done by candle light. Finally, at a late hour, they reach the quarters, sleepy and overcome with the long day's toil. Then a fire must be kindled in the cabin, the corn ground in the small hand-mill, and supper, and dinner for the next day in the field, prepared. All that is allowed them is corn and bacon, which is given out at the corncrib and smoke-house every Sunday morning. Each one receives, as his weekly allowance, three and a half pounds of bacon, and corn enough to make a peck of meal. That is all – no tea, coffee, sugar, and with the exception of a very scanty sprinkling now and then, no salt....

An hour before day light the horn is blown. Then the slaves arouse, prepare their breakfast, fill a gourd with water, in another deposit their dinner of cold bacon and corn cake, and hurry to the field again. It is an offense invariably followed by a flogging, to be found at the quarters after daybreak. Then the fears and labors of another day begin; and until its close there is no such thing as rest....

In the month of January, generally, the fourth and last picking is completed. Then commences the harvesting of corn.... Ploughing, planting, picking cotton, gathering the corn, and pulling and burning stalks, occupies the whole of the four seasons of the year. Drawing and cutting wood, pressing cotton, fattening and killing hogs are but incidental labors.

Source: Solomon Northrup, *Twelve Years a Slave: Narrative of Solomon Northrup* (Auburn, N.Y., 1853).

2 Charles Ball, a Slave in Maryland, South Carolina, and Georgia, Compares Working Conditions on Tobacco and Cotton Plantations (1858)

"The general features of slavery are the same everywhere"

> *For 40 years, Charles Ball toiled as a slave in Maryland, South Carolina, and Georgia, and, according to his autobiography, managed to escape twice. In the following selection, he describes the regimen on a tobacco plantation.*

In Maryland and Virginia, although the slaves are treated with so much rigour, and oftimes with so much cruelty, I have seen instances of the greatest tenderness of feeling on the part of their owners. I, myself, had three masters in Maryland, and I cannot say now, even after having resided so many years in a state where slavery is not tolerated, that either of them (except the last, who sold me to the Georgians, and was an unfeeling man,) used me worse than they had a moral right to do, regarding me merely as an article of property, and not entitled to any rights as a man, political or civil.

My mistresses, in Maryland, were all good women; and the mistress of my wife, in whose kitchen I spent my Sundays and many of my nights, for several years, was a lady of most benevolent and kindly feelings. She was a true friend to me, and I shall always venerate her memory. . . .

If the proprietors of the soil in Maryland and Virginia, were skillful cultivators – had their lands in good condition – and kept no more slaves on each estate, than would be sufficient to work the soil in a proper manner, and kept up the repairs of the place – the condition of the coloured people would not be, by any means, a comparatively unhappy one. I am convinced, that in nine cases in ten, the hardships and suffering of the coloured population of lower Virginia, are attributable to the poverty and distress of its owners. In many instances, an estate scarcely yields enough to feed and clothe the slaves in a comfortable manner, without allowing any thing for the support of the master and family; but it is obvious, that the family must first be supported, and the slaves must be content with the surplus – and this, on a poor, old, worn out tobacco plantation, is often very small, and wholly inadequate to the comfortable sustenance of the hands, and they are called. There, in many places, nothing is allowed to the poor Negro, but his peck of corn per week, without the sauce of a salt herring, or even a little salt itself. . . .

The general features of slavery are the same everywhere; but the utmost rigour of the system, is only to be met with, on the cotton plantations of Carolina and Georgia, or in the rice fields which skirt the deep swamps and morasses of the southern rivers. In the tobacco fields of Maryland and Virginia, great cruelties are practiced – not so frequently by the owners, as by the overseers of the slaves; but yet, the tasks are not so excessive as in the cotton region, nor is the press of labour so incessant throughout the year. It is true, that from the period when the tobacco plants are set in the field, there is no resting time until it is housed; but it is planted out about the first of May, and must be cut and taken out of the field before the frost comes. After it is hung and dried, the labor of stripping and preparing it for the hogshead in leaf, or of manufacturing it into twist, is comparatively a work of leisure and ease. Besides, on almost every plantation the hands are able to complete the work of preparing the tobacco by January, and sometimes earlier; so that the winter months, form some sort of respite from the toils of the year. The people are obliged, it is true, to occupy themselves in cutting wood for the house, making rails and repairing fences, and in clearing new land, to raise the tobacco plants for the next year; but as there is usually time enough, and to spare, for the completion of all this work, before the season arrives for setting the plants in the field; the men are seldom flogged much, unless they are very lazy or negligent, and the women are allowed to remain in the house, in the very cold, snowy, or rainy weather. . . .

In Maryland I never knew a mistress or a young mistress, who would not listen to the complaints of the slaves. It is true, we were always obliged to approach the door of the mansion, with our hats in our hands, and the most subdued and beseeching language in our mouths – but, in return, we generally received words of kindness, and very often a redress of our grievances; though I have known very great ladies, who would never grant any request from the plantation hands, but always referred them and their petitions to their master, under a pretence, that they could not meddle with things that did not belong to the house. The mistresses of the great families, generally gave mild language to the slaves; though they sometimes sent for the overseer and have them severely flogged; but I have never heard any mistress, in either Maryland or Virginia, indulge in the low, vulgar and profane vituperations, of which I was myself the object, in Georgia, for many years, whenever I came into the presence of my mistress. Flogging – though often severe and excruciating in Maryland, is not practiced with the order, regularity and system, to which it is often reduced in the South. On the Potomac, if a slave gives offence, he is generally chastised on the spot, in the field where he is at work, as the overseer always carried a whip – sometimes a twisted cow-hide, sometimes a kind of horse-whip, and very often a simple hickory switch or gad, cut in the adjoining woods. For stealing meat, or other provisions, or for any of the higher offences, the slaves are stripped, tied up by the hands – sometimes by the thumbs – and whipped at the quarter – but many times, on a large tobacco plantation, there is not more than one of these regular whippings in a week – though on others, where the master happens to be a bad man, or a drunkard – the back of the unhappy Maryland slaves, is seamed with scars from his neck to his hips.

Source: Charles Ball, *Fifty Years in Chains; or, the Life of an American Slave* (New York, 1858).

3 Josiah Henson, a Maryland Slave, Describes Slave Housing, Diet, and Clothing (1877)

"We lodged in log huts"

Josiah Henson spent 30 years on a plantation in Montgomery County, Maryland, before he escaped slavery and became a Methodist preacher, abolitionist, lecturer, and founder of a cooperative colony of former slaves in Canada. His memoirs, published in 1849, provided Harriet Beecher Stowe with her model of Uncle Tom. Here, he describes living conditions on his plantation.

My earliest employments were, to carry buckets of water to the men at work, and to hold a horse-plough, used for weeding between the rows of corn. As I grew older and taller, I was entrusted with the care of master's saddle-horse. Then a hoe was put into my hands, and I was soon required to do the day's work of a man; and it was not long before I could do it, at least as well as my associates in misery.

A description of the everyday life of a slave on a southern planta-tion illustrates the character and habits of the slave and the slaveholder, created and perpetuated by their relative position. The principal food of those upon my master's plantation consisted of corn-meal and salt herrings; to which was added in summer a little buttermilk, and the few vegetables which each might raise for himself and his family, on the little piece of ground which was assigned to him for the purpose, called a truck-patch.

In ordinary times we had two regular meals in a day: breakfast at twelve o'clock, after laboring from daylight, and supper when the work of the remainder of the day was over. In harvest season we had three. Our dress was of tow-cloth; for the children, nothing but a shirt; for the older ones a pair of pantaloons or a gown in addition, according to the sex. Besides these, in the winter a round jacket or overcoat, a wool-hat once in two or three years, for the males, and a pair of coarse shoes once a year.

We lodged in log huts, and on the bare ground. Wooden floors were an unknown luxury. In a single room were huddled, like cattle, ten or a dozen persons, men, women, and children. All ideas of refinement and decency were, of course, out of the question. We had neither bedsteads, nor furniture of any description. Our beds were collections of straw and old rags, thrown down in the corners and boxed in with boards; a single blanket the only covering. Our favourite way of sleeping, however, was on a plank, our heads raised on an old jacket and our feet toasting before the smoulder-ing fire. The wind whistled and the rain and snow blew in through the cracks, and the damp earth soaked in the moisture till the floor was miry as a pig-sty. Such were our houses. In these wretched hovels were we penned at night, and fed by day; here were the children born and the sick – neglected.

Source: Josiah Henson, *Uncle Tom's Story of His Life: An Autobiography of the Rev. Josiah Henson* (London, 1877).

4 Francis Henderson, Who Was a Slave near Washington, D.C., Describes Living Conditions Under Slavery (1856)

"My ... bedstead consisted of a board wide enough to sleep on"

Francis Henderson was 19 when he managed to escape from a slave plantation outside of Washington, D.C., in 1841. Here, he describes conditions on his plantation.

Our houses were but log huts – the tops partly open – ground floor – rain would come through. My aunt was quite an old woman, and had been sick several years; in rains I have seen her moving from one part of the house to the other, and rolling her bedclothes about to try to keep dry – everything would be dirty and muddy. I lived in the house with my aunt. My bed and bedstead consisted of a board wide enough to sleep on – one end on a stool, the other placed near the fire. My pillow consisted of my jacket – my covering was whatever I could get. My bedtick was the board itself. And this was the way the single men slept – but we were comfortable in this way of sleeping, being used to it. I only remember having but one blanket from my owners up to the age of nineteen, when I ran away.

Our allowance was given weekly – a peck of sifted corn meal, a dozen and a half herrings, two and a half pounds of pork. Some of the boys would eat this up in three days – then they had to steal, or they could not perform their daily tasks. They would visit the hog-pen, sheep-pen, and granaries. I do not remember one slave but who stole some things – they were driven to it as a matter of necessity. I myself did this – many a time have I, with others, run among the stumps in chase of a sheep, that we might have something to eat.... In regard to cooking, sometimes many have to cook at one fire, and before all could get to the fire to bake hoe cakes, the overseer's horn would sound: then they must go at any rate. Many a time I have gone along eating a piece of bread and meat, or herring broiled on the coals – I never sat down at a table to eat except at harvest time, all the time I was a slave. In harvest time, the cooking is done at the great house, as the hands they have are wanted in the field. This was more like people, and we liked it, for we sat down then at meals. In the summer we had one pair of linen trousers given us – nothing else; every fall, one pair of woolen pantaloons, one woolen jacket, and two cotton shirts.

My master had four sons in his family. They all left except one, who remained to be a driver. He would often come to the field and accuse the slave of having taken so and so. If we denied it, he would whip the grown-up ones to make them own it. Many a time, when we didn't know he was anywhere around, he would be in the woods watching us – first thing we would know, he would be sitting on the fence looking down upon us, and if any had been idle, the young master would visit him with blows. I have known him to kick my aunt, an old woman who had raised and nursed him, and I have seen him punish my sisters awfully with hickories from the woods.

The slaves are watched by the patrols, who ride about to try to catch them off the quarters, especially at the house of a free person of color. I have known the slaves to stretch clothes lines across the street, high enough to let the horse pass, but not the rider; then the boys would run, and the patrols in full chase would be thrown off by running against the lines. The patrols are poor white men, who live by plundering and stealing, getting rewards for runaways, and setting up little shops on the public roads. They will take whatever the slaves steal, paying in money, whiskey, or whatever the slaves want. They take pigs, sheep, wheat, corn – any thing that's raised they encourage the slaves to steal: these they take to market next day. It's all speculation – all a matter of self-interest, and when the slaves run away, these same traders catch them if they can, to get the reward. If the slave threatens to expose his traffic, he does not care – for the slave's word is good for nothing–it would not be taken.

Source: Benjamin Drew, *A North-Side View of Slavery* (Boston, 1856).

5 A South Carolina Slave, Jacob Stroyer, Recalls the Material Conditions of Slave Life (1898)

"Most of the cabins … were built … to contain two families"

One of 15 children, Jacob Stroyer was born on a plantation 28 miles from Columbia, South Carolina, in 1849. After the Civil War he became an African Methodist Episcopal minister, serving in Salem, Massachusetts.

Most of the cabins in the time of slavery were built so as to contain two families; some had partitions, while others had none. When there were no partitions each family would fit up its own part as it could; sometimes they got old boards and nailed them up, stuffing the cracks with rags; when they could not get boards they hung up old clothes. When the family increased the children all slept together, both boys and girls, until one got married; then a part of another cabin was assigned to that one, but the rest would have to remain with their mother and father, as in childhood, unless they could get with some of their relatives or friends who had small families, or unless they were sold; but of course the rules of modesty were held in some degrees by the slaves, while it could not be expected that they could entertain the highest degree of it, on account of their condition. A portion of the time the young men slept in the apartment known as the kitchen, and the young women slept in the room with their mother and father. The two families had to use one fireplace. One who was accustomed to the way in which the slaves lived in their cabins could tell as soon as they entered whether they were friendly or not, for when they did not agree the fires of the two families did not meet on the hearth, but there was a vacancy between them, that was a sign of disagreement. In a case of this kind, when either of the families stole a hog, cow or sheep from the master, he had to carry it to some of his family, for fear of being betrayed by the other family. On one occasion a man, who lived with one unfriendly, stole a hog, killed it and carried some of the meat home. He was seen by some one of the other family, who reported him to the overseer, and he gave the man a severe whipping. . . .

No doubt you would like to know how the slaves could sleep in their cabins in summer, when it was so very warm. When it was too warm for them to sleep comfortably, they all slept under trees until it grew too cool, that is along in the month of October. Then they took up their beds and walked.

Source: Jacob Stroyer, *My Life in the South* (enlarged edition; Salem, Mass., 1898).

6 A Former Virginia Slave, James Martin, Remembers a Slave Auction (1937)

"The slaves are put in stalls like . . . cattle"

James Martin, born on a Virginia plantation in 1847, was 90 years old when he was interviewed by the Works Progress Administration in 1937. After the Civil War he moved to Texas, where he served in the 9th US Cavalry and later worked as a cowboy. Here, he describes a slave auction.

The slaves are put in stalls like the pens they use for cattle – a man and his wife with a child on each arm. And there's a curtain, sometimes just a sheet over the front of the stall, so the bidders can't see the "stock" too soon. The overseer's standin' just outside with a big black snake whip and a pepperbox pistol in his belt. Across the square a little piece, there's a big platform with steps leadin' to it.

Then, they pulls up the curtain, and the bidders is crowdin' around. Them in back can't see, so the overseer drives the slaves out to the platform, and he tells the ages of the slaves and what they can do. They have white gloves there, and one of the bidders takes a pair of globes and rubs his fingers over a man's teeth, and he says to the overseer, "You call this buck twenty years old? Why there's cut worms in his teeth. He's forty years old, if he's a day." So they knock this buck down for a thousand dollars. They calls the men "bucks" and the women "wenches."

When the slaves is on the platform – what they calls the "block" – the overseer yells, "Tom or Jason, show the bidders how you walk." Then, the slave steps across the platform, and the biddin' starts.

At these slave auctions, the overseer yells, "Say, you bucks and wenches, get in your hole. Come out here." Then, he makes 'em hop, he makes 'em trot, he makes 'em jump. "How much," he yells, "for this buck? A thousand? Eleven hundred? Twelve hundred dollars?" Then the bidders makes offers accordin' to size and build.

Source: George P. Rawick, ed., *The American Slave: A Composite Autobiography* (Westport, Conn., 1972).

7   Elizabeth Keckley, Born into Slavery in Virginia, Describes a Slave Sale (1868)

"I witnessed, for the first time, the sale of a human being"

Born in slavery in Virginia about 1818, Elizabeth Keckley knew both Abraham Lincoln and Jefferson Davis. Mary Todd Lincoln called her "my best and kindest friend." Keckley worked as a household servant and as a dressmaker. In 1855, she gained her freedom by purchasing herself and her son for $1,200, funds raised by her customers.

During the Civil War, Keckley's son died fighting for the Union Army in Missouri. In 1864, she became president of the Contraband Relief Association, which provided relief to the fugitive slaves (known as "contraband") who fled behind Union lines. Here, she describes a slave sale.

When I was about seven years old I witnessed, for the first time, the sale of a human being. We were living at Prince Edward, in Virginia, and master had just purchased his hogs for the winter, for which he was unable to pay in full. To escape from his embarrassment it was necessary to sell one of the slaves. Little Joe, the son of the cook, was selected as the victim. His mother was ordered to dress him up in his Sunday clothes, and send him to the house. He came in with a bright face, was placed in the scales, and was sold, like the hogs, at so much per pound. His mother was kept in ignorance of the transaction, but her suspicions were aroused. When her son started for Petersburgh in the wagon, the truth began to dawn upon her mind, and she pleaded piteously that her boy should not be taken from her; but master quieted her by telling her that he was simply going to town with the wagon, and would be back in the morning.

Morning came, but little Joe did not return to his mother. Morning after morning passed, and the mother went down to the grave without ever seeing her child again. One day she was whipped for grieving for her lost boy. Colonel Burwell never liked to see one of his slaves wear a sorrowful face, and those who offended in this particular way were always punished. Alas! the sunny face of the slave is not always an indication of sunshine in the heart. Colonel Burwell at one time owned about seventy slaves, all of which were sold, and in a majority of instances wives were separated from husbands and children from their parents.

Source: Elizabeth Keckley, *Behind the Scenes, or, Thirty years a Slave, and Four Years in the White House* (New York, 1868).

Discussion Questions

1. How would you describe slaves' working conditions and their diet, clothing, and housing?
2. How did slaves' conditions of life vary in geographical areas where different crops were raised?
3. What took place at a slave sale?

Chapter 5   "Nobody Knows the Trouble I've Seen": Visual History of Slavery

In order to truly understand slavery's human meaning – its severity, brutality, and cruelties – it is essential to analyze all kinds of evidence. In general, historians emphasize written documents – letters, diaries, account books, and plantation records. In recent years, however, growing attention has been paid to visual evidence – paintings, engravings, and advertisements for slave sales or for the return of fugitive slaves. These images help us visualize slavery's oppressive realities in ways that written documents often cannot. The images allow us to picture day-to-day life in bondage and to envisage the dress and demeanor of enslaved African Americans. Many of these images are deeply disturbing, forcing us to confront harsh realities about the Middle Passage, slave punishment, or auctions that we often prefer to avoid.

Visual images, however, are not simply objective representations of reality. These images are rich cultural texts that radiate emotions and often carry profound political implications. To interpret these images, we need to explore their cultural and ideological meaning. We must assess their creator's intentions and ask how these images were understood by those who viewed them. Some questions we might ask are suggested at the end of the chapter.

1 The Inspection and Sale of an African Captive Along the West African Coast (1854)

This 1854 engraving depicts the inspection and sale of an African captive along the West African coast. Would you regard this as a basically objective representation of the process of enslavement? Which group would find this image most supportive of their views: slaveholders or abolitionists?

INSPECTION AND SALE OF A NEGRO.

Figure 1 The inspection and sale of an African captive along the West African coast, 1854.
Source: Brantz Meyer, *Captain Canot; or, Twenty Years of an African Slaver* (New York, 1854). Library of Congress, Call Number LOT 4422-A-1, Reproduction Number LC-USZ62–15392.

2 An Illustration of the Layout of a Slave Ship (1807)

On this ship, adult men were allotted space 6' in length and 16" in breadth. Boys were allowed 5' in length and 14" in breadth, adult women 5' 10" by 16"; and girls, 4' by 12".

The height between the ship's decks was just 5' 8". On some ships, shelves were erected between decks, reducing the head room to just 2' 6".

The men were fastened together with handcuffs and leg irons. When weather was favorable, they were allowed about 8 hours on deck, but when the weather was foul, the were only allowed about 15 minutes on the main deck.

Figure 2 An illustration of the layout of a slave ship, 1807.
Source: "Remarks on the Slave-Trade" [Philadelphia, 1807]. Library of Congress, Printed Ephemera Collection; Portfolio 156, Folder 41.

3 Enslaved Africans on the Deck of a Slave Ship (1860)

The transatlantic voyage lasted at least five weeks and sometimes as long as three months. During the sixteenth and seventeenth centuries, shipboard death rates ran as high as 25 percent or more. By the late eighteenth century, rates had fallen to about 10 percent, remaining twice the rate for white immigrants. Insurrections occurred on about one voyage in ten.

This illustration depicts the treatment of 510 Africans on board the bark Wildfire, *which was apprehended while trying to smuggle slaves into the United States in 1860. The freed captives were then transported to Liberia.*

Figure 3   Enslaved Africans on the deck of a slave ship, 1860.
Source: "The Africans of the Slave Bark 'Wildfire,'" *Harper's Weekly*, June 2, 1860.

4 Two Slave Sale Advertisements (1859, c.1780s)

Although the first African captives apparently arrived in British North America in 1619, large-scale imports from Africa began in the early eighteenth century. Between 1716 and 1740, slave traders brought approximately 85,000 African captives into the colonies, with about half taken to Virginia. A second wave of imports took place between 1751 and 1775, when about 115,000 slaves were brought into the colonies, two-thirds of whom arrived in South Carolina. In the 1780s and 1790s, Spanish planters brought some 25,000 slaves into Louisiana. At the very beginning of the nineteenth century, prior to the enactment in 1808 of the previous year's ban on the African slave trade, another 40,000 slaves were imported into Charleston, South Carolina. An unknown number of slaves arrived in the colonies after the African slave trade was banned.

Some slave sale advertisements reveal the disregard with which slave family ties were respected. An 1859 Savannah, Georgia, advertisement states "slaves will be sold separate, or in lots, as best suits the purchaser." This same ad, transcribed here, allows us to explore naming patterns as well as the correlation between slaves' age, gender, health, skills, and prices.

No.	Name	Age	Remarks	Price
1	Lunesta	27	Prime Rice Planter	$1,275,00
2	Violet	16	Housework & nursemaid	900.00
3	Lizzie	30	Rice, unsound	300.00
4	Minda	27	Cotton, Prime woman	1,200.00
5	Adam	28	Cotton, Prime young man	1,100.00
6	Abel	41	Rice Hand, Eyesight Poor	675.00
7	Tanney	22	Prime cotton Hand	950.00
8	Flementina	39	Good Cook, stiff knee	400.00
9	Lanney	34	Prime Cotton Hand	1,000.00
10	Sally	10	Handy in Kitchen	675.00
11	Maccabey	35	Prime Man, Fair Carpenter	980.00
12	Dorcas Judy	25	Seamstress, Hand in the House	800.00
13	Happy	60	Blacksmith	575.00
14	Mowden	15	Prime Cotton Boy	700.00
15	Bills	21	Handy with Mules	900.00
16	Theopolis	39	Rice Hand, Gets Fits	575.00
17	Coolidge	29	Rice Hand and Blacksmith	1,275.00
18	Bessie	69	Infirm, Sews	250.00
19	Infant	1	Strong Likely Boy	400.00
20	Samson	41	Prime Man, Good with Stock	975.00
21	Callie May	27	Prime Woman, Rice	1,000.00

22	Honey	14	Prime Girl, Hearing Poor	850.00
23	Angelina	16	Prime Girl, House or Field	1,000.00
24	Virgil	21	Prime Field Hand	1,100.00
25	Tom	40	Rice Hand, Lame Leg	750.00
26	Noble	11	Handy Boy	900.00
27	Judge Lesh	55	Prime Blacksmith	800.00
28	Booster	43	Fair Mason, Unsound	600.00
29	Big Kate	37	Housekeeper and Nurse	950.00
30	Melie Ann	19	Housework, Smart Yellow Girl	1,250.00
31	Deacon	26	Prime Rice Hand	1,000.00
32	Coming	19	Prime Cotton Hand	1,000.00
33	Mabel	47	Prime Cotton Hand	800.00
34	Uncle Tim	60	Fair Hand with Mules	600.00
35	Abe	27	Prime Cotton Hand	1,000.00
36	Tennes	29	Prime Rice Hand and Coachman	1,250.00

Source: "Credit Sale of a Choice Gang of 41 SLAVES!," Slave Sale Broadside, 1823–52, Chicago Historical Society.

Figure 4   Slave sale advertisement, c.1780s.
Source: Photograph of newspaper advertisement from the 1780s(?) for the sale of slaves at Ashley Ferry outside of Charleston, South Carolina. Library of Congress, Call Number: LOT 4422-A-1, Reproduction Number: LC-USZ62–10293.

5 A Fugitive Slave Advertisement (1774)

Colonial newspapers frequently contained announcements of slave sales and requests for overseers as well as ads for runaway slaves. These advertisements, though brief in length, are filled with valuable information.

The fugitive slave ad included in this advertisement, which was published July 25, 1774, in Savannah, Georgia, states:

RUN AWAY the 20th of May last from John Forbes, Esq's plantation in St. John's parish, TWO NEGROES, named BILLY and QUAMINA, of the Guinea Country, and speak good English. Billy is lusty and well made, about 5 feet 10 or 11 inches high, of a black complection [complexion], has lost some of his upper teeth, and had on when he went away a white negroe cloth jacket and trowsers [trousers] of the same. Quamina is stout and well made, about 5 feet 10 or 11 inches high, very black, has his country marks on his face, had on when he went away a jacket, trowsers, and robbin [ribbon?] of white negroe cloth. Whoever takes up said Negroes, and deliver them to me at the above plantation, or to the Warden of the Work-House in Savannah, shall receive a reward of 20 s[hillings]. besides what the law allows.

DAVIS AUSTIN.

Additional advertisements for fugitive slaves can be found on the Virginia Runaways website, http://etext.lib.virginia.edu/subjects/runaways, which contains dozens of ads placed in Virginia newspapers between 1736 and 1790 for the return of escaped slaves and servants.

After reading each ad, answer the following questions for each runaway:

1. What does the advertisement say about the fugitive's personal characteristics and physical appearance, including the runaway's:

gender	age
complexion	height
hair style	whiskers
clothing	marital status
name	ailments or disabilities

2. Is the description of the fugitive detailed or vague? Does it seem to reflect a great deal of knowledge about the fugitive?
3. Does the fugitive speak English?
4. Does the fugitive have an African or an English name?
5. Does the fugitive have any special skills?
6. Does the advertisement offer any clues about the psychology or demeanor?
7. Does the fugitive have any scars?
8. How did the fugitive manage to escape?
9. Did the fugitive run away alone or in a group?
10. Who, if anyone, assisted in the escape?

11. At what time of the day and year did fugitive escape?
12. What goods, if any, did the fugitive escape with?
13. Where was the fugitive headed?
14. What reward was offered?
15. Is the fugitive armed?

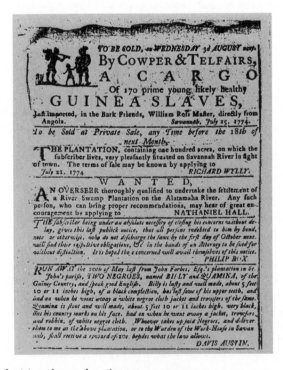

Figure 5   A fugitive slave advertisement, 1774.
Source: Savannah, July 25, 1774. Copyprint of a broadside. Prints and Photographs Division. Reproduction Number: LC-USZ63–16876 (1–2) http://lcweb. loc.gov/exhibits/odyssey/archive/01/01020001r.jpg.

6 An Illustration of a Slave Auction at Richmond, Virginia (1856)

This illustration, from a London newspaper in 1856, depicts an enslaved woman being auctioned off before a crowd of men. What does this image suggest about the attitude of the men participating in the auction?

Figure 6 An illustration of a slave auction at Richmond, Virginia, 1856.
Source: Illustration from the *Illustrated London News*, September 27, 1856, p. 315. Library of Congress, Call Number, LOT 4422-A-1, Reproduction Number, LC-USZ62–15398.

7 Five Generations of a Slave Family (c.1850s)

Despite sale and family separation, enslaved African Americans succeeded in maintaining strong familial and kinship ties. Even though slave marriages lacked legal sanction, these unions proved to be durable and slave parents and children received support from a network of kin and non-kin. Nevertheless, slavery imposed harsh pressures on family life. As many as half of all slave children grew up apart from their father, either because he resided on another plantation or because he was white. During their teens or early twenties, a majority of slave adolescents were sold apart from their families. It is notable that this photograph does not portray a single young adult male.

Figure 7   Five generations of a slave family, c.1850s.
Source: "Five generations on Smith's plantation, Beaufort, South Carolina."

Digital ID: ppmsc 00057. Reproduction Number: LC-B8171–152-A (b&w film copy neg.). Repository: Library of Congress Prints and Photographs Division.

8 An Engraving Illustrating Nat Turner's Insurrection (c.1831)

Although Nat Turner's revolt was far smaller in scale than insurrections that took place in Haiti, Jamaica, and Demerara, it exerted an immense impact on American society. The uprising, which involved from 60 to 80 slaves and left about 60 whites dead, touched off panics in many parts of the South, which resulted in the killings of scores of blacks. The revolt led some state legislatures to make it a crime to teach slaves to read or write, and the Virginia legislature actually debated whether slavery should continue to be legal in the state. Because the revolt took place just eight months after William Lloyd Garrison's militant antislavery newspaper, the Liberator, *appeared, many white southerners blamed the abolitionist movement for somehow contributing to the insurrection. Meanwhile, abolitionists noted that the insurrection utterly disproved the contention of slavery apologists that slaves were contented.*

Does the following illustration suggest that Nat Turner and his followers were deranged murderers or oppressed people fighting for their freedom? What, if anything, does the image convey about the nature of slavery or of the reasons for slave resistance?

Figure 8 An engraving illustrating Nat Turner's insurrection, c.1831.
Source: Library of Congress Rare Book and Special Collections Division, Digital ID: cph 3a39248, Reproduction Number: LC-USZ62–38902.

9 A Plantation Manual Offers Detailed Instructions to Overseers about How They Are to Treat Nursing Mothers (1857–1858)

This page from the plantation manual of US senator James Henry Hammond of South Carolina, transcribed below, offers detailed instructions to overseers about how they are to treat nursing mothers. It also specifies work arrangements for the elderly and for pregnant slaves. Hammond, who warned the North against threatening the South – declaring "You dare not make war on cotton – no power on earth dares make war upon it. Cotton is king" – not only took a slave woman and later her daughter as his mistresses, but also records in his diary having relations with four adolescent nieces.

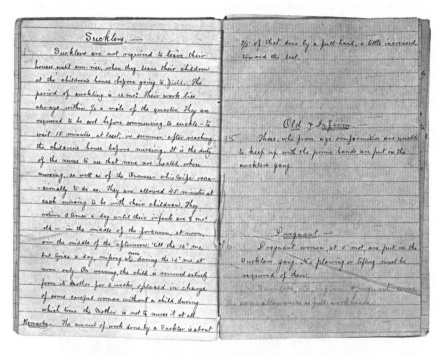

Figure 9   A plantation manual offers detailed instructions to overseers about how they are to treat nursing mothers, 1857–1858.
Source: Library of Congress, Plantation manual, 1857–58. James Henry Hammond. James Henry Hammond Papers (container 43). Manuscript Division. LC-MS-24695-1.

Sucklers [nursing mothers]. –

Sucklers are not required to leave their houses until sun-rise, when they leave their children at the children's house before going to field. The period of suckling is 12 mo[nth]s. Their work lies always within ½ a mile of the quarter. They are required to be cool before commencing to suckle – to wait 15 minutes, at least, in summer, after reaching the children's house before nursing. It is the duty of the nurse to see that none are heated when nursing, as well as of the Overseer & his wife occasionally to do so. They are allowed 45 minutes at each nursing to be with their children. They return 3 times a day until their infants are 8 mo[nth]s old – in the middle of the forenoon, at noon, & in the middle of the afternoon: 'till the 12th mo[nth] but twice a day, missing at noon: during the 12th mo[nth] at noon only. On weaning, the child is removed entirely from its mother for 2 weeks, & placed in charge of some careful woman without a child, during which time the mother is not to nurse it at all.

Remarks. – The amount of work done by a Suckler is about 3/5s of that done by a full-hand, a little increased toward the last.

Old & Infirm. –
Those, who from age infirmities are unable to keep up with the prime hands are put in the suckler's gang.

Pregnant. –
Pregnant women, at 5 mo[nth]s, are put in the suckler's gang. No plowing or lifting must be required of them.

10 African Americans in Baltimore Celebrate the Ratification of the Fifteenth Amendment, Extending the Vote to Black Men (1870)

This lithograph's central image shows a parade in Baltimore, Maryland, celebrating the ratification of the Fifteenth Amendment, extending the vote to African American men. Surrounding the parade scene are portraits of President Ulysses S. Grant, Vice President Schulyer S. Colfax, Martin R. Delany, a physician, author, abolitionist, and early black nationalist, the abolitionist Frederick Douglass, and Mississippi Senator Hiram R. Revels, as well as of Abraham Lincoln and John Brown.

Many of the images carry an inscription. The Bible is described as "Our Charter of Rights" and a scene of a minister preaching to his congregation is labeled "The Holy Ordinances of Religion are Free" An image of a classroom is inscribed "Education will prove the Equality of the Races"; a wedding ceremony is captioned "Liberty Protects the Marriage Altar"; and a family scene illustrates how "Freedom unites the Family Circle." An image of a black officer commanding his troops is captioned "We will protect our Country as it defends our Rights" and three men carry a banner labeled "We Unite [in] the Bonds of Fellowship."

Figure 10   African Americans in Baltimore celebrate the ratification of the Fifteenth Amendment, extending the vote to black men, 1870.
Source: Thomas Kelly, "The Fifteenth Amendment, Celebrated May 19th 1870" (New York, 1870). Library of Congress. LC-USZC4-2399 (color film copy transparency) LC-USZ62-36272 (b&w film copy neg.). http://memory.loc. gov/master/pnp/cph/3g00000/3g02000/3g02300/3g02399u.tif on the Library of Congress website.

Discussion Questions

1. What was the function of a particular image? Was it intended to document the realities of slavery or was it intended to persuade?
2. What emotions does the image evoke and what issues, ideas, or conflicts does it reveal?
3. Does the image provide an accurate representation of slavery or is the picture it presents sentimentalized, sanitized, or distorted?
4. Do the images portray slaves as realistic individuals or as caricatures? Are enslaved African Americans depicted as powerless and passive or as assertive individuals who were able to create a culture supportive of human dignity within the confines of slavery?

Chapter 6   "O Mother Don't You Weep": Women, Children, and Families

She was called Isabella when she was born into slavery around 1797 in New York's Hudson River Valley. Years later, she adopted a new name. As Sojourner Truth she became a legend in the struggle to abolish slavery and extend equal rights to women.

The youngest of 10 or 12 children, she grew up in a single room in a dark and damp cellar, sleeping on straw on top of loose boards. She served as a household slave in New York State, and was sold five times. One owner beat her so savagely that her arms and shoulders bore scars for the rest of her life.

She bore a fellow slave five children, only to see at least three of her offspring sold away. In 1826, just a year before slavery was finally abolished in the state, she fled after her owner broke a promise to free her and her husband. She took refuge with a farm family that later bought her freedom.

She moved to New York City, carrying only a bag of clothing and 25 cents. There she supported herself as a domestic servant. It was a period of intense religious excitement, and although she lacked formal schooling, Isabella began to preach at camp meetings and on street corners. Convinced that God had called on her to wander the country and boldly speak out the truth, she adopted the name Sojourner Truth. Her fame as a preacher, singer, and orator spread quickly and three incidents became the stuff of legend. During the late 1840s, when Frederick Douglass, the fugitive slave who became one of the country's best-known abolitionists, expressed doubt about the possibility of ending slavery peacefully, she replied: "Frederick, is God dead?" In 1858, when a hostile audience insisted that the six-foot-tall orator spoke too powerfully to be a woman, she reportedly bared her breasts before them.

She is best known today for a speech that she reportedly gave in 1851 before a woman's rights convention in Akron, Ohio. According to an account published 12 years after the event, she demanded that Americans recognize that impoverished African American women were women too, reportedly saying: "I could work as much and eat as much as a man – when I could get it – and bear de lash as well! And a'n't I a woman?"

Sojourner Truth's life illustrates many of slavery's worst horrors: abuse, deprivation, exploitation, and family breakup. But her example also reveals extraordinary resilience and strength. In understanding the treatment of women, children, and families in bondage, we must recognize the extreme forms of oppression that enslaved African Americans lived under, but also their remarkable ability to resist slavery's dehumanizing pressures especially through family and kinship relationships.

1 Harriet Jacobs Describes Her Efforts to Escape Verbal, Physical, and Sexual Abuse (1861)

"this narrative is no fiction"

For far too long, two topics – the history of slavery and the history of men in slavery – were virtually synonymous. In recent years, however, women's distinctive experience under slavery has grown more and more visible. Long shrouded by cultural caricatures, which obscured the realities of enslaved women's lives, the history of enslaved women has revealed a complexity that was hidden behind stereotypes of the loyal, deferential mammy, or the seductive, highly sexual Jezebel.

The subject of women in slavery is awash with controversy. One set of debates involved the issue of whether the slave family was more mother-centered (or matricentric or matrifocal) than free families. Another set of debates has arisen over whether slave women were worse off than their male counterparts – whether they were the "slaves of slaves" – or whether slave women were more equal to slave men than white women were to white men. These were not merely academic controversies. A 1965 government report, The Negro Family: The Case for National Action, *generated a firestorm of controversy when it asserted that slavery had emasculated black men, stripping them of an opportunity to head households or to protect their wives and children from abuse.*

Women's experience under slavery differed in significant ways from that of free women and of enslaved men, and the strategies that women adopted to resist slavery were different from male slaves'. At a time when an emerging urban middle class upheld a gender ideal in which married women were not to engage in labor outside the home, enslaved women were involved in many different kinds of work: as field hands, domestic servants, and active participants in local markets. Slave women had a prominent role in certain kinds of labor, not only domestic service and cooking, making and mending clothes, and tending garden plots, but rice cultivation, textile manufacture, and various forms of handicrafts. Enslaved women also dominated marketing of foodstuffs and items manufactured by slaves.

Enslaved women played crucial roles within slave families and within the broader slave community, transmitting knowledge about healing, serving as midwives during childbirth, and overseeing courtship. Not only were they primarily responsible for the day-to-day care of infants and children, they played active roles in religion, health care, and the transmission of cultural legacies, values, and practical knowledge to children.

African American women developed a conception of womanhood that differed profoundly from that which predominated among white Americans during the early nineteenth century. This was a definition that combined work and family life, and which anticipates the conception of womanhood that prevails today. At the same time, compared to gender relations among whites in the pre-Civil War South, male–female relations among blacks appear to have been less hierarchical and patriarchal and more egalitarian, defined less in terms of control than of complementary roles. This pattern of gender relations may have had African roots, as women played a critical role in raising food crops in many west and central African societies.

"Slavery is terrible for men, but it is far more terrible for women," Harriet Jacobs wrote in 1861, under the pen name Linda Brent. Jacobs was the author of the most widely read woman's slave narrative, the thinly veiled autobiographical Incidents in the Life of a Slave Girl. *"I have not exaggerated the wrongs inflicted by Slavery," Jacobs told her readers. "Only by experience can any one realize how deep, and dark, and foul is that pit of abominations."*

Born into slavery in rural North Carolina in 1813, she was sent, following her mistress's death, to live with a cruel and abusive doctor, James Norcom. Refusing to submit to his sexual advances, 15-year-old Jacobs sought protection by beginning a sexual relationship with an unmarried white neighbor, Samuel Tredwell Sawyer (who later became a member of Congress), with whom she had two children. She asks her readers to refuse to judge her harshly, and to realize how few options she had.

To escape the doctor's persistent threats and verbal and physical abuse, Jacobs hid in a cramped attic in her grandmother's shed, nine feet long, seven feet wide, and just three feet high at its tallest point. She spent much of her time for nearly seven years in this cramped, uninsulated space, peering through cracks in the walls to catch a glimpse of her children.

In 1842, Jacobs was smuggled to Philadelphia aboard a schooner, and supported herself as a nursemaid. Ten years later, her employer purchased her freedom for $300, provoking deep ambivalence, since Jacobs never wanted to see herself as owned by another person. "I am deeply grateful to the generous friend who procured [my freedom]," she wrote, "but I despise the miscreant who demanded payment for what never rightfully belonged to him or his."

During the Civil War, Jacobs raised money from Quakers and women's rights activists, and used the funds to provide clothing, blankets, and other supplies for ex-slaves who fled to contraband camps behind Union lines. She worked as a seamstress, cook, boarding house operator, and founder of a school for African Americans.

Jacobs's narrative of her life is quite different from Frederick Douglass's, and the differences may be related to gender. Unlike Frederick Douglass, whose autobiographies reveal little about his family of birth or of marriage, Jacobs stresses the people who were important in her life, including her grandmother, brother and half brother, and son and daughter. Although Jacobs, like Douglass, stresses the importance of maintaining her independence in the face of her master's attempts to force her into submission, she must struggle to retain control over her own body.

READER, be assured this narrative is no fiction. I am aware that some of my adventures may seem incredible; but they are, nevertheless, strictly true. I have not exaggerated the wrongs inflicted by Slavery; on the contrary, my descriptions fall far short of the facts. I have concealed the names of places, and given persons fictitious names. I had no motive for secrecy on my own account, but I deemed it kind and considerate towards others to pursue this course.

I wish I were more competent to the task I have undertaken. But I trust my readers will excuse deficiencies in consideration of circumstances. I was born and reared in Slavery; and I remained in a Slave State twenty-seven years. Since I have been at the North, it has been necessary for me to work diligently for my own support, and the education of my children. This has not left me much leisure to make up for the loss of early opportunities to improve myself, and it has compelled me to write these pages at irregular intervals, whenever I could snatch an hour from household duties.

... I do earnestly desire to arouse the women of the North to a realizing sense of the condition of two millions of women at the South, still in bondage, suffering what I suffered, and most of them far worse. I want to add my testimony to that of abler pens to convince the people of the Free States what Slavery really is. Only by experience can any one realize how deep, and dark, and foul is that pit of abominations. May the blessing of God rest on this imperfect effort in behalf of my persecuted people!

* * *

A SMALL shed had been added to my grandmother's house years ago. Some boards were laid across the joists at the top, and between these boards and the roof was a very small garret, never occupied by any thing but rats and mice. It was a pent roof, covered with nothing but shingles, according to the southern custom for such buildings. The garret was only nine feet long and seven wide. The highest part was three feet high, and sloped down abruptly to the loose board floor. There was no admission for either light or air. My uncle Philip, who was a carpenter, had very skilfully made a concealed trap-door, which communicated with the storeroom. He had been doing this while I was waiting in the swamp. The storeroom opened upon a piazza. To this hole I was conveyed as soon as I entered the house. The air was stifling; the darkness total. A bed had been spread on the floor. I could sleep quite comfortably on one side; but the slope was so sudden that I could not turn on the other without hitting the roof. The rats and mice ran over my bed; but I was weary, and I slept such sleep as the wretched may, when a tempest has passed over them. Morning came. I knew it only by the noises I heard; for in my small den day and night were all the same. I suffered for air even more than for light. But I was not comfortless. I heard the voices of my children. There was joy and there was sadness in the sound. It made my tears flow. How I longed to speak to them! I was eager to look on their faces; but there was no hole, no crack, through which I could peep. This continued darkness was oppressive. It seemed horrible to sit or lie in a cramped position day after day, without one gleam of light. Yet I would have chosen this, rather than my lot as a slave, though white people considered it an easy one; and it was so compared with the fate of others. I was never cruelly overworked; I was never lacerated with the whip from head to foot; I was never so beaten and bruised that I could not turn from one side to the other; I never had my heel-strings cut to prevent my running away; I was never chained to a log and forced to drag it about, while I toiled in the fields from morning till night; I was never branded with hot iron, or torn by bloodhounds. On the contrary, I had always been kindly treated, and tenderly cared for, until I came into the hands of Dr. Flint. I had never wished for freedom till then. But though my life in slavery was comparatively devoid of hardships, God pity the woman who is compelled to lead such a life!

My food was passed up to me through the trap-door my uncle had contrived; and my grandmother, my uncle Phillip, and aunt Nancy would seize such opportunities as they could, to mount up there and chat with me at the opening. But of course this was not safe in the daytime. It must all be done in darkness. It was impossible for me to move in an erect position, but I crawled about my den for exercise. One day I hit my head against something, and found it was a gimlet. My uncle had left it sticking there when he made the trap-door. I was as rejoiced as Robinson Crusoe could have been at finding such a treasure. It put a lucky thought into my head. I said to myself, "Now I will have some light. Now I will see my children." I did not dare to begin my work during the daytime, for fear of attracting attention. But I groped round; and having found the side next the street, where I could frequently see my children, I stuck the gimlet in and waited for evening. I bored three rows of holes, one above another; then I bored out the interstices between. I thus succeeded in making one hole about an inch long and an inch broad. I sat by it till late into the night, to enjoy the little whiff of air that floated in. In the morning I watched for my children. The first person I saw in the street was Dr. Flint. I had a shuddering, superstitious feeling that it was a bad omen. Several familiar faces passed by. At last I heard the merry laugh of children, and presently two sweet little faces were looking up at me, as though they knew I was there, and were conscious of the joy they imparted. How I longed to tell them I was there!

Source: Linda Brent [Harriet Jacobs], *Incidents in the Life of a Slave Girl* (Boston, 1861).

2 Bethany Veney Describes How She Aborted a Slave Sale (1889)

"certain tricks that I could resort to"

Enslaved women had fewer opportunities to travel long distances, and were highly vulnerable to sexual abuse. Nevertheless, slave women also developed their own distinctive forms of resistance to slavery. To be sure fewer women than men ran away to the North, but many fled shorter distances (to neighboring plantations or nearby woods and swamps), held clandestine religious services and social gatherings, and engaged in a variety of forms of day-to-day resistance, including tool-breaking or acts of disrespect toward masters and mistresses. Above all, cultural resistance – through the preservation of cultural traditions and the celebration of distinctive cultural rituals – proved to be a particularly valuable way to resist the dehumanizing pressures of slavery.

Born into slavery in Virginia around 1815, one of five children, Bethany Veney knew nothing about her father and was orphaned when her mother died when she was nine. Twice married, she described her first marriage ceremony in moving language. She said that she did not want to make her husband "promise that we would always be true to each other as the white people do in their marriage service, because I knew that at any time our masters could compel us to break such a promise."

Shifted from one master to another, she was eventually bought by a speculator, who took her to Richmond, to sell her for a profit. In this excerpt, she describes a slave sale that she witnessed and her successful effort to stave off her own sale.

In 1858, a northern visitor purchased her and her son for $775. She accompanied the visitor to Providence, Rhode Island, where she worked as his household servant. She later moved with the man's family to Worcester, Massachusetts.

Arrived in Richmond, we were again shut up in jail, all around which was a very high fence, so high that no communication with the outside world was possible. I say we, for there was a young slave girl whom McCoy had taken with me to the Richmond market. The next day, as the hour for the auction drew near, Jailer O'Neile came to us, with a man, whom he told to take us along to the dressmaker and to charge her to "fix us up fine." This dressmaker was a most disagreeable woman, whose business it was to array such poor creatures as we in the gaudiest and most striking attire conceivable, that, when placed upon the auction stand, we should attract the attention of all present, if not in one way, why, in another. She put a white muslin apron on me, and a large cape, with great pink bows on each shoulder, and a similar rig also on Eliza. Thus equipped, we were led through a crowd of rude men and boys to the place of sale, which was a large open space on a prominent square, under cover.

I had been told by an old negro woman certain tricks that I could resort to, when placed upon the stand, that would be likely to hinder my sale; and when the doctor, who was employed to examine the slaves on such occasions, told me to let him see my tongue, he found it coated and feverish, and, turning from me with a shiver of disgust, said he was obliged to admit that at that moment I was in a very bilious condition. One after another of the crowd felt of my limbs, asked me all manner of questions, to which I replied in the ugliest manner I dared; and when the auctioneer raised his hammer, and cried, "How much do I hear for this woman?" the bids were so low I was ordered down from the stand, and Eliza was called up in my place.

Poor thing! there were many eager bids for her; for, for such as she, the demands of slavery were insatiable.

Source: Bethany Veney, *The Narrative of Bethany Veney, A Slave Woman* (Boston, 1889).

3 Susie King Taylor Escapes to Freedom During the Civil War (1902)

"the white people did not want slaves to go over to the Yankees"

During the Civil War, slave women's ability to resist slavery was particularly evident. Tens of thousands of slave women and their children courageously fled their plantations and took refuge behind Union lines.

Born into slavery on the Georgia Sea Islands in 1848, Susie Baker (later known as Susie King Taylor) was six when she and a brother began to live with her maternal grandmother in Savannah. At a secret school run by a free black woman, she learned to read and write. For two years, she wrote, "We went every day about nine o'clock, with our books wrapped in paper to prevent the police or white persons from seeing them. We went in, one at a time." Later, she received additional instruction from another free black woman, a white playmate, and her grandmother's landlord's son.

In April 1862, an uncle led Susie and his own family to a Sea Island under Union control. Although she was only 14, she became a laundress for the 33rd US Colored troops, one of the Union Army's first black regiments, and led a day school for 40 African American children and a night school for adults. She also nursed wounded soldiers. At first, the wounded and bloody soldiers shocked her, but soon she grew accustomed to the sight. "It seems strange," she later wrote, "how our aversion to suffering is overcome in war. How we are able to see the most sickening sights and instead of turning away, how we hurry to assist in alleviating their pain."

During the war, she married Edward King, a sergeant from Darien, Georgia. Following the war, Susie Baker King, who was then 17, went back to Savannah with her husband, but her husband soon died. She then opened a school for African American children.

About this time [in 1860] I had been reading so much about the "Yankees" I was very anxious to see them. The whites would tell their colored people not to go to the Yankees, for they would harness them to carts and make them pull the carts around, in place of horses. I asked grandmother, one day, if this was true. She replied, "Certainly not!" that the white people did not want slaves to go over to the Yankees, and told them these things to frighten them. "Don't you see those signs pasted about the streets? one reading, 'I am a rattlesnake; if you touch me I will strike!' Another reads, 'I am a wild-cat! Beware,' etc. These are warnings to the North; so don't mind what the white people say." I wanted to see these wonderful "Yankees" so much, as I heard my parents say the Yankee was going to set all the slaves free. Oh, how those people prayed for freedom! I remember, one night, my grandmother went out into the suburbs of the city to a church meeting, and they were fervently singing this old hymn, –

> "Yes, we all shall be free,
> Yes, we all shall be free,
> Yes, we all shall be free,
> When the Lord shall appear,"

– when the police came in and arrested all who were there, saying they were planning freedom, and sang "the Lord," in place of "Yankee," to blind any one who might be listening. Grandmother never forgot that night, although she did not stay in the guard-house, as she sent to her guardian, who came at once for her; but this was the last meeting she ever attended out of the city proper.

On April 1, 1862, about the time the Union soldiers were firing on Fort Pulaski, I was sent out into the country to my mother. I remember what a roar and din the guns made. They jarred the earth for miles. The fort was at last taken by them. Two days after the taking of Fort Pulaski, my uncle took his family of seven and myself to St. Catherine Island. We landed under the protection of the Union fleet, and remained there two weeks, when about thirty of us were taken aboard the gunboat P –, to be transferred to St. Simon's Island; and at last, to my unbounded joy, I saw the "Yankee."

After we were all settled aboard and started on our journey, Captain Whitmore, commanding the boat, asked me where I was from. I told him Savannah, Ga. He asked if I could read; I said, "Yes!" "Can you write?" he next asked. "Yes, I can do that also," I replied, and as if he had some doubts of my answers he handed me a book and a pencil and told me to write my name and where I was from. I did this; when he wanted to know if I could sew. On hearing I could, he asked me to hem some napkins for him. He was surprised at my accomplishments (for they were such in those days), for he said he did not know there were any negroes in the South able to read or write. He said, "You seem to be so different from the other colored people who came from the same place you did." "No!" I replied, "the only difference is, they were reared in the country and I in the city, as was a man from Darien, Ga., named Edward King." That seemed to satisfy him, and we had no further conversation that day on the subject.

... After I had been on St. Simon's about three days, Commodore [John R.] Goldsborough heard of me, and came to Gaston Bluff to see me. I found him very cordial. He said Captain Whitmore had spoken to him of me, and that he was pleased to hear of my being so capable, etc., and wished me to take charge of a school for the children on the island. I told him I would gladly do so, if I could have some books. He said I should have them, and in a week or two I received two large boxes of books and testaments from the North. I had about forty children to teach, beside a number of adults who came to me nights, all of them so eager to learn to read, to read above anything else.

Source: Susie King Taylor, *Reminiscences of My Life in Camp with the 33d United States Colored Troops Late 1st S.C. Volunteers* (Boston, 1902).

4 Jacob Stroyer Recalls the Formative Experiences of His Childhood (1898)

"I cannot do anything for you"

At a time when the urban middle class was freeing its children from work responsibilities, prolonging and intensifying their family ties, and devoting an increasing number of their years to formal schooling, a slave childhood was a world apart. It was a world of poverty, privation, punishment, and early physical labor. Still, through the strength of their kinship and community ties and the force of their character, enslaved children grappled with the harsh day-to-day realities of slavery, made them more bearable, and ultimately succeeded in transcending slavery's traumas.

Even worse than slavery's physical severities were its psychological cruelties. Children grew up fearful of family separation. They felt an intense sense of powerlessness and quickly came to recognize that their parents were unable to protect them from slavery's hardships. Many, like Frederick Douglass, felt that slavery's greatest evil was the systematic deprivation of knowledge about one's ancestry, about reading, writing, and even one's birth date. Slavery, he later wrote in My Bondage and My Freedom, *his 1855 autobiography, "made my brothers and sisters strangers to me; it converted the mother that bore me into a myth; it shrouded my father in mystery, and left me without an intelligible beginning in the world." Slavery, in his view, had robbed him not merely of the attributes of childhood, but of certain defining elements of a human identity.*

Worse yet, slavery instilled in some children a profound sense of inferiority and shame. Thomas Jones, who spent his childhood in slavery in North Carolina, described his memory of growing up under slavery in his 1862 narrative of his life: "My recollections of early life are associated with poverty, suffering and shame. I was made to feel, in my boyhood's first experience, that I was inferior and degraded, and that I must pass through life in a dependent and suffering condition."

Yet for all of slave childhood's horrors, enslaved boys and girls nonetheless succeeded in "stealing" a childhood. They devised games that prepared them psychologically for the traumas of whippings and family separation. A surprisingly large number succeeded in learning how to read and write. Above all, they contributed to their family's well-being by supplementing their meager diets and assisting in their parents' work activities. For all its deprivations, childhood within bondage promoted an early sense of personal responsibility and strong communal loyalties.

In the following selection, Jacob Stroyer describes growing up under slavery. Note the ways that some slave children sought to imitate the behavior of their white owners and the ways that slave owners undermined the authority of slave parents.

Gilbert was a cruel [slave] boy. He used to strip his fellow Negroes while in the woods, and whip them two or three times a week, so that their backs were all scarred, and threatened them with severer punishments if they told; this state of things had been going on for quite a while. As I was a favorite with Gilbert, I always managed to escape a whipping, with the promise of keeping the secret of the punishment of the rest.... But finally, one day, Gilbert said to me, "Jake," as he used to call me, "you am a good boy, but I'm gwine to wip you some to-day, as I wip dem toder boys." Of course I was required to strip off my only garment, which was an Osnaburg linen shirt, worn by both sexes of the Negro children in the summer. As I stood trembling before my merciless superior, who had a switch in his hand, thousands of thoughts went through my little mind as to how to get rid of the whipping. I finally fell upon a plan which I hoped would save me from a punishment that was near at hand.... I commenced reluctantly to take off my shirt, at the same time pleading with Gilbert, who paid no attention to my prayer.... Having satisfied myself that no mercy was to be found with Gilbert, I drew my shirt off and threw it over his head, and bounded forward on a run in the direction of the sound of the [nearby] carpenters. By the time he got from the entanglement of my garment, I had quite a little start of him.... As I got near to the carpenters, one of them ran and met me, into whose arms I jumped. The man into whose arms I ran was Uncle

Benjamin, my mother's uncle.... I told him that Gilbert had been in the habit of stripping the boys and whipping them two or three times a week, when we went into the woods, and threatened them with greater punishment if they told.... Gilbert was brought to trial, severely whipped, and they made him beg all the children to pardon him for his treatment to them.

[My] father ... used to take care of horses and mules. I was around with him in the barn yard when but a very small boy; of course that gave me an early relish for the occupation of hostler, and I soon made known my preference to Col. Singleton, who was a sportsman, and an owner of fine horses. And, although I was too small to work, the Colonel granted my request; hence I was allowed to be numbered among those who took care of the fine horses and learned to ride. But I soon found that my new occupation demanded a little more than I cared for.

It was not long after I had entered my new work before they put me upon the back of a horse which threw me to the ground almost as soon as I had reached his back. It hurt me a little, but that was not the worst of it, for when I got up there was a man standing near with a switch in hand, and he immediately began to beat me. Although I was a very bad boy, this was the first time I had been whipped by anyone except father and mother, so I cried out in a tone of voice as if I would say, this is the first and last whipping you will give me when father gets hold of you.

When I had got away from him I ran to father with all my might, but soon found my expectation blasted, as father very coolly said to me, "Go back to your work and be a good boy, for I cannot do anything for you." But that did not satisfy me, so on I went to mother with my complaint and she came out to the man who had whipped me; he was a groom, a white man master had hired to train the horses. Mother and he began to talk, then he took a whip and started for her, and she ran from him, talking all the time. I ran back and forth between mother and him until he stopped beating her. After the fight between the groom and mother, he took me back to the stable yard and gave me a severe flogging. And, although mother failed to help me at first, still I had faith that when he had taken me back to the stable yard, and commenced whipping me, she would come and stop him, but I looked in vain, for she did not come.

Then the idea first came to me that I, with my dear father and mother and the rest of my fellow Negroes, were doomed to cruel treatment through life, and was defenseless. But when I found that father and mother could not save me from punishment, as they themselves had to submit to the same treatment, I concluded to appeal to the sympathy of the groom, who seemed to have full control over me; but my pitiful cries never touched his sympathy. . . .

One day, about two weeks after Boney Young [the white man who trained horses for Col. Singleton] and mother had the conflict, he called me to him. . . . When I got to him he said, "Go and bring me the switch, sir." I answered, "yes, sir," and off I went and brought him one . . . [and] he gave me a first-class flogging. . . .

When I went home to father and mother, I said to them, "Mr. Young is whipping me too much now, I shall not stand it, I shall fight him." Father said to me, "You must not do that, because if you do he will say that your mother and I advised you to do it, and it will make it hard for your mother and me, as well as for yourself. You must do as I told you, my son: do your work the best you can, and do not say anything." I said to father, "But I don't know what I have done that he should whip me; he does not tell me what wrong I have done, he simply calls me to him and whips me when he gets ready." Father said, "I can do nothing more than to pray to the Lord to hasten the time when these things shall be done away; that is all I can do."

Source: Jacob Stroyer, *My Life in the South* (enlarged edition; Salem, Mass., 1898).

5 James W. C. Pennington Analyzes the Impact of Slavery upon Childhood (1849)

"the want of parental care and attention"

Despite the threat of sale and separation, African American parents did succeed in instilling a strong sense of family identity in their children. Fathers purchased or made gifts for their children and passed down craft skills to their sons. To sustain a sense of identity over time, slave parents commonly named their eldest son for fathers and paternal grandfathers.

The fragility of the nuclear slave family gave special significance to the extended kinship group. By the mid-eighteenth century, the enslaved had created dense networks of family and surrogate families. Slave children were encouraged to refer to older slaves as "aunt" and "uncle" and to younger slaves as "sister" and "brother." Kin, including aunts, uncles, nephews, nieces, cousins, and in-laws, as well as friends, served as substitute parents in the event of family separation. Together, the bonds of family and the extended kin group sustained African American children through the travails of slavery.

In 1849, James W. C. Pennington, the minister of a Presbyterian church in New York City and the recipient of a degree from the University of Heidelberg in Germany, published a narrative of his life that revealed the astonishing news that he was a fugitive slave and a former blacksmith from Maryland. In his account of his life, Pennington offers the following reflections on the impact of slavery upon slave children.

My feelings are always outraged when I hear [ministers] speak of "kind masters," – "Christian masters," – "the mildest form of slavery," – "well fed and clothed slaves," as extenuations of slavery; I am satisfied they either mean to pervert the truth, or they do not know what they say. The being of slavery, its soul and body, lives and moves in the chattel principle, the property principle, the bill of sale principle; the cart-whip, starvation, and nakedness, are its inevitable consequences to a greater or less extent, warring with the dispositions of men. . . .

Another evil of slavery [is] . . . the want of parental care and attention. My parents were not able to give any attention to their children during the day. I often suffered much from hunger and other similar causes. To estimate the sad state of a slave child, you must look at it as a helpless human being thrown upon the world without the benefit of its natural guardians. It is thrown into the world without a social circle to flee to for hope, shelter, comfort, or instruction. The social circle, with all its heaven-ordained blessings, is of the utmost importance to the tender child; but of this, the slave child, however tender and delicate, is robbed.

There is another source of evil to slave children, which I cannot forbear to mention here, as one which early embittered my life, – I mean the tyranny of the master's children. My master had two sons, about the ages and sizes of my older brother and myself. We were not only required to recognize these young sirs as our young masters, but they felt themselves to be such; and, in consequence of this feeling, they sought to treat us with the same air of authority that their father did the older slaves.

Another evil of slavery that I felt severely about this time, was the tyranny and abuse of the overseers. These men seem to look with an evil eye upon children. I was once visiting a menagerie, and being struck with the fact, that the lion was comparatively indifferent to every one around his cage, while he eyed with peculiar keenness a little boy I had; the keeper informed me that such was always the case. Such is true of those human beings in the slave states, called overseers. They seem to take pleasure in torturing the children of slaves, long before they are large enough to be put at the hoe, and consequently under the whip.

We had an overseer, named Blackstone; he was an extremely cruel man to the working hands. He always carried a long hickory whip, a kind of pole.

He kept three or four of these in order, that he might not at any time be without one.

I once found one of these hickories lying in the yard, and supposing that he had thrown it away, I picked it up, and boy-like, was using it for a horse; he came from the field, and seeing me with it, fell upon me with the one he then had in his hand, and flogged me most cruelly. From that, I lived in constant dread of that man; and he would show how much he delighted in cruelty by chasing me from my play with threats and imprecations. I have lain for hours in a wood, or behind a fence, to hide from his eye....

When I was nine years of age, myself and my brother were hired out from home; my brother was placed with a pump-maker, and I was placed with a stone-mason. We were both in a town some six miles from home. As the men with whom we lived were not slaveholders, we enjoyed some relief from the peculiar evils of slavery. Each of us lived in a family where there was no other Negro.

The slaveholders in that state [Maryland] often hire the children of their slaves out to non-slaveholders, not only because they save themselves the expense of taking care of them, but in this way they get among their slaves useful trades. They put a bright slave-boy with a tradesman, until he gets such a knowledge of the trade as to be able to do his own work, and then he takes him home. I remained with the stonemason until I was eleven years of age: at this time I was taken home. This was another serious period in my childhood; I was separated from my older brother, to whom I was much attached; he continued at his place, and not only learned the trade to great perfection, but finally became the property of the man with whom he lived, so that our separation was permanent, as we never lived nearer after, than six miles.

Source: James W. C. Pennington, *The Fugitive Blacksmith or, Events in the History of James W. C. Pennington* (2nd edition; London, 1849).

6 Lunsford Lane Describes the Moment When He First Recognized the Meaning of Slavery (1842)

"I discovered the difference between myself and my master's white children"

As they remembered their lives in bondage, former slaves invariably recalled a moment in their childhood when they were first forced to confront the harsh realities of slavery. For one former Louisiana slave that moment came when

*her mistress whipped her for saying "to missis, 'My mother sent me.' We were
not allowed to call our mammies 'mother.' It was too near the way of the white
folks." For other ex-slaves, the shock of recognition came upon seeing their
parents whipped or upon confronting the fact that their parents were unable to
protect them from punishment from a master or an overseer.*

*For a Virginia slave known only as Charles, the crucial moment came when
his white playmates first began to treat him as a slave. In 1864, his master's
son, Moncure D. Conway, recalled that moment. "It is customary in nearly all
households in the South for the white and black children connected with each
other to play together," he wrote. "The trial ... comes when the young
Negroes who have hitherto been on this democratic footing with the young
whites are presently deserted by their ... companions, who enter upon school
life ... ceasing to associate with their swarthy comrades any longer, [they]
meet them in the future with the air of the master." Charles responded with
bitterness and defiance. He set fire to the family's house and was subsequently
sold to the deep South.*

*Lunsford Lane, who grew up on a plantation near Raleigh, North Carolina,
manufactured pipes and tobacco and succeeded in saving enough money to
buy his own freedom and purchase his wife and seven children. Here, he
describes his experiences as a slave child.*

My father was a slave to a near neighbor. The apartment where I was born
and where I spent my childhood and youth was called "the kitchen,"
situated some fifteen or twenty rods from the "great house." Here the
house servants lodged and lived, and here the meals were prepared for the
people in the mansion. . . .

My infancy was spent upon the floor, in a rough cradle, or sometimes in
my mother's arms. My early boyhood in playing with the other boys and
girls, colored and white, in the yard, and occasionally doing such little
matters of labor as one of so young years could. I knew no difference
between myself and the white children; nor did they seem to know any in
turn. Sometimes my master would come out and give a biscuit to me, and
another to one of his own white boys; but I did not perceive the difference
between us. I had no brothers or sisters, but there were other colored
families living in the same kitchen, and the children playing in the same
yard with me and my mother. . . .

When I began to work, I discovered the difference between myself and my
master's white children. They began to order me about, and were told to do
so by my master and mistress. I found, too, that they had learned to read,
while I was not permitted to have a book in my hand. To be in possession of
anything written or printed, was regarded as an offence. And then there was

the fear that I might be sold away from those who were dear to me, and conveyed to the far South. I had learned that being a slave I was subject to the worst (to us) of all calamities; and I knew of others in similar situations to myself, thus sold away. My friends were not numerous; but in proportion as they were few they were dear; and the thought that I might be separated from them forever, was like that of having the heart wrenched from its socket; while the idea of being conveyed to the far South, seemed infinitely worse than the terrors of death.

Source: Lunsford Lane, *The Narrative of Lunsford Lane* (Boston, 1842).

7 Laura Spicer Learns that Her Husband, Who Had Been Sold Away, Has Taken Another Wife (1869)

"it never was our wishes to be separated"

Families under slavery existed under conditions of extreme hardship, including the constant threat of separation from loved ones. Following the Civil War, an English traveler, William Macrae, heard a former slave respond bitterly to the remark that his former master had been kind to his slaves. "Kind! I was dat man's slave; and he sold my wife, and he sold my two chill'en . . . Kind!, yes, he gib me corn enough, and he gib me pork enough, and he neber gib me one lick wid de whip, but whar's my wife? – whar's my chill'en? Take away de pork, I say; take away de corn, I can work and raise dese for myself; but gib me back de wife of my bosom, and gib me back my poor chill'en as was sold away."

Certainly, many owners believed that it was in their own self-interest to encourage stable family lives. They knew that stable families raised slave morale, reduced the likelihood of slaves running away, and encouraged a high slave birth rate. Thus, many slaveholders promoted stable families by participating in slave marriage ceremonies, providing slave families with separate garden plots, prohibiting divorce, and severely punishing adultery.

But slave owners also regarded slaves as a form of property that might be sold at any time. In conducting marriages, slaveholders pointedly omitted any words that indicated that slave unions were perpetual. A former slave, Matthew Jarrett, noted that masters would never say "What God done jined, cain't no man pull asunder." Instead, they "jus' say, 'Now you married.'" A slave preacher thought slave owners should conclude the ceremony with the words: "till death or buckra [master] do you part."

Many slave spouses resided on separate farms or plantations. Millie Barber's parents lived five miles apart, and her father could only visit his family if he received permission from his owner. As this former South Carolina slave later recalled: "My pa have to git a pass to come to see my mammy. He come

*sometimes widout de pass. Patrollers catch him way up de chimney hidin' one
night; they stripped him right befo' mammy and give him thirty-nine lashes."
After purchasing new slaves, some masters required them to take new
husbands or wives. A former Louisiana slave, Stephen Jordon, described the
torment that this could cause: "I myself had my wife on another plantation.
The woman my master gave me had a husband on another plantation. Every
thing was mixed up. My other wife had two children for me, but the woman
master gave me had no children. We were put in the same cabin, but both of us
cried, me for my old wife and she for her old husband."*

*When he and his wife were sold apart, Laura Spicer's husband remarried,
thinking that he would never see her again. After the Civil War, however,
Laura found him, prompting anguish and confusion.*

I don't know whether I have told you Laura Spicers story. She was sold from
her husband some years ago, and he, hearing she was dead, married again.
He has had a wavering inclination to again unite his fortunes with hers; and
she has received a letter from him in which he said, "I read you letters over
and over again. I keep them always in my pocket. If you are married I don't
ever want to see you again." And yet, in some of his letters, he says,
"I would much rather you would get married to some good man, for
every time I gits a letter from you it tears me all to pieces. The reason why
I have not written you before, in a long time, is because your letters
disturbed me so very much. You know I love my children. I treats them
good as a Father can treat his children; and I do a good deal of it for you.
I was sorry to hear that Lewellyn, my poor little son, have had such bad
health. I would come and see you, but I know you could not bear it. I want
to see you and I don't want to see you. I love you just as well as I did the last
day I saw you, and it will not do for you and I to meet. I am married, and my
wife have two children, and if you and I meets it would make a very
dissatisfied family."

Some of the children are with the mother and the father writes, "Send me
some of the children's hair in a separate paper with their names on the
paper. Will you please git married, as long as I am married. My dear, you
know the Lord know both of our hearts. You know it never was our wishes
to be separated from each other, and it never was our fault. Oh, I can see
you so plain, at any-time, I had rather anything to have happened to me
most than ever have been parted from you and the children. As I am, I do
not know which I love best, you or Anna. If I was to die, today or
tomorrow, I do not think I would die satisfied till you tell me you will
try and marry some good, smart man that will take good care of you and
the children; and do it because you love me; and not because I think more

of the wife I have got than I do of you. The woman is not born that feels as near to me as you do. You feel this day like myself. Tell them [the children] they must remember they have a good father and one that cares for them and one that thinks about them every day. – My heart did ache when reading you very kind and interesting letter. Laura I do not think that I have change any at all since I saw you last – I thinks of you and my children every day of my life. Laura I do love you the same. My love to you never have failed. Laura, truly, I have got another wife, and I am very sorry, that I am. You feels and seems to me as much like my dear loving wife, as you ever did Laura."

Source: Unsigned and undated letter (1869?). Chase Papers, American Antiquarian Society, Worcester, Mass.

8 An Overseer Attempts to Rape Josiah Henson's Mother (1877)

"the overseer . . . sent my mother away . . . to a retired place"

Nothing provided greater ammunition for critics of slavery than the outrages committed on slave families. Southern law did not recognize or protect slave marriages or slave family ties. Slave owners were free to sell husbands from wives and parents from children and to sexually exploit slave wives or daughters.

The sexual abuse of slave women aroused great fury within the slave community. Josiah Henson describes his father's reaction to an overseer's attempt to molest his mother.

I was born June 15th, 1789, in Charles County, Maryland, on a farm belonging to Mr. Francis Newman, about a mile from Port Tobacco. My mother was a slave of Dr. Josiah McPherson, but hired to the Mr. Newman to whom my father belonged. The only incident I can remembered which occurred while my mother continued on Mr. Newman's farm, was the appearance one day of my father with his head bloody and his back lacerated. He was beside himself with mingled rage and suffering. The explanation I picked up from the conversation of others only partially explained the matter to my mind; but as I grew older I understood it all. It seemed the overseer had sent my mother away from the other field hands to a retired place, and after trying persuasion in vain, had resorted to force to accomplish a brutal purpose. Her screams aroused my father at his distant work, and running up, he found his wife struggling with the man. Furious at the sight, he sprung upon him like a tiger. In a moment the overseer was down, and, mastered by rage, my father would have killed him but for the entreaties of my mother, and the overseer's own promise that nothing should ever be said of the matter. The promise was kept – like most promises of the cowardly and debased – as long as the danger lasted.

The laws of slave states provide means and opportunities for revenge so ample, that miscreants like him never fail to improve them. "A nigger has struck a white man;" that is enough to set a whole county on fire; no question is asked about the provocation. The authorities were soon in pursuit of my father. The fact of the sacrilegious act of lifting a hand against the sacred temple of a white man's body ... this was all it was necessary to establish. And the penalty followed: one hundred lashes on the bare back, and to have the right ear nailed to the whipping-post, and then severed from the body. For a time my father kept out of the way, hiding in the woods, and at night venturing into some cabin in search of food. But at length the strict watch set baffled all his efforts. His supplies cut off, he was fairly starved out, and compelled by hunger to come back and give himself up.

The day for the execution of the penalty was appointed. The Negroes from the neighboring plantations were summoned, for their moral improvement, to witness the scene. A powerful blacksmith named Hewes laid on the stripes. Fifty were given, during which the cries of my father might be heard a mile, and then a pause ensued. True, he had struck a white man, but as valuable property he must not be damaged. Judicious men felt his pulse. Oh! he could stand the whole. Again and again the thong fell on his lacerated back. His cries grew fainter and fainter, till a feeble groan was the only response to his final blows. His head was then thrust against the post, and his right ear fastened to it with a tack; a swift pass of a knife, and the bleeding member was left sticking to the place. Then came a hurrah from the degraded crowd, and the exclamation, "That's what he's got for striking a white man." A few said, "it's a damned shame;" but the majority regarded it as but a proper tribute to their offended majesty. . . .

Previous to this affair my father, from all I can learn, had been a good-humored and light-hearted man, the ringleader in all fun at corn-huskings and Christmas buffoonery. His banjo was the life of the farm, and all night long at a merry-making would he play on it while the other Negroes danced. But from this hour he became utterly changed. Sullen, morose, and dogged, nothing could be done with him. The milk of human kindness in his heart was turned to gall. He brooded over his wrongs. No fear or threats of being sold to the far south – the greatest of all terrors to the Maryland slave – would render him tractable. So off he was sent to Alabama. What was his fate neither my mother nor I have ever learned. . . .

For two or three years my mother and her young family of six children had resided on [Dr McPherson's] estate; and we had been in the main very happy. . . .

Our term of happy union as one family was now, alas! at an end. Mournful as was the Doctor's death to his friends it was a far greater calamity to us. The estate and the slaves must be sold and the proceeds divided among the heirs. We were but property – not a mother, and the children God had given her.

Common as are slave-auctions in the southern states, and naturally as a slave may look forward to the time when he will be put upon the block, still the full misery of the event – of the scenes which precede and succeed it – is never understood till the actual experience comes. The first sad announcement that the sale is to be; the knowledge that all ties of the past are to be sundered; the frantic terror at the idea of being "sent south;" the almost certainty that one member of a family will be torn from another; the anxious scanning of purchasers' faces; the agony at parting, often forever, with husband, wife, child – these must be seen and felt to be fully understood. Young as I was then, the iron entered into my soul. The remembrance of the breaking up of McPherson's estate is photographed in its minutest features in my mind. The crowd collected around the stand, the huddling group of Negroes, the examination of muscle, teeth, the exhibition of agility, the look of the auctioneer, the agony of my mother – I can shut my eyes and see them all.

My brothers and sisters were bid off first, and one by one, while my mother, paralyzed by grief, held me by the hand. Her turn came, and she was bought by Isaac Riley of Montgomery County. Then I was offered to the assembled purchasers. My mother, half distracted by the thought of parting forever from all her children, pushed through the crowd, while the bidding for me was going on, to the spot where Riley was standing. She fell at his feet and clung to his knees, entreating him in tones that a mother only could command, to buy her baby as well as herself, and spare to her one, at least of her little ones. Will it, can it be believed that this man, thus appealed to, was capable not merely of turning a deaf ear to her supplication, but of disengaging himself from her with such violent blows and kicks, as to reduce her to the necessity of creeping out of his reach, and mingling the groan of bodily suffering with the sob of a breaking heart? As she crawled away from the brutal man I heard her sob out, "Oh, Lord Jesus, how long, how long shall I suffer this way!" I must have been then between five and six years old. I seem to see and hear my poor weeping mother now. This was one of my earliest observations of men; an experience which I only shared with thousands of my race, the bitterness of which to any individual who suffers it cannot be diminished by the frequency of its recurrence, while it is dark enough to overshadow the whole after-life with something blacker than a funeral pall.

Source: Josiah Henson, *Uncle Tom's Story of His Life: An Autobiography of the Rev. Josiah Henson* (London, 1877).

9 Lewis Clarke Discusses the Impact of Slavery on Family Life (1846)

"there is but little ... scruple about separating families"

Despite the possibility of disruption, enslaved African Americans were intensely committed to their families. To perpetuate a sense of family identity, slave parents named their children after ancestors or relatives. The strength of slave family ties is also suggested by the number of advertisements for runaway slaves that indicate that the fugitives were seeking to visit family members who lived on separate plantations.

Surviving slave letters provide a graphic record of the strength of slave families. In 1858, after learning that he was going to be sold away from his family, a Georgia slave named Abream Scriven wrote the following words to his wife: "My dear wife for you and my Children my pen cannot Express the griffe I feel to parted from you all.... I remain your truly husband until Death." In 1833, a Tennessee slave named George Pleasant expressed similar sentiments to his wife, who lived in North Carolina: "I hope with gods helpe that I may be abble to rejoys with you on the earth and In heaven lets meet when [God] will."

Lewis Clarke, the son of a Scottish weaver and a slave mother, was born in Kentucky in 1815. Despite an agreement that she was to be freed upon her husband's death, Clarke's mother and her nine children remained in slavery. After he learned that he was going to be sold in New Orleans, Clarke successfully fled through Ohio across Lake Erie to Canada in 1841. In an account of his life published in 1846, he provided answers to questions he was frequently asked about the impact of slavery upon slave families.

[Question] Are families often separated? How many such cases have you personally known?

[Answer] – I never knew a whole family to live together till all were grown up in my life. There is almost always, in every family, some one or more keen and bright, or else sullen and stubborn slave, whose influence they are afraid of on the rest of the family, and such a one must take a walking ticket to the south.

There are other causes of separation. The death of a large owner is the occasion usually of many families being broken up. Bankruptcy is another cause of separation, and the hard-heartedness of a majority of slave-holders another and a more fruitful cause than either or all the rest. Generally there is but little more scruple about separating families than there is with a man who keeps sheep in selling off the lambs in the fall. On one plantation where I lived, there was an old slave named Paris. He was from fifty to sixty years old, and a very honest and apparently pious slave. A slave-trader came along one day, to gather hands for the south. The old master ordered the waiter or coachman to take Paris into the back room pluck out all his gray hairs, rub his face with a greasy towel, and then had him brought forward and sold for a young man. His wife consented to go with him, upon a promise from the trader that they should be sold together, with their youngest child, which she carried in her arms. They left two behind them, who were only from four to six or eight years of age. The speculator collected his drove, started for the market, and, before he left the state, he sold that infant child to pay one of his tavern bills, and took the balance in cash. . . .

[Question] Have you ever known a slave mother to kill her own children?

[Answer] There was a slave mother near where I lived, who took her child into the cellar and killed it. She did it to prevent being separated from her child. Another slave mother took her three children and threw them into a well, and then jumped in with them, and they were all drowned. Other instances I have frequently heard of. At the death of many and many a slave child, I have seen the two feelings struggling in the bosom of a mother – joy, that it was beyond the reach of the slave monsters, and the natural grief of a mother over her child. In the presence of the master, grief seems to predominate; when away from them, they rejoice that there is one whom the slave-killer will never torment.

Source: *Interesting Memoirs and Documents Relating to American Slavery, and the Glorious Struggle Now Making for Complete Emancipation* (London, 1846).

Discussion Questions

1. How did women's experience of slavery differ from that of men?
2. How did women resist slavery and how and why did their strategies differ from men's?
3. Based on these accounts, would you say that the experience of slave women was essentially similar to or different than that of men?
4. How did a slave childhood differ from that of a southern white child?
5. How did parents seek to provide their children with guidance and protection?
6. Did slave children lack a childhood as we would define it today?
7. What stresses did slavery impose upon slave families?
8. What was the relationship between the slave family and the larger slave community?
9. How did slave spouses cope with the pressures that slavery inflicted upon their families?

Chapter 7   "Go Home to My Lord and Be Free": Religion

Some slaveholders were quite open in their belief that religion could serve as a valuable mechanism of social control, instilling submissiveness and conscientiousness within slaves. An 1845 pamphlet by George Washington Bethune asserted that Christianity could promote "good will," "meekness," "patience," "truth and faithfulness." But Christian religion also had another face, emphasizing judgment, equality, and liberation. As one white observer in Georgia, Emily P. Burke, commented in an 1850 book, the slaves believe "that in the life to come there will also be white people and black people; but then the white people will be slaves, and they shall have the dominion over them."

During the seventeenth century, slave owners were reluctant to Christianize their slaves for fear that baptized slaves would have to be set free. They also worried that the Christian notion of the spiritual equality of all human beings would lead slaves to demand their freedom. Many slaves rejected Christianity because of, as one white observer, Thomas Secker, the bishop of London, put it in 1741, a "Fondness they have for their old Heathenish Rites, and the strong Prejudice they must have against Teachers from among those, whom they serve so unwillingly."

By the second quarter of the eighteenth century, a growing number of slaveholders concluded that Christianity would make slaves more docile and conscientious, by placing them "under strong Obligations to perform [their] duties with the greatest Diligence and Fidelity . . . from a Sense of Duty to God, and the Belief and Expectation of a future account," as Edmund Gibson, the bishop of London, wrote in 1727. The process of converting slaves to Christianity began in earnest during the Great Awakening of the 1730s and 1740s and then accelerated in the late eighteenth century.

Within the Baptist and Methodist churches, slaves began to create a hybrid African American form of Christianity, blending Christian rituals and beliefs with elements of west African culture. The result, as Albert J. Raboteau has shown, was a religion with its own distinctive forms of preaching and worship, characterized by rhythmic sermons, "shouting" and other ecstatic behavior induced by spiritual possession, and forms of singing and dancing influenced by slaves' African traditions.

On individual plantations, slaves held informal or secret prayer meetings, apart from the influence of their masters. Here slave preachers conducted baptisms, weddings, and funerals, and slaves sang spirituals, which blended Christian hymns and psalms with African styles and gave expression to the slaves' intense desire for freedom and transcendence. Slave religion, in turn, existed alongside folk traditions with African roots, like witchcraft, herbalism, and conjuration (which involved supernatural spells and charms) that addressed needs unmet by Protestant Christianity.

1 Olaudah Equiano, from Eastern Nigeria, Describes West African Religious Beliefs and Practices (1789)

"the strong analogy ... in the manners ... of my countrymen, and those of the Jews"

> *Religion played a central role in the cultures of west Africa. In this extract from his memoirs, Olaudah Equiano describes Ibo religion in present-day eastern Nigeria and observes that certain aspects of African religious belief resemble those found in Judaism and Christianity.*

As to religion, the natives believe that there is one Creator of all things, and that he lives in the sun, and is girded round with a belt, that he may never eat or drink; but according to some, he smokes a pipe, which is our own favorite luxury. They believe he governs events, especially our deaths or captivity; but, as for the doctrine of eternity, I do not remember to have ever heard of it: some however believe in the transmigration of souls in a certain degree. Those spirits, which are not transmigrated, such as their dear friends or relations, they believe always attend them, and guard them from the bad spirits of their foes. For this reason, they always, before eating, as I have observed, put some small portion of the meat, and pour some of their drink, on the ground for them; and they often make oblations of the blood of beasts or fowls at their graves. I was very fond of my mother, and almost constantly with her. When she went to make these oblations at her mother's tomb, which was a kind of small solitary thatched house, I sometimes attended her. There she made her libations, and spent most of the night in cries and lamentation....

We compute the year from the day on which the sun crosses the line; and, on its setting that evening, there is a general shout throughout the land; at least, I can speak from my own knowledge, throughout our vicinity. The people at the same time made a great noise with rattles not unlike the basket rattles used by children here, though much larger, and hold up their hands to heaven for a blessing. It is then the greatest offerings are made; and those children whom our wise men foretell will be fortunate are then presented to different people.... They have many offerings, particularly at full moons, generally two at harvest, before the fruits are taken out of the ground; and, when any young animals are killed, sometimes they offer up part of them as a sacrifice....

We practiced circumcision like the Jews, and made offerings and feasts on that occasion in the same manner as they did. Like them also our children were named from some event, some circumstance, or fancied foreboding, at the time of their birth. I was named Olaudah, which, in our language, signifies vicissitude, or fortune; also one favored, and having a loud voice, and well spoken. I remember we never polluted the name of the object of our adoration; on the contrary, it was always mentioned with the greatest reverence; and we were totally unacquainted with swearing, and all those terms of abuse and reproach which find their way so readily and copiously into the language of more civilized people. The only expressions of that kind I remember were "May you rot, or may you swell, or may a beast take you."

I have before remarked, that the natives of this part of Africa are extremely cleanly. This necessary habit of decency was with us a part of religion, and therefore we had many purifications and washings.... Those that touched the dead at any time were obliged to wash and purify themselves before they could enter a dwelling house. Every woman too, at certain times, was forbidden to come into a dwelling-house, or touch any person, or anything we eat. I was so fond of my mother I could not keep from her, or avoid touching her at some of those periods, in consequence of which I was obliged to be kept out with her in a little house made for that purpose, till offering was made, and then we were purified.

Though we had no places of public worship, we had priests and magicians, or wise men. I do not remember whether they had different offices, or whether they were united in the same persons, but they were held in great reverence by the people. They calculated our time and foretold events.... They wore their beards; and, when they died, they were succeeded by their sons. Most of their implements and things of value were interred along with them. Pipes and tobacco were also put into the grave with the corpse, which was always perfumed and ornamented; and animals were offered in sacrifice to them. None accompanied their funerals, but those of the same profession or tribe. These buried them after sunset, and always returned from the grave by a different way from that which they went.

These magicians were also our doctors or physicians. They practiced bleeding by cupping; and were very successful in healing wounds and expelling poisons. They had likewise some extraordinary method of discovering jealousy, theft, and poisoning; the success of which no doubt they derived from the unbounded influence over the credulity and superstition of the people. I do not remember what those methods were, except that as to poisoning I recollect an instance or two, which I hope it will not be deemed impertinent here to insert, as it may serve as a kind of specimen of the rest, and is still used by the Negroes in the West Indies. A young woman had been poisoned, but it was not known by whom: the doctor ordered the corpse to be taken up by some persons, and carried to the grave. As soon as the bearers had raised it on their shoulders, they seemed seized with some sudden impulse, and ran to fro, unable to stop themselves. At last, after having passed through a number of thorns and prickly bushes unhurt, the corpse fell from them close to a house, and defaced it in the fall; and the owner being taken up, he immediately confessed the poisoning. . . .

Such is the imperfect sketch my memory has furnished me with of the manner and customs of a people among whom I first drew my breath. And here I cannot forbear suggesting what has long struck me very forcibly, namely, the strong analogy which even by this sketch, imperfect as it is, appears to prevail in the manners and customs of my countrymen, and those of the Jews, before they reached the Land of Promise. . . . Like the Israelites in their primitive state, our government was conducted by our chiefs, our judges, our wise men, and elders; and the head of a family with us enjoyed a similar authority over his household with that which is ascribed to Abraham and the other patriarchs. The law of retaliation obtained almost universally with us as with them: and even their religion appeared to have shed upon us a ray of its glory, though broken and spent in its passage, or eclipsed by the cloud with which time, tradition, and ignorance, might have enveloped it: for we had our circumcision (a rule I believe peculiar to that people): we had also our sacrifices and burnt-offerings, our washings and purifications, on the same occasion as they had.

Source: Olaudah Equiano, *The Interesting Narrative of the Life of Olaudah Equiano or Gustavus Vassa the African* (London, 1789).

2 Charles Ball, a Slave in Maryland, Remembers a Slave Funeral, which Incorporated Traditional African Customs (1837)

"I assisted ... to inter the infant"

> *During the early nineteenth century, some slaves continued to draw upon west African religious customs in burying the dead. In this selection, Charles Ball, a slave in western Maryland, describes a slave funeral.*

I assisted her and her husband to inter the infant ... and its father buried with it, a small bow and several arrows; a little bag of parched meal; a miniature canoe, about a foot long, and a little paddle, (with which he said it would cross the ocean to his own country) a small stick, with an iron nail, sharpened and fastened into one end of it; and a piece of white muslin, with several curious and strange figures painted on it in blue and red, by which, he said, his relations and countrymen would know the infant to be his son, and would receive it accordingly, on its arrival amongst them ... He cut a lock of hair from his head, threw it upon the dead infant, and closed the grave with his own hands. He then told us the God of his country was looking at him, and was pleased with what he had done.

Source: Charles Ball, *Slavery in the United States: A Narrative of the Life and Adventures of Charles Ball, A Black Man* (New York, 1837).

3 Peter Randolph, a Former Virginia Slave, Describes the Religious Gatherings Slaves Held Outside of Their Masters' Supervision (1893)

"the slaves assemble in the swamps"

> *Peter Randolph, who grew up in slavery on a plantation in Prince George County, Virginia, received his freedom in 1847 following his owner's death, and then served as an antislavery agent, a newspaper editor, and a Baptist minister in the North and in Canada. Following the Civil War, he served as minister in the Ryland or Old African Baptist Church in Richmond, Virginia. This selection describes the disparity between the version of Christianity that masters taught to the slaves and the version that slaves taught to themselves.*

Many say the Negroes receive religious education – that Sabbath worship is instituted for them as for others, and were it not for slavery, they would die in their sins – that really, the institution of slavery is a benevolent missionary enterprise. Yes, they are preached to, and I will give my readers some faint glimpses of these preachers, and their doctrines and practices.

In Prince George County there were two meeting-houses intended for public worship. Both were occupied by the Baptist denomination. These houses were built by William and George Harrison, brothers ... that their slaves might go there on the Sabbath and receive instruction, such as slave-holding ministers would give. The prominent preaching to the slaves was, " 'Servants, obey your masters'. Do not steal or lie, for this is very wrong. Such conduct is sinning against the Holy Ghost, and is base ingratitude to your kind masters, who feed, clothe and protect you...." I should think, when making such statements, the slaveholders would feel the rebuke of the Apostle and fall down and be carried out from the face of day, as were Ananias and Sapphira, when they betrayed the trust committed to them, or refused to bear true testimony in regard to that trust.

There was another church, about fourteen miles from the one just men-tioned. It was called "Brandon's church", and there the white Baptists worshiped....

There was one Brother Shell who used to preach. One Sabbath, while exhorting the poor, impenitent, hard-hearted, ungrateful slaves, so much beloved by their masters, to repentance and prayerfulness, while entreating them to lead good lives, that they might escape the wrath (of the lash) to come, some of his crocodile tears overflowed his cheek.... But, my readers, Monday morning, Brother Shell was afflicted with his old malady, hardness of heart, so that he was obliged to catch one of the sisters by the throat, and give her a terrible flogging.

The like of this is the preaching, and these are the men that spread the Gospel among the slaves. Ah! such a Gospel had better be buried in oblivion, for it makes more heathens than Christians. Such preachers ought to be forbidden by the laws of the land ever to mock again at the blessed religion of Jesus, which was sent as a light to the world....

Not being allowed to hold meetings on the plantation, the slaves assemble in the swamps, out of reach of the patrols. They have an understanding among themselves as to the time and place of getting together. This is often done by the first one arriving breaking boughs from the trees, and bending them in the direction of the selected spot. Arrangements are then made for conducting the exercises. They first ask each other how they feel, the state of their minds, etc. The male members then select a certain space, in separate groups, for their division of the meeting. Preaching in order, by the brethren;

then praying and singing all round, until they generally feel quite happy. The speaker usually commences by calling himself unworthy, and talks very slowly, until, feeling the spirit, he grows excited, and in a short time, there fall to the ground twenty or thirty men and women under its influence. Enlightened people call it excitement; but I wish the same was felt by everybody, so far as they are sincere.

The slave forgets all his sufferings, except to remind others of the trials during the past week, exclaiming: "Thank God, I shall not live here always!" Then they pass from one to another, shaking hands, and bidding each other farewell, promising, should they meet no more on earth, to strive and meet in heaven, where all is joy, happiness and liberty. As they separate, they sing a parting hymn of praise.

Sometimes the slaves meet in an old log-cabin, when they find it necessary to keep a watch. If discovered, they escape, if possible; but those who are caught often get whipped. Some are willing to be punished thus for Jesus' sake. Most of the songs used in worship are composed by the slaves themselves, and describe their own sufferings. Thus:

> "Oh, that I had a bosom friend,
> To tell my secrets to,
> One always to depend upon
> In everything I do!"

> "How do I wander, up and down!
> I seem a stranger, quite undone;
> None to lend an ear to my complaint,
> No one to cheer me, though I faint."

Some of the slaves sing –

> "No more rain, no more snow,
> No more cowskin on my back!"

Then they change it by singing –

> "Glory be to God that rules on high."

In some places, if the slaves are caught praying to God, they are whipped more than if they had committed a great crime. The slaveholders will allow the slaves to dance, but do not want them to pray to God. Sometimes, when a slave, on being whipped, calls upon God, he is forbidden to do so, under threat of having his throat cut, or brains blown out. Oh, reader! this seems very hard – that slaves cannot call on their Maker, when the case most needs it. Sometimes the poor slave takes courage to ask his master to let him pray, and is driven away, with the answer, that if discovered praying, his back will pay the bill.

Source: Peter Randolph, *Slave Cabin to the Pulpit* (Boston, 1893).

4 Henry Bibb, Who Toiled in Slavery in Kentucky, Louisiana, and Arkansas, Discusses "Conjuration" (1849)

"Many ... believe in what they call 'conjuration'"

Henry Bibb, born to a white father and a slave mother in Shelby County, Kentucky, in 1815, was held in slavery in Kentucky, Louisiana, and in present-day Arkansas. In 1837, he escaped through Ohio and Michigan into Canada. In this selection, he describes slaves' notions of conjuration that existed alongside Christianity.

In 1833, I had some very serious religious impressions, and there was quite a number of slaves in that neighborhood, who felt very desirous to be taught to read the Bible. There was a Miss Davis, a poor white girl, who offered to teach a Sabbath School for the slaves, notwithstanding public opinion and the law was opposed to it. Books were furnished and she commenced the school; but the news soon got to our owners that she was teaching us to read. This caused quite an excitement in the neighborhood. Patrols were appointed to go and break it up the next Sabbath. They were determined that we should not have a Sabbath School in operation. For slaves this was called an incendiary movement.

The Sabbath is not regarded by a large number of the slaves as a day of rest. They have no schools to go to; no moral nor religious instruction at all in many localities where there are hundreds of slaves. Hence they resort to some kind of amusement. Those who make no profession of religion, resort to the woods in large numbers on that day to gamble, fight, get drunk, and break the Sabbath. This is often encouraged by slaveholders. When they wish to have a little sport of that kind, they go among the slaves and give them whiskey, to see them dance, "pat juber" [a dance involving intense bodily movement], sing and play on the banjo. Then get them to wrestling, fighting, jumping, running foot races, and butting each other like sheep. This is urged on by giving them whiskey; making bets on them; laying chips on one slave's head, and daring another to tip it off with his hand; and if he tipped it off, it would be called an insult, and cause a fight. Before fighting, the parties choose their seconds to stand by them while fighting; a ring or a circle is formed to fight in, and no one is allowed to enter the ring while they are fighting, but their seconds, and the white gentlemen. They are not allowed to fight a duel, nor to use weapons of any kind. The blows are made by kicking, knocking, and butting with their heads; they grab each other by their ears, and jam their heads together like sheep. If they are likely to hurt each other very bad, their masters would rap them with their walking canes, and make them stop. After fighting they make friends, shake hands, and take a dram together, and there is no more of it.

But this is all principally for want of moral instruction. This is where they have no Sabbath Schools; no one to read the Bible to them; no one to preach the gospel who is competent to expound the Scriptures, except slaveholders. And the slaves, with but few exceptions, have no confidence at all in their preaching, because they preach a pro-slavery doctrine. They say, "Servants be obedient to your masters; – and he that knoweth his master's will and doeth it not, shall be beaten, with many stripes; –" means that God will send them to hell, if they disobey their masters. This kind of preaching has driven thousands into infidelity. They view themselves as suffering unjustly under the lash, without friends, without protection of law or gospel, and the green-eyed monster tyranny staring them in the face. They know that they are destined to die in that wretched condition, unless they are delivered by the arm of Omnipotence. And they cannot believe or trust in such a religion, as above named. . . .

There is much superstition among the slaves. Many of them believe in what they call "conjuration," tricking, and witchcraft; and some of them pretend to understand the art, and say that by it they can prevent their masters from exercising their will over their slaves. Such are often applied to by others, to give them power to prevent their masters from flogging them. The remedy is most generally some kind of bitter root; they are directed to chew it and spit towards their masters when they are angry with the slaves. At other times they prepare certain kinds of powders, to sprinkle about their masters' dwellings. This is all done for the purpose of defending themselves in some peaceable manner, although I am satisfied that there is no virtue at all in it. . . .

[A conjurer] said if I would pay him a small sum, he would prevent my being flogged. After I had paid him, he mixed up some alum, salt and other stuff into a powder, and said I must sprinkle it about my master, if he should offer to strike me; this would prevent him. He also gave me some kind of bitter root to chew, and spit towards him, which would certainly prevent my being flogged. According to order I used his remedy, and for some cause I was let pass without being flogged that time.

I had then great faith in conjuration and witchcraft. I was led to believe that I could do almost as I pleased, without being flogged. So on the next Sabbath my conjuration was fully tested by my going off, and staying away until Monday morning, without permission. When I returned home, my master declared that he would punish me for going off; but I did not believe that he could do it, while I had this root and dust; and as he approached me, I commenced talking saucy to him. But he soon convinced me that there was no virtue in them. He became so enraged at me for saucing him, that he grasped a handful of switches and punished me severely, in spite of all my roots and powders....

I wanted to be well thought of by [young women], and would go to great lengths to gain their affection. I had been taught by the old superstitious slaves, to believe in conjuration, and it was hard for me to give up the notion, for all I had been deceived by them. One of these conjurers, for a small sum, agreed to teach me to make any girl love me that I wished. After I had paid him, he told me to get a bull frog, and take a certain bone out of the frog, dry it, and when I got a chance I must step up to any girl whom I wished to make love me, and scratch her somewhere on her naked skin with this bone, and she would be certain to love me, and would follow me in spite of herself; no matter who she might be engaged to, nor who she might be walking with.

So I got me a bone for a certain girl, whom I knew to be under the influence of another young man. I happened to meet her in the company of her lover, one Sunday evening, walking out; so when I got a chance, I fetched her a tremendous rasp across her neck with this bone, which made her jump. But in place of making her love me, it only made her angry with me. She felt more like running after me to retaliate on me for thus abusing her, than she felt like loving me.

Source: Henry Bibb, *Narrative of the Life and Adventures of Henry Bibb, An American Slave* (New York, 1849).

Discussion Questions

1. Did religion encourage accommodation to slavery or did it help slaves resist bondage?
2. What did many enslaved African Americans find attractive in Christianity?
3. In what ways may enslaved African Americans have influenced the nature of early nineteenth-century American Protestantism?

Chapter 8   "Oppressed So Hard They Could Not Stand": Punishment

Dr John Wesley Monette, an apologist for slavery, rejected the charge that whipping slaves was cruel and barbaric. He acknowledged that anyone unacquainted with the lash, "hearing the loud sharp crack of the whip upon the naked skin, would almost tremble for the life of the poor sufferer." But, he assured his readers, there was no reason for anxiety. "After hearing fifty or one hundred stripes thus being laid on," one would "find the skin not broken, and not a drop of blood drawn from him!" Indeed, he insisted, a buckskin whip's end was so soft that one "could scarcely hurt a child with it." He acknowledged that a lashing "stings, or 'burns' the skin smartly," but, he added, it "does not bruise it." Though slave owners tried to disguise this fact, they relied on physical punishment to force slaves to toil for long hours and meager rewards.

Though slave owners, like Monette, tried to deny – or obscure – the cruelty of slavery, the fact remains that slave management was based on fear.

A Georgia slave owner maintained that "the surest and best method of managing Negroes, is to love them." "If we love our horse ... he will become gentle, docile and obedient," he observed. "Why will it not have the same effect upon slaves." Many slaveholders offered a variety of rewards and incentives; they gave slaves small garden patches on which they could raise their own crops, distributed gifts, and offered cash bonuses and special holidays to particularly diligent slaves. A few masters actually made profit-sharing agreements with slaves.

Yet even the most humane masters balanced the hope of reward with the threat of punishment. A slave owner might deny disobedient or unproductive slaves passes off the plantation or reduce their rations. One Maryland planter forced a slave to eat worms that she had failed to pick off a tobacco plant. One farmer described his approach to discipline: "I do not punish often, but I seldom let an offense pass." He disciplined children by "pulling an ear, or a sound box." He placed adults in solitary confinement within a windowless "hewed log house, with a good substantial door, lock and key."

Ultimately a master's authority rested on the threat of physical pain. To discipline slaves, plantation owners set up private jails, confined slaves in stocks, and shackled them with chains and iron collars. It was the whip, however, that became the defining symbol of slavery. As James Henry Hammond, a South Carolina governor and US senator, wrote in his plantation manual, "the highest punishment must not exceed 100 lashes in one day and to that extent only in extreme cases. In general 15 to 20 lashes will be a sufficient flogging."

1 Frederick Douglass, a Fugitive Slave from Maryland, Describes the Circumstances that Prompted Masters to Whip Slaves (1845)

"matters for which a slave may be whipped"

Perhaps the nineteenth century's staunchest advocate of equal rights, Frederick Douglass was born into slavery on Maryland's eastern shore in 1818, the son of a slave woman and an unknown white man. While toiling as a ship's caulker, he taught himself to read. After he escaped from slavery at the age of 20, he became the abolitionist movement's most effective orator and published an influential anti-slavery newspaper, the North Star. *In this excerpt from one of his three autobiographies, he describes the circumstances that prompted slave owners to whip slaves.*

A mere look, word, or motion, – a mistake, accident, or want of power, – are all matters for which a slave may be whipped at any time. Does a slave look dissatisfied? It is said, he has the devil in him, and it must be whipped out. Does he speak loudly when spoken to by his master? Then he is getting high-minded, and should be taken down a button-hole lower. Does he forget to pull off his hat at the approach of a white person? Then he is wanting in reverence, and should be whipped for it. Does he ever venture to vindicate his conduct, when censured for it? Then he is guilty of impudence, – one of the greatest crimes of which a slave can be guilty. Does he ever venture to suggest a different mode of doing things from that pointed out by his master? He is indeed presumptuous, and getting above himself. ...

Source: Frederick Douglass, *Narrative of the Life of Frederick Douglass, An American Slave* (3rd English edition; Leeds, 1846).

2 Elizabeth Keckley of Virginia Describes a Lashing She Received (1868)

"What have I done that I should be so punished?"

From slavery in Virginia, Elizabeth Keckley would go on to become Mary Todd Lincoln's closest confidante. After 30 years in bondage, she succeeded in buying freedom for herself and her son. In this excerpt from her autobiography, she describes how she responded when her master tried to whip her.

When I was about fourteen years old I went to live with my master's eldest son, a Presbyterian minister. His salary was small, and he was burdened with a helpless wife, a girl that he had married in the humble walks of life. She was morbidly sensitive, and imagined that I regarded her with contemptuous feelings because she was of poor parentage. I was their only servant, and a gracious loan at that. They were not able to buy me, so my old master sought to render them assistance by allowing them the benefit of my services. From the very first I did the work of three servants, and yet I was scolded and regarded with distrust.

The years passed slowly, and I continued to serve them, and at the same time grew into strong, healthy womanhood. I was nearly eighteen when we removed from Virginia to Hillsboro', North Carolina, where young Mr. Burwell took charge of a church. The salary was small, and we still had to practise the closest economy. Mr. Bingham, a hard, cruel man, the village schoolmaster, was a member of my young master's church, and he was a frequent visitor to the parsonage. She whom I called mistress seemed to be desirous to wreak vengeance on me for something, and Bingham became her ready tool.

During this time my master was unusually kind to me; he was naturally a good-hearted man, but was influenced by his wife. It was Saturday evening, and while I was bending over the bed, watching the baby that I had just hushed into slumber, Mr. Bingham came to the door and asked me to go with him to his study. Wondering what he meant by his strange request, I followed him, and when we had entered the study he closed the door, and in his blunt way remarked: "Lizzie, I am going to flog you." I was thunderstruck, and tried to think if I had been remiss in anything. I could not recollect of doing anything to deserve punishment, and with surprise exclaimed: "Whip me, Mr. Bingham! what for?"

"No matter," he replied, "I am going to whip you, so take down your dress this instant."

Recollect, I was eighteen years of age, was a woman fully developed, and yet this man coolly bade me take down my dress. I drew myself up proudly, firmly, and said: "No, Mr. Bingham, I shall not take down my dress before you. Moreover, you shall not whip me unless you prove the stronger. Nobody has a right to whip me but my own master, and nobody shall do so if I can prevent it."

My words seemed to exasperate him. He seized a rope, caught me roughly, and tried to tie me. I resisted with all my strength, but he was the stronger of the two, and after a hard struggle succeeded in binding my hands and tearing my dress from my back. Then he picked up a rawhide, and began to ply it freely over my shoulders. With steady hand and practised eye he would raise the instrument of torture, nerve himself for a blow, and with fearful force the rawhide descended upon the quivering flesh. It cut the skin, raised great welts, and the warm blood trickled down my back. Oh God! I can feel the torture now – the terrible, excruciating agony of those moments. I did not scream; I was too proud to let my tormentor know what I was suffering. I closed my lips firmly, that not even a groan might escape from them, and I stood like a statue while the keen lash cut deep into my flesh.

As soon as I was released, stunned with pain, bruised and bleeding, I went home and rushed into the presence of the pastor and his wife, wildly exclaiming: "Master Robert, why did you let Mr. Bingham flog me? What have I done that I should be so punished?"

"Go away," he gruffly answered, "do not bother me."

I would not be put off thus. "What have I done? I will know why I have been flogged."

I saw his cheeks flush with anger, but I did not move. He rose to his feet, and on my refusing to go without an explanation, seized a chair, struck me, and felled me to the floor. I rose, bewildered, almost dead with pain, crept to my room, dressed my bruised arms and back as best I could, and then lay down, but not to sleep. No, I could not sleep, for I was suffering mental as well as bodily torture. My spirit rebelled against the unjustness that had been inflicted upon me, and though I tried to smother my anger and to forgive those who had been so cruel to me, it was impossible. It seems that Mr. Bingham had pledged himself to Mrs. Burwell to subdue what he called my "stubborn pride."

Source: Elizabeth Keckley, *Behind the Scenes, or, Thirty Years a Slave, and Four Years in the White House* (New York, 1868).

3 John Brown, Born into Slavery in Virginia, Has Bells and Horns Fastened on His Head (1855)

"fixed bells and horns on my head"

> *John Brown (who was unrelated to the Harpers Ferry raider) was born into slavery in Southampton County, Virginia, and later toiled in Georgia and Louisiana. Here he describes the methods of discipline employed by one of his owners.*

To prevent my running any more, Stevens fixed bells and horns on my head. This is not by any means an uncommon punishment. I have seen many slaves wearing them. A circle of iron, having a hinge behind, with a staple and padlock before, which hang under the chin, is fastened round the neck. Another circle of iron fits quite close round the crown of the head. The two are held together in this position by three rods of iron, which are fixed in each circle. These rods, or horns, stick out three feet above the head, and have a bell attached to each. The bells and horns do not weigh less than twelve to fourteen pounds. When Stevens had fixed this ornament on my head, he turned me loose, and told me I might run off now if I liked.

I wore the bells and horns, day and night, for three months, and I do not think any description I could give of my sufferings during this time would convey anything approaching to a faint idea of them. Let alone that their weight made my head and neck ache dreadfully, especially when I stooped to my work. At night I could not lie down to rest, because the horns prevented my stretching myself, or even curling myself up; so I was obliged to sleep crouching. Of course it was impossible for me to attempt to remove them, or to get away, though I still held to my resolution to make another venture as soon as I could see my way of doing it.

Source: John Brown, *Slave Life in Georgia: A Narrative of the Life, Sufferings, and Escape of John Brown, A Fugitive Slave, Now in England* (London, 1855).

4 William Wells Brown, a Missouri Slave Driver, Is Tied Up in a Smokehouse (1847)

"I was tied up in the smokehouse"

One of the nation's first black novelists and historians, William Wells Brown was born in Lexington, Kentucky, in 1816 and raised in Missouri. After serving as a slave driver, he was hired out to transport slaves to the New Orleans slave market, but managed to escape. Here, he describes the punishments he encountered while he was a slave in Missouri.

My mother was hired out in the city, and I was also hired out there to Major Freeland, who kept a public house. He was formerly from Virginia, and was a horse-racer, cock-fighter, gambler, and withal an inveterate drunkard. There were ten or twelve servants in the house, and when he was present, it was cut and slash – knock down and drag out. In his fits of anger, he would take up a chair, and throw it at a servant; and in his more rational moments, when he wished to chastise one, he would tie them up in the smokehouse, and whip them; after which, he would cause a fire to be made of tobacco stems, and smoke them. This he called "Virginia play."

I complained to my master of the treatment which I received from Major Freeland; but it made no difference. He cared nothing about it, so long as he received the money for my labor. After living with Major Freeland five or six months, I ran away, and went into the woods back of the city; and when night came on, I made my way to my master's farm, knowing that if Mr. Haskell, the overseer, should discover me, I should be again carried back to Major Freeland; so I kept in the woods. One day, while in the woods, I heard the barking and howling of dogs, and in a short time they came so near that I knew them to be the bloodhounds of Major Benjamin O'Fallon. He kept five or six, to hunt runaway slaves with.

As soon as I was convinced that it was them, I knew there was no chance of escape. I took refuge in the top of a tree and the hounds were soon at its base, and there remained until the hunters came up in a half or three quarters of an hour afterwards. There were two men with the dogs, who, as soon as they came up, ordered me to descend. I came down, was tied, and taken to St. Louis jail. Major Freeland soon made his appearance, and took me out, and ordered me to follow him, which I did. After we returned home I was tied up in the smokehouse, and was very severely whipped. After the major had flogged me to his satisfaction, he sent out his son Robert, a young man eighteen or twenty years of age, to see that I was well smoked. He made a fire of tobacco stems, which soon set me to coughing and sneezing. This, Robert told me, was the way his father used to do to his slaves in Virginia. After giving me what they conceived to be a decent smoking, I was untied and again set to work.

Source: William Wells Brown, *Narrative of William W. Brown, A Fugitive Slave* (Boston, 1847).

5 Moses Roper, a Slave in Georgia and the Carolinas, Is Punished for Attempting to Run Away (1837)

"Among the instruments of torture employed"

> *Moses Roper, who was born into slavery in Caswell County, North Carolina, lived in North and South Carolina and in Georgia before he successfully fled to the North and then to England. In this selection from his autobiography, he describes the punishment he faced after he tried unsuccessfully to run away.*

My master gave me a hearty dinner, the best he ever did give me; but it was to keep me from dying before he had given me all the flogging he intended. After dinner he took me up to the log-house, stripped me quite naked, fasted a rail up very high, tied my hands to the rail, fastened my feet together, put a rail between my feet, and stood on the end of it to hold me down; the two sons then gave me fifty lashes, the son-in-law another fifty, and Mr. Gooch himself fifty more.

While doing this his wife came out, and begged him not to kill me, the first act of sympathy I ever noticed in her. When I called for water, they brought a pail-full and threw it over my back ploughed up by the lashes. After this, they took me to the blacksmith's shop, got two large bars of iron, which they bent around my feet, each bar weighing twenty pounds, and put a heavy log-chain on my neck....

Among the instruments of torture employed, I here describe one: – This is a machine used for packing and pressing cotton. By it he hung me up by the hands, a horse, and at times, a man moving round the screw and carrying it up and down, and pressing the block into a box into which the cotton is put. At this time he hung me up for a quarter of an hour. I was carried up ten feet from the ground.... After this torture, I stayed with him several months, and did my work very well. It was about the beginning of 1832, when he took off my irons, and being in dread of him, he having threatened me with more punishment, I attempted again to escape from him. At this time I got into North Carolina: but a reward having been offered for me, a Mr. Robinson caught me, and chained me to a chair, upon which he sat up with me all night, and next day proceeded home with me. This was Saturday. Mr. Gooch had gone to church, several miles from his house. When he came back, the first thing he did was to pour some tar upon my head, then rubbed it all over my face, took a torch with pitch on, and set it on fire; he put it out before it did me very great injury, but the pain which I endured was the most excruciating, nearly all my hair having been burnt off. On Monday, he puts irons on me again, weighing nearly fifty pounds. He threatened me again on the Sunday with another flogging; and on the Monday morning, before daybreak, I got away again, with my irons on, and was about three hours going a distance of two miles. I had gone a good distance, when I met with a coloured man, who got some wedges, and took my irons off. However, I was caught again, and put into prison in Charlotte, where Mr. Gooch came, and took me back to Chester. He asked me how I got my irons off. They having been got off by a slave, I would not answer his question, for fear of getting the man punished. Upon this he put the fingers of my hands into a vice, and squeezed all the nails off. He then had my feet put on an anvil, and ordered a man to beat my toes, till he smashed some of my nails off. The marks of this treatment still remain upon me, some of my nails never having grown perfect since.

Source: Moses Roper, *Narrative of the Adventures and Escape of Moses Roper* (London, 1837).

6 A Kentucky Slave, Lewis Clarke, Describes the Implements His Mistress Used to Beat Him (1846)

"her invention was wonderfully quick"

As a slave child in Kentucky, Lewis Clarke was frequently whipped by his mistress. Here, he describes the implements she used to punish him.

[My mistress's] instruments of torture were ordinarily the raw hide, or a bunch of hickory-sprouts seasoned in the fire and tied together. But if these were not at hand, nothing came amiss. She could relish a beating with a chair, the broom, tongs, shovel, shears, knife-handle, the heavy heel of her slipper, or a bunch of keys; her zeal was so active in these barbarous inflictions, that her invention was wonderfully quick, and some way of inflicting the requisite torture was soon found.

One instrument of torture is worthy of particular description. This was an oak club, a foot and a half in length, and an inch and a half square. With this delicate weapon she would beat us upon the hands and upon the feet until they were blistered. This instrument was carefully preserved for a period of four years. Every day, for that time, I was compelled to see that hated tool of cruelty lying in the chair by my side. The least degree of delinquency, either in not doing all the appointed work, or in look or behavior, was visited with a beating from this oak club. That club will always be a prominent object in the picture of horrors of my life of more than twenty years of bitter bondage. . . .

Mrs. Banton, as is common among slave-holding women, seemed to hate and abuse me all the more, because I had some of the blood of her father in my veins. There are no slaves that are so badly abused, as those that are related to some of the women, or the children of their own husband; it seems as though they never could hate these quite bad enough.

Source: *Interesting Memoirs and Documents Relating to American Slavery, and the Glorious Struggle Now Making for Complete Emancipation* (London, 1846).

Discussion Questions

1. Abolitionists charged that slavery depended on the infliction of physical punishment. Do you think they were correct? Or could the slave South have outlawed whipping and other cruel punishments?
2. What actions prompted slave owners to inflict such barbarous punishments?
3. Do you think such punishments were effective?

Chapter 9   "Let My People Go": Resistance and Flight

Four times during the first 31 years of the nineteenth century, American slaves organized insurrections against slavery. In 1800, a 24-year-old Virginia slave named Gabriel, a blacksmith, led a march of perhaps 50 armed slaves on Richmond. The plot failed when a storm washed out the road to Richmond, giving the Virginia militia time to arrest the rebels. White authorities executed Gabriel and 25 other conspirators.

In 1811 in Louisiana, between 180 and 500 slaves led by Charles Deslondes, a free mulatto from Haiti, marched on New Orleans, armed with axes and other weapons. Slave owners retaliated by killing 82 blacks and placing the heads of 16 leaders on pikes.

In 1822, a former slave named Denmark Vesey apparently devised a scheme to take over Charleston, South Carolina, on a summer Sunday when many whites would be vacationing outside the city. Vesey, who had been born in either Africa or the Caribbean in the late 1760s, had won a lottery, purchased his freedom, and opened a carpenter's shop. The decision by Charleston authorities to close the city's independent African church led Vesey to organize his conspiracy. Before the revolt could take place, however, a slave betrayed Vesey's plans. The authorities proceeded to arrest 131 blacks and hang 37.

The bloodiest slave revolt in American history took place in 1831 when Nat Turner, a Baptist preacher, led a force of between 60 and 80 slaves on a rampage through Southampton County in southern Virginia, leaving more than 50 whites dead. White authorities retaliated by killing about 100 blacks. Twenty more slaves, including Turner, were later executed.

Recognizing that open revolt against slavery was futile, most slaves expressed their opposition to slavery in more subtle ways. There was day-to-day resistance, acts that undercut slavery's economic efficiency, such as sabotage, stealing, malingering, murder, arson, and infanticide. There was also flight, running away sometimes to freedom in the North, but more frequently over shorter distances, into swamps or wooded areas or southern cities. Also highly significant was cultural resistance, the use of religion and various cultural rituals and practices as a way to resist slave masters' efforts to strip enslaved African Americans of a distinctive identity. These acts of resistance most commonly occurred when a master or overseer overstepped customary bonds. Through these acts, slaves established a right to proper treatment and forced those owners who considered themselves to be paternalistic to live up to their obligations.

1 Frederick Douglass Resists a Slave Breaker (1845)

"cowardice departed, bold defiance took its place"

Frederick Douglass believed that slave owners employed a variety of techniques to break slaves' spirits. These included the denial of education, the threat of sale, and the provision of liquor. In the most serious instances of resistance, some slave owners turned a slave over to a "Negro-breaker." In this selection, Douglass describes his battles with a man his master hired to beat him into submission.

If at any one time of my life more than another, I was made to drink the bitterest dregs of slavery, that time was during the first six months of my stay with Mr. [Edward] Covey. We were worked in all weathers. It was never too hot or too cold; it could never rain, blow, hail, or snow too hard for us to work in the field. Work, work, work was scarcely more the order of the day than of the night. The longest days were too short for him, and the shortest nights too long for him. I was somewhat unmanageable when I first went there, but a few months of this discipline tamed me. Mr. Covey succeeded in breaking me. I was broken in body, soul, and spirit. My natural elasticity was crushed, my intellect languished, the disposition to read departed, the cheerful spark that lingered about my eye died; the dark night of slavery closed in upon me; and behold a man transformed into a brute!

Sunday was my only leisure time. I spent this in a sort of beast-like stupor, between sleep and wake, under some large tree. At times I would rise up, a flash of energetic freedom would dart through my soul, accompanied with a faint gleam of hope that flickered for a moment, and then vanished. I sank down again, mourning over my wretched condition. I was sometimes prompted to take my life and that of Covey, but was prevented by a combination of hope and fear....

You have seen how a man was made a slave; you shall see how a slave was made a man. On one of the hottest days of the month of August, 1833, Bill Smith, William Hughes, a slave named Eli, and myself were engaged in fanning wheat.... The work was simple, requiring strength rather than intellect; yet, to one entirely unused to such work, it came very hard. About three o'clock of that day, I broke down; my strength failed me; I was seized with a violent aching of the head, attended with extreme dizziness; I trembled in every limb....

Mr. Covey was at the house, about one hundred yards from the treading-yard where we were fanning. On hearing the fan stop, he left immediately, and came to the spot where we were. He hastily enquired what the matter was. Bill answered that I was sick, and there was no one to bring wheat to the fan. I had by this time crawled away under the side of the post and rail-fence by which the yard was enclosed, hoping to find relief by getting out of the sun. He then asked where I was. He was told by one of the hands. He came to the spot, and after looking at me awhile, asked me what was the matter. I told him as well as I could, for I scarce had strength to speak. He then gave me a savage kick in the side, and told me to get up. I tried to do so, but fell back in the attempt. He gave me another kick, and again told me to rise. I again tried, and succeeded in gaining my feet: but, stopping to get the tub with which I was feeding the fan, I again staggered and fell. While down in this situation, Mr. Covey took up the hickory slat with which Hughes had been striking off the half-bushel measure, and with it gave me a heavy blow upon the head, making a large wound, and the blood ran freely; and with this, again told me to get up. I made no effort to comply, having now made up my mind to let him do his worst. In a short time after receiving this blow, my head grew better. Mr. Covey had now left me to my fate. At this moment I resolved to go to my master, enter a complaint, and ask his protection. In order to [do] this, I must that afternoon walk seven miles; and this, under the circumstances, was truly a severe undertaking. I was exceedingly feeble; made so as much by the kicks and blows which I received, as by the severe fit of sickness to which I had been subjected. I, however, watched my chance, while Covey was looking in an opposite direction, and started for St. Michael's. I succeeded in getting a considerable distance on my way to the woods, when Covey discovered me, and called after me to come back, threatening what he would do if I did not come. I disregarded both his calls and his threats, and made my way to the woods as fast as my feeble state would allow; and thinking I might be overhauled by him if I kept the road, I walked through the woods, keeping far enough from the road to avoid detection, and near enough to prevent losing my way. I had not gone far, before my little strength again failed me. I could go no farther. I fell down, and lay for a considerable time. The blood was yet oozing from the wound on my head. For a time I thought I should bleed to death, and think now that I should have done so, but the blood so matted my hair as to stop the wound. After lying there about three quarters of an hour, I nerved myself up again, and started on my way, through bogs and briers, barefooted and bareheaded, tearing my feet sometimes at nearly every step; and after a journey of about seven miles, occupying some five hours to perform it, I arrived at master's store. I then presented an appearance enough to affect any but a heart of iron. From the crown of my head to my feet, I was covered with blood. My hair was all clotted with dust and blood, my shirt was stiff with briers and thorns, and were also covered with blood. I supposed I looked like a man who had escaped a den of wild beasts, and barely escaped them. In this state I appeared before my master, humbly entreating him to interpose his authority for my protection. I told him all the circumstances as well as I could, and it seemed, as I spoke, at times to affect him. he would then walk the floor, and seek to justify Covey by saying he expected I deserved it. He asked me what I wanted. I told him to let me get a new home; that as sure as I lived with Mr. Covey again, I should live with but to die with him; that Covey would surely kill me – he was in a fair way for it. Master Thomas ridiculed the idea that there was any danger of Mr. Covey's killing me, and said that he knew Mr. Covey; that he was a good man, and that he could not think of taking me from him; that should he do so, he would lose the whole year's wages; that I belonged to Mr. Covey for one year, and that I must go back to him, come what might; and that I must not trouble him with any more stories, or that he would get hold of me. After threatening me thus, he gave me a very large dose of salts, telling me that I might remain in St. Michael's that night, (it being quite late,) but that I must be off back to Mr. Covey's early in the morning; and that if I did not, he would get hold of me, which meant that he would whip me. I remained all night, and according to his orders, I started off to Covey's in the morning (Saturday morning) wearied in body and broken in spirit. I got no supper that night, or breakfast that morning. I reached Covey's about nine o'clock; and just as I was getting over the fence that divided Mrs. Kemp's fields from ours, out ran Covey with his cowskin, to give me another whipping. Before he could reach me, I succeeded in getting to the cornfield; and as the corn was very high, it afforded me the means of hiding. He seemed very angry, and searched for me a long time. My behaviour was altogether unaccountable. He finally gave up the chase, thinking, I suppose, that I must come home for something to eat;

he would give himself no further trouble in looking for me. I spent that day mostly in the woods, having the alternative before me, – to go home and be whipped to death, or stay in the woods and be starved to death. That night, I fell in with Sandy Jenkins, a slave with whom I was somewhat acquainted. Sandy had a free wife, who lived about four miles from Mr. Covey's; and it being Saturday, he was on his way home to see her. I told him my circumstances, and he very kindly invited me to go home with him. I went home with him, and talked this whole matter over, and got his advice as to what course it was best for me to pursue. I found Sandy an old adviser. He told me, with great solemnity, I must go back to Covey; but that before I went, I must go with him into another part of the woods, where there was a certain root, which, if I would take some of it with me, carrying it always on my right side, would render it impossible for Mr. Covey, or any other white man, to whip me. He said he had carried it for years; and since he had done so, he had never received a blow, and never expected to, while he carried it. I at first rejected the idea, that the simple carrying of a root in my pocket would have any such effect as he had said, and was not disposed to take it; but Sandy impressed the necessity with such earnestness, telling me it could do no harm, if it did not good. To please him, I at length took the root, and, according to his direction, carried it upon my right side. This was Sunday morning. I immediately started for home; and upon entering the yard gate, out came Mr. Covey on his way to meeting. He spoke to me very kindly, bade me drive the pigs from a lot near by, and passed toward the church. Now this singular conduct of Mr. Covey really made me begin to think that there was something in the root which Sandy had given me; and had it been any other day than Sunday, I could have attributed the conduct to no other cause than the influence of that root; and as it was, I was half inclined to think the root to be something more than I at first had taken it to be. All went well till Monday morning. On this morning, the virtue of the root was fully tested. Long before daylight, I was called to go and rub, curry, and feed the horses. I obeyed, and was glad to obey. But whilst thus engaged, whilst in the act of throwing down some blades from the loft, Mr. Covey entered the stable with a long rope; and just as I was half way out of the loft, he caught hold of my legs, and was about tying me. As soon as I found what he was up to, I gave a sudden spring, and as I did so, he holding to my legs, I was brought sprawling on the stable floor. Mr. Covey seemed now to think he had me, and could do what he pleased; but at this moment – from whence came the spirit I don't know – I resolved to fight; and suiting my action to the resolution, I seized Covey hard by the throat; and as I did so, I rose. He held on to me, and I to him. My resistance was so entirely unexpected, that Covey seemed taken all aback. He trembled like a leaf. This gave me assurance, and I held him uneasy, causing the blood to run where I touched him with the ends of my fingers. Mr. Covey soon called out to Hughes for help. Hughes came, and, while Covey held me, attempted to tie my right hand. While he was in the act of doing so, I watched my chance, and gave him a heavy kick close under the ribs. This kick fairly sickened Hughes, so that he left me in the hands of Mr. Covey. This kick had the effect of not only weakening Hughes, but Covey also. While he saw Hughes bending over with pain, his courage quailed. He asked me if I meant to persist in my resistance. I told him I did, come what might; that he had used me like a brute for six months, and that I was determined to be used so no longer. With that, he strove to drag me to a stick that was lying just out of the stable door. He meant to knock me down. But just as he was leaning over to get the stick, I seized him with both hands by his collar, and brought him by a sudden snatch to the ground. By this time, Bill came. Covey called upon him for assistance, Bill wanted to know what he could do. Covey said, "Take hold of him, take hold of him!" Bill said his master hired him out to work, and not to help to whip me; so he left Covey and myself to fight our own battle out. We were at it for nearly two hours. Covey at length let me go, puffing and blowing at a great rate, saying that if I had not resisted, he would not have whipped me half so much. The truth was, that he had not whipped me at all. I considered him as getting entirely the worst end of the bargain; for he had drawn no blood from me, but I had from him. The whole six months afterwards, that I spent with Mr. Covey, he never laid the weight of his finger upon me in anger. He would occasionally say, he didn't want to get hold of me again. "No," thought I, "you need not; for you will come off worse than you did before."

This battle with Mr. Covey was the turning-point in my career as a slave. It rekindled the few expiring embers of freedom, and revived within me a sense of my own manhood. It recalled the departed self-confidence, and inspired me again with a determination to be free. The gratification afforded by the triumph was a full compensation for whatever else might follow, even death itself. He only can understand the deep satisfaction which I experienced, who had himself repelled by force the bloody arm of slavery. I felt as I never felt before. It was a glorious resurrection from the tomb of slavery to the heaven of freedom. My long-crushed spirit rose, cowardice departed, bold defiance took its place; and now I resolved that, however long I might remain a slave in form, the day had passed forever when I could be a slave in fact. I did not hesitate to let it be known of me, that the white man who expected to succeed in whipping, must also succeed in killing me.

From this time I was never again what might be called fairly whipped, though I remained a slave four years afterwards. I had several fights, but was never whipped.

It was for a long time a matter of surprise to me why Mr. Covey did not immediately have me taken by the constable to the whipping-post, and there regularly whipped for the crime of raising my hand against a white man in defence of myself. And the only explanation I can now think of does not entirely satisfy me; but such as it is, I will give it. Mr. Covey enjoyed the most unbounded reputation for being a first-rate overseer and Negro-breaker. It was of considerable importance to him. That reputation was at stake; and had he sent me – a boy of sixteen years old – to the whipping-post, his reputation would have been lost; so, to save his reputation, he suffered me to go unpunished.

Source: Frederick Douglass, *Narrative of the Life of Frederick Douglass, An American Slave* (Boston, 1845).

2 Nat Turner, a Baptist Preacher in Virginia, Describes His Revolt Against Slavery (1831)

"the last should be first"

On August 22, 1831, Nat Turner, along with five followers, launched the most famous slave revolt in American history. Within a day, his band of insurgents had swollen to between 60 and 80 (including at least four free men of color), and killed between 55 and 58 whites, including 15 women and at least 23 children. For nine weeks Turner eluded capture. He was captured on October 30, put on trial, and executed on November 11, 1831. Fifty-two slaves were put on trial and 17 were eventually executed.

In the wake of the rebellion, Virginia passed a series of laws intended to prevent another insurrection. These included laws that forbade teaching slaves to read and write, barred blacks from carrying firearms, and prohibited blacks from holding religious services without a white minister present. The rebellion also sparked a serious debate within Virginia's legislature over the future of slavery. A proposal to gradually abolish slavery within the state was defeated.

To understand why Turner led his revolt, we turn to his "confessions," which a white attorney, Thomas C. Gray, claimed that Turner had dictated to him. According to this document, Turner stated that his owner was "kind ..., and placed the greatest confidence in me." But a series of visions convinced him that he had been called by God to lead a rebellion.

Sir – You have asked me to give a history of the motives which induced me to undertake the late insurrection, as you call it – To do so I must go back to the days of my infancy. . . . In my childhood a circumstance occurred which made an indelible impression on my mind, and laid the groundwork of that enthusiasm, which has terminated so fatally to many, both white and black, and for which I am about to atone at the gallows. . . . Being at play with other children, when three or four years old, I was telling them something, which my mother overhearing, said it had happened before I was born . . . others being called on were greatly astonished . . . and caused them to say in my hearing, I surely would be a prophet. . . .

For two years [I] prayed continually, whenever my duty would permit – and then again I had [a] . . . revelation, which fully confirmed me in the impression that I was ordained for some great purpose, in the hands of the Almighty. . . .

About this time [around 1825] I had a vision – and I saw white spirits and black spirits engaged in battle, and the sun was darkened – the thunder rolled in the Heavens, and blood flowed in streams. . . .

And on the 12th of May, 1828, I heard a loud noise in the heavens, and the Spirit instantly appeared to me and said the Serpent was loosened, and Christ had laid down the yoke he had borne for the sins of men, and that I should take it on and fight against the Serpent, for the time was fast approaching when the first should be last and the last should be first.

[Question] Do you not find yourself mistaken now?

[Answer] Was not Christ crucified? And by signs in the heavens that it would be made known to me when I should commence the great work – and until the first sign appeared, I should conceal if from the knowledge of men – And on the appearance of the sign (the eclipse of the sun last February), I should arise and prepare myself, and slay my enemies with their own weapons. And immediately on the sign appearing in the heavens, the seal was removed from my lips, and I communicated the great work laid out before me to do, to four in whom I had the greatest confidence (Henry, Hark, Nelson, and Sam) – It was intended by us to have begun the work of death on the 4th of July last – Many were the plans formed and rejected by us, and it affected my mind to such a degree, that I fell sick, and the time passed without our coming to any determination how to commence – Still forming new schemes and rejecting them, when the sign appeared again, which determined me not to wait longer.

Since the commencement of 1830, I had been living with Mr. Joseph Travis, who was to me a kind master, and placed the greatest confidence in me: in fact, I had no cause to complain of his treatment of me. On Saturday evening, the 20th of August, it was agreed between Henry, Hark, and myself, to prepare a dinner the next day for the men we expected, and then to concert a plan, as we had not yet determined on any. Hark, on the following morning, brought a pig, and Henry brandy, and being joined by Sam, Nelson, Will and Jack, they prepared in the woods a dinner, where, about three o'clock, I joined them. . . .

I saluted them on coming up, and asked Will how came he there, he answered, his life was worth no more than others, and his liberty as dear to him. I asked him if he thought to obtain it? He said he would, or lose his life. This was enough to put him in full confidence. Jack, I knew, was only a tool in the hands of Hark, it was quickly agreed we should commence at home (Mr. J. Travis') on that night, and until we had armed and equipped ourselves, and gathered sufficient force, neither age nor sex was to be spared (which was invariably adhered to). We remained at the feast, until about two hours in the night, when we went to the house and found Austin; they all went to the cider press and drank, except myself. On returning to the house Hark went to the door with an axe, for the purpose of breaking it open, as we knew we were strong enough to murder the family, if they were awakened by the noise; but reflecting that it might create an alarm in the neighborhood, we determined to enter the house secretly, and murder them whilst sleeping. Hark got a ladder and set it against the chimney, on which I ascended, and hoisting a window, entered and came down stairs, unbarred the door, and removed the guns from their places. It was then observed that I must spill the first blood. On which, armed with a hatchet, and accompanied by Will, I entered my master's chamber, it being dark, I could not give a death blow, the hatchet glanced from his head, he sprang from the bed and called his wife, it was his last word, Will laid him dead, with a blow of his axe, and Mrs. Travis shared the same fate, as she lay in bed. The murder of this family, five in number, was the work of a moment, not one of them awoke; there was a little infant sleeping in a cradle, that was forgotten, until we had left the house and gone some distance, when Henry and Will returned and killed it; we got here, four guns that would shoot and several old muskets, with a pound or two of powder. We remained some time at the barn, where we paraded; I formed them in a line as soldiers, and . . . marched them off to Mr. Salthul Francis', about six hundred yards distant. Sam and Will went to the door and knocked. Mr. Francis asked who was there, Sam replied it was him, and he had a letter for him, on which he got up and came to the door; they immediately seized him, and dragging him out a little from the door, he was dispatched by repeated blows on the head; there was no other white person in the family. We started from there for Mrs. Reese's, maintaining the most perfect silence on our march, where finding the door unlocked, we entered, and murdered Mrs. Reese in her bed, while sleeping; her son awoke, but it was only to sleep the sleep of death, he had only time to say who is that, and he was no more. From Mrs. Reese's we went to Mrs. Turner's, a mile distant, which we reached about sunrise, on Monday morning. Henry, Austin, and Sam, went to the still, where, finding Mr. Peebles, Austin shot him, and the rest of us went to the house; as we approached, the family discovered us, and shut the door. Vain hope! Will, with one stroke of his axe opened it, and we entered and found Mrs. Turner and Mrs. Newsome in the middle of a room, almost frightened to death. Will immediately killed Mrs. Turner, with one blow of his axe. I took Mrs. Newsome by the hand, and with the sword I had when I was apprehended, I struck her several blows over the head, but not being able to kill her, as the sword was dull. Will turning around and discovering it, dispatched her also. A general destruction of property and search for money and ammunition, always succeeded the murders. By this time my company amounted to fifteen, and nine men mounted, who started for Mrs. White-head's.... As we approached the house we discovered Mr. Richard White-head standing in the cotton patch, near the lane fence; we called him over into the lane, and Will, the executioner, was near at hand, with his fatal axe, to send him to an untimely grave.... As I came around to the door I saw Will pulling Mrs. Whitehead out of the house, and at the step he nearly severed her head from her body, with his broad axe. Miss Margaret, when I discovered her, had concealed herself in the corner... on my approach she fled, but was soon overtaken, and after repeated blows with a sword, I killed her by a blow on the head, with a fence rail....

'Twas my object to carry terror and devastation wherever we went.... I sometimes got in sight in time to see the work of death completed, viewed the mangled bodies as they lay, in silent satisfaction, and immediately started in quest of other victims – Having murdered Mrs. Waller and ten children, we started for Mr. William Williams' – having killed him and two little boys that were there; while engaged in this, Mrs. Williams fled and got some distance from the house, but she was pursued, overtaken, and compelled to get up behind one of the company, who brought her back, and after showing her the mangled body of her lifeless husband, she was told to get down and lay by his side, where she was shot dead....

Our number amounted now to fifty or sixty, all mounted and armed with guns, axes, swords, and clubs.... We were met by a party of white men, who had pursued our blood-stained track.... The white men, eighteen in number, approached us in about one hundred yards, when one of them fired.... I then ordered my men to fire and rush them; the few remaining stood their ground until we approached within fifty yards, when they fired and retreated.... As I saw them re-loading their guns, and more coming up than I saw at first, and several of my bravest men being wounded, the other became panick struck and squandered over the field; the white men pursued and fired on us several times....

All deserted me but two, (Jacob and Nat,) we concealed ourselves in the woods until near night, when I sent them in search of Henry, Sam, Nelson, and Hark, and directed them to rally all they could, at the place where had had our dinner the Sunday before, where they would find me, and I accordingly returned there as soon as it was dark and remained until Wednesday evening, when discovering white men riding around the place as though they were looking for someone, and none of my men joining me, I concluded Jacob and Nat had been taken, and compelled to betray me. On this I gave up all hope for the present; and on Thursday night after having supplied myself with provisions from Mr. Travis' I scratched a hole under a pile of fence rails in a field, where I concealed myself for six weeks, never leaving my hiding place but for a few minutes in the dead of night to get water which was very near.... I know not how long I might have led this life, if accident had not betrayed me, a dog in the neighborhood passing by my hiding place one night while I was out, was attracted by some meat I had in my cave, and crawled in and stole it, and was coming out just as I returned. A few nights after, two Negroes having started to go hunting with the same dog, and passed that way, the dog came again to the place, and having just gone out to walk about, discovered me and barked, on which thinking myself discovered, I spoke to them to beg concealment. On making myself known they fled from me. Knowing when they would betray me, I immediately left my hiding place, and was pursued almost incessantly until I was taken a fortnight afterwards by Mr. Benjamin Phipps, in a little hole I had dug out with my sword, for the purpose of concealment, under the top of a fallen tree.

Source: Nat Turner, *The Confessions of Nat Turner, the Leader of the Late Insurrection in Southampton, Va.* (Baltimore, 1831).

3 Harriet Tubman, a Former Maryland Slave, Sneaks into the South to Free Slaves (1872)

"Time and again she made successful visits to Maryland on the Underground Rail Road"

It is among the most famous images in American literature: a slave mother, a baby in her arms and pursued by snarling dogs, leaps from ice floe to ice floe, in a desperate attempt to cross the Ohio River to freedom. Immortalized in Harriet Beecher Stowe's Uncle Tom's Cabin, *this scene was based on a real-life incident in 1838. A slave mother, whose name is unknown, fled her plantation after she learned of her master's plans to sell her apart from her husband and other children.*

Although this woman slipped into the freezing water three times, she and her infant did succeed in reaching the Ohio shore. An abolitionist fed them, provided a change of clothes, and escorted the runaways to the home of a minister, who helped them go further north. We know about this incident because it was recorded by a slave catcher, who was so impressed by the woman's courage that he decided not to pursue her.

The Underground Railroad – the covert network that helped fugitives escape slavery – contains some of the most amazing stories in American history. There was Henry "Box" Brown, who, with the help of an abolitionist doctor, was nailed into a wooden crate and shipped to Philadelphia, and whose story is told in reading 8 below. There were Ellen and William Craft of Georgia, who disguised themselves as a male slave owner (the role assumed by the light-skinned Ellen Craft) accompanied by his slave.

The Underground Railroad acquired its name in the 1840s, at the time that the nation's railroads were rapidly expanding. The name is somewhat misleading. It was not a railroad, nor did it run underground, except metaphorically. Contrary to legend, which speaks of "stations" and "conductors," the Underground Railroad did not consist of a formalized or centralized structure. Although there were safe houses, guides, and pathways, there were no maps or timetables. Rather, the Underground Railroad was a loose network of individuals and groups that facilitated the flight of slaves to the North and to Canada.

The most famous of all the guides leading slaves to freedom was Harriet Tubman, the "Black Moses," who made 12 or possibly 13 trips, liberating about 70 individuals from slavery. Born Araminta "Minty" Ross in 1822 on Maryland's eastern shore, not far from Frederick Douglass's birthplace, she saw two sisters sold and underwent repeated whippings, incidents that fueled her hunger for freedom. In 1849, she left her husband, escaped from slavery, and made her way to Philadelphia. During the 1850s, she became legendary for rescuing slaves in her native Maryland, and appeared frequently on the antislavery lecture circuit. John Brown consulted her before his fateful raid on Harpers Ferry, Virginia. In 1860, she orchestrated the escape of Charles Nalle, a fugitive slave New York authorities wanted to ship back to Virginia.

Her success was wonderful. Time and again she made successful visits to Maryland on the Underground Rail Road, and would be absent for weeks at a time, running daily risks while making preparations for herself and her passengers. Great fears were entertained for her safety, but she seemed wholly devoid of personal fear. The idea of being captured by slave-hunters or slave-holders, seemed never to enter her mind. She was apparently proof against all adversaries. While she thus maintained utter personal indifference, she was much more watchful with regard to those she was piloting. Half of her time, she had the appearance of one asleep, and would actually sit down by the road-side and go fast asleep when on her errands of mercy through the South, yet, she would not suffer one of her party to whimper once, about "giving out and going back," however wearied they might be by the hard travel day and night. She had a very short and pointed rule or law of her own, which implied death to any who talked of giving out and going back. Thus, in an emergency she would give all to understand that "times were very critical and therefore no foolishness would be indulged in on the road." That several who were rather weak-kneed and faint-hearted were greatly invigorated by Harriet's blunt and positive manner and threat of extreme measures, there could be no doubt.

After having once enlisted, "They had to go through or die." Of course Harriet was supreme, and her followers generally had full faith in her, and would back up any word she might utter. So when she said to them that "a live runaway could do great harm by going back, but that a dead one could tell no secrets," she was sure to have obedience. Therefore, none had to die as traitors on the "middle passage." It is obvious enough, however, that her success in going into Maryland as she did, was attributable to her adventurous spirit and utter disregard of consequences. Her like it is probable was never known before or since.

Source: William Still, *The Underground Railroad* (Philadelphia, 1872).

4 Harriet Tubman's Life and Methods for Liberating Slaves (1863, 1865)

"the most remarkable woman of this age"

> *This account of Harriet Tubman's life and her success in helping slaves escape from bondage describes the religious faith that motivated her efforts and the detailed planning that she undertook to liberate slaves.*
>
> *During the Civil War, she served as a scout, spy, and nurse for the Union army in South Carolina, where she assisted the 54th Massachusetts Volunteer Infantry, the African American regiment that was the subject of the film* Glory. *In June 1863, she guided Union gunboats up South Carolina's Combahee River, helping to liberate over 700 slaves in a single night. Over the next 30 years she was active in the women's rights movement and battled for a Union pension, which she finally received in 1892, making her one of only a handful of women rewarded for service during the Civil War. She died in 1913, the year that Rosa Parks, another civil rights pioneer, was born.*

One of the teachers lately commissioned by the New-England Freedmen's Aid Society is probably the most remarkable woman of this age. That is to say, she has performed more wonderful deeds by the native power of her own spirit against adverse circumstances than any other. She is well known to many by the various names which her eventful life has given her; Harriet Garrison, Gen. Tubman, &c.; but among the slaves she is universally known by her well earned title of Moses, – Moses the deliverer. She is a rare instance, in the midst of high civilization and intellectual culture, of a being of great native powers, working powerfully, and to beneficent ends, entirely untaught by schools or books.

Her maiden name was Araminta Ross. She is the granddaughter of a native African, and has not a drop of white blood in her veins. She was born in 1820 or 1821, on the Eastern Shore of Maryland....

She seldom lived with her owner, but was usually "hired out" to different persons. She once "hired her time," and employed it in the rudest farming labors, ploughing, carting, driving the oxen, &c., to so good advantage that she was able in one year to buy a pair of steers worth forty dollars.

When quite young she lived with a very pious mistress; but the slave-holder's religion did not prevent her from whipping the young girl for every slight or fancied fault. Araminta found that this was usually a morning exercise; so she prepared for it by putting on all the thick clothes she could procure to protect her skin. She made sufficient outcry, however, to convince her mistress that her blows had full effect; and in the afternoon she would take off her wrappings, and dress as well as she could. When invited into family prayers, she preferred to stay on the landing, and pray for herself; "and I prayed to God," she says "to make me strong and able to fight and that's what I've allers prayed for ever since...."

In her youth she received a severe blow on her head from a heavy weight thrown by her master at another slave, but which accidentally hit her. The blow produced a disease of the brain which was severe for a long time, and still makes her very lethargic.... She was married about 1844 to a free colored man named John Tubman, but never had any children. Owing to changes in her owner's family, it was determined to sell her and some other slaves; but her health was so much injured, that a purchaser was not easily found. At length she became convinced that she would soon be carried away, and she decided to escape. Her brothers did not agree with her plans, and she walked off alone, following the guidance of the brooks, which she had observed to run North....

She remained two years in Philadelphia working hard and carefully hoarding her money. Then she hired a room, furnished it as well as she could, bought a nice suit of men's clothes, and went back to Maryland for her husband. But the faithless man had taken to himself another wife. Harriet did not dare venture into her presence, but sent word to her husband where she was. He declined joining her. At first her grief and anger were excessive ... but finally she thought ... "if he could do without her, she could without him," and so "he dropped out of her heart," and she determined to give her life to brave deeds. Thus all personal aims died out of her heart; and with her simple brave motto, "I can't die but once," she began the work which has made her Moses, – the deliverer of her people. Seven or eight times she has returned to the neighborhood of her former home, always at the risk of death in the most terrible forms, and each time has brought away a company of fugitive slaves, and led them safely to the free States, or to Canada. Every time she went, the dangers increased. In 1857, she brought away her old parents, and, as they were too feeble to walk, she was obliged to hire a wagon, which added greatly to the perils of the journey. In 1860 she went for the last time, and among her troop was an infant whom they were obliged to keep stupefied with laudanum to prevent its outcries. ...

She always came in the winter when the nights are long and dark, and people who have homes stay in them. She was never seen on the plantation herself; but appointed a rendezvous for her company eight or ten miles distant, so that if they were discovered at the first start she was not compromised. She started on Saturday night; the slaves at that time being allowed to go away from home to visit their friends – so that they would not be missed until Monday morning. Even then they were supposed to have loitered on the way, and it would often be late on Monday afternoon before the flight would be certainly known. If by any further delay the advertisement was not sent out before Tuesday morning, she felt secure of keeping ahead of it; but if it were, it required all her ingenuity to escape. She resorted to various devices, she had confidential friends all along the road. She would hire a man to follow the one who put up the notices, and take them down as soon as his back was turned. She crossed creeks on railroad bridges by night, she hid her company in the woods while she herself not being advertised went into the towns in search of information. ...

The expedition was governed by the strictest rules. If any man gave out, he must be shot. "Would you really do that?" she was asked. "Yes," she replied, "if he was weak enough to give out, he'd be weak enough to betray us all, and all who had helped us; and do you think I'd let so many die just for one coward man." "Did you ever have to shoot any one?" she was asked. "One time," she said, "a man gave out on the second night; his feet were sore and swollen, he couldn't go any further; he'd rather go back and die, if he must." They tried all arguments in vain, bathed his feet, tried to strengthen him, but it was of no use, he would go back. Then she said, "I told the boys to get their guns ready, and shoot him. They'd have done it in a minute; but when he heard that, he jumped right up and went on as well as any body...."

When going on these journeys she often lay alone in the forests all night. Her whole soul was filled with awe of the mysterious Unseen Presence, which thrilled her with such depths of emotion, that all other care and fear vanished. Then she seemed to speak with her Maker "as a man talketh with his friend;" her child-like petitions had direct answers, and beautiful visions lifted her up above all doubt and anxiety into serene trust and faith. No man can be a hero without this faith in some form; the sense that he walks not in his own strength, but leaning on an almighty arm. Call it fate, destiny, what you will, Moses of old, Moses of to-day, believed it to be Almighty God.

Source: *Commonwealth*, July 17, 1863; *Freeman's Record*, March 1865.

5 Levi Coffin, the "President" of the Underground Railroad, Assists Fugitives to Escape Slavery (1876)

"Seldom a week passed without our receiving passengers"

The story of the Underground Railroad is enveloped in myths. Many people assume that the song "Follow the Drinking Gourd" offered directions to runaways. In fact, the song was first published in 1928, 63 years after slavery's abolition, and it acquired its current music and lyrics only in 1947. Nor is there evidence that escape routes were inscribed on quilts.

Between the 1780s, when the northern states began to abolish slavery and the free black population began to rise, and 1860, a growing number of northerners, black and white, assisted fugitives fleeing across the Mason–Dixon line and the Ohio River. Among the best known was the black activist David Ruggles of New York City, who may have helped over 600 former slaves achieve freedom. Other key figures include Jermain Loguen, an African American leader in Syracuse, New York, who openly published his address in local newspapers in a bid to help fugitives; George DeBaptiste, a black barber in Madison, Indiana; and Levi Coffin, a white North Carolina-raised Quaker who lived for two decades in Newport (now Fountain City), Indiana.

Coffin was called the Underground Railroad's president. After moving to Newport in 1826, he and his wife Catherine provided food and shelter to fugitives seeking freedom. He explained his commitment to assisting fugitives with these words: "The Bible, in bidding us to feed the hungry and clothe the naked, said nothing about color, and I should try to follow out the teachings of that good book." Following the Civil War, he was a leading figure in the Western Freedmen's Aid Society, which provided food, clothing, medical

services, and schooling to former slaves. He described his role in the
Underground Railroad in his Reminiscences, *published in 1876, the year*
before his death.

Soon after we located at Newport [Indiana], I found that we were on a line
of the U.G.R.R. [Underground Railroad]. Fugitives often passed through
that place, and generally stopped among the colored people.... I learned
that the fugitive slaves who took refuge with these people were often
pursued and captured, the colored people not being very skillful in conceal-
ing them, or shrewd in making arrangements to forward them to Canada ...
I was willing to receive and aid as many fugitives as were disposed to come
to my house. I knew that my wife's feelings and sympathies regarding this
matter were the same as mine, and that she was willing to do her part....

In the winter of 1826–27, fugitives began to come to our house, and as it
became more widely known on different routes that the slaves fleeing from
bondage would find a welcome and shelter at our house, and be forwarded
safely on their journey, the number increased. Friends in the neighborhood,
who had formerly stood aloof from the work, fearful of the penalty of the
law, were encouraged to engage in it when they saw the fearless manner in
which I acted, and the success that attended my efforts.

... the Underground Railroad business increased as time advanced, and it
was attended with heavy expenses, which I could not have borne had not
my affairs been prosperous. I found it necessary to keep a team and a wagon
always at command, to convey the fugitive slaves on their journey. Sometimes, when we had large companies, one or two other teams and wagons
were required. These journeys had to be made at night, often through deep
mud and bad roads, and along by ways that were seldom traveled. Every
precaution to evade pursuit had to be used, as the hunters were often on the
track, and sometimes ahead of the slaves....

I soon became extensively known to the friends of the slaves, at different
points on the Ohio River, where fugitives generally crossed, and to those
northward of us on the various routes leading to Canada.... Three principal lines from the South converged at my house: one from Cincinnati, one
from Madison, and one from Jeffersonville, Indiana. The roads were always
in running order, the connections were good, the conductors active and
zealous, and there was no lack of passengers. Seldom a week passed without
our receiving passengers by the mysterious road.

Source: Levi Coffin, *Reminiscences of Levi Coffin* (Cincinnati, 1876).

6 A Maryland Slave, Margaret Ward, Follows the North Star to Freedom (1879)

"she would not be whipped, she would rather die"

> *Altogether, it appears that between 100,000 and 130,000 fugitives escaped to the North or Canada between 1790 and 1860. Most of these runaways came from states bordering the North, like Maryland and Kentucky. It seems likely that an even larger number fled to southern towns and cities. Most runaways, however, were unable to escape permanently. Instead, they fled for a temporary period and ultimately returned to their plantation after a period of negotiation. Flight was often triggered by the threat of a sale, excessive punishment, or violation of accepted rules (for example, involving access to garden plots or opportunities to visit across plantations or religious ceremonies or burials).*
>
> *Running away ultimately depended on the audacity and ingenuity of individual African Americans. They had to borrow or forge passes, devise disguises, locate hiding places, or stow away on boats or trains. Here, we learn how Margaret Ward and her infant son Samuel Ringgold Ward, slaves from Maryland, succeeded in following the North Star to freedom.*

At sixteen she went to live with her young mistress, who was married to a planter in that fertile country known as the "Eastern Shore." At eighteen Margaret was a large woman, tall and well formed, her complexion black as jet, her countenance always pleasant, though she seldom laughed. She talked but little, even to those of her own race. At twenty years of age she became the wife of a worthy young man to whom she had given her best affections. Not long after, her young master became very angry with her for what he called stubbornness and resistance to his will, and threatened to chastise her by whipping – a degradation that she had always felt that she could not submit to, and yet to obey her master in the thing he demanded would be still worse. She therefore told him that she would not be whipped, she would rather die, and gave him warning that any attempt to execute his threat would surely result in the death of one of them. He knew her too well to risk the experiment, and decided to punish her in another way. He sold her husband, and she saw him bound in chains and driven off with a large drove of men and women for the New Orleans market. He then put her in the hands of a brutal overseer, with directions to work her to the extent of her ability on a tobacco plantation, which command was enforced up to the day of the birth of her child. At the end of one week she was driven again to the field and compelled to perform a full task, having at no time any abatement of her work on account of her situation, with exception of one week. It was the custom on the plantation to establish nurseries, presided over by old, broken down slaves, where mothers might leave their infants, but this privilege was denied to Margaret. She was obliged to leave her child under the shade of a bush in the field, returning to it but twice during the long day. On returning to the child one evening she found it apparently senseless, exhausted with crying, and a large serpent lying across it. Although she felt that it would be better for both herself and child if it were dead, yet a mother's heart impelled her to make an effort to save it, and by caressing him and careful handling she resuscitated it.

As soon as she heard its feeble, wailing cry, she made a vow to deliver her boy from the cruel power of slavery or die in the attempt, and falling prostrate, she prayed for strength to perform her vow, and for grace and patience to sustain her in her suffering, toil, and hunger; then pressing her child to her bosom, she fled with all the speed of which she was capable toward the North Star. Having gone a mile or two, she heard something pursuing her; on looking round she saw Watch, the old house dog. Watch was a large mastiff, somewhat old, and with him Margaret had ever been a favorite, and since she had been driven to the field, Watch often visited her at her cabin in the evening. She feared it would not be safe to allow Watch to go with her, but she could not induce him to go back, so she resumed her flight, accompanied by her faithful escort. At break of day she hid herself on the border of a plantation and soon fell asleep.

Toward evening she was aroused by the noise made by the slaves returning to their quarters, and seeing an old woman lingering behind all the others, she called her, told her troubles, and asked for food. The old woman returned about midnight with a pretty good supply of food, which Margaret divided with Watch, and then started on, taking the north star for her guide. The second day after she left, the Overseer employed a hunter with his dogs to find her. . . .

Margaret had been missed at roll call the morning after her flight, but the Overseer supposed she was hiding near the place for a day or two, and that hunger would soon drive her up; therefore, when the hunter started, he led the old dog, expecting to find her in an hour or two, but not overtaking her the first day, on the next morning, he let his hounds loose, intending to follow on horseback, guided by their voices. About noon, the old dog struck the track at the place where Margaret had made her little camp the day before, and she bounded off with fresh vigor, leaving the man and the younger dogs beyond sight and hearing. The young dogs soon lost the track where Margaret forded the streams, and the old dog was miles away, leaving the hunter without a guide to direct him.

Margaret had been lying in the woods on the bank of a river, intending to start again as soon as it was dark, when she was startled by the whining and nervous motions of old Watch, and listening, she heard the hoarse ringing bay of a blood-hound. Although she had expected that she would be hunted with dogs, and recalled over and over again the shocking accounts related by Overseers to the slaves, of fugitives overtaken and torn in pieces by the same Spanish blood-hounds, she had not, until now, realized the horrors of her situation. She expected to have to witness the destruction of her child by the savage brute, and then be torn in pieces herself. Meanwhile, old Watch lay with his nose between his feet, facing the coming foe. The hound, rendered more fierce by the freshness of the track, came rushing headlong with nose to the ground, scenting her prey, and seemed not to see old Watch, until, leaping to pass over him, she found her wind-pipe suddenly collapsed in the massive jaws of the old mastiff. The struggle was not very noisy, for Watch would not even growl, and the hound could not, for it was terribly energetic. The hound made rapid and persuasive gestures with her paws and tail, but it was of no use, the jaws of old Watch relaxed not until all signs of life in his enemy had ceased. Margaret came back from the river, and would have embraced her faithful friend, but fearing that a stronger pack was following, she hastily threw the dead hound into the river and pursued her journey.

Within a few hours after her providential escape by the aid of her faithful friend, old Watch, from the fangs of the slave hunter's hound, she fell into the hands of friends, who kept her secreted until she could be sent into a free State; while there, she learned about the pursuit by the hunter, and that he never knew what became of his best hound. After the chase was abandoned, she, through a regular line, similar to our Underground Railroad, was sent to Philadelphia and then to New York, where she became a celebrated nurse, and always befriended the poor of all colors and all nationalities.

Source: Eber Pettit, *Sketches in the History of the Underground Railroad* (Fredonia, N.Y., 1879).

7 Frederick Douglass Borrows a Sailor's Papers to Escape Slavery (1855, 1895)

"A new World burst upon my agitated vision"

For many years, Frederick Douglass refused to disclose how he had succeeded in fleeing slavery. From two sources, which are brought together in the following reading, we learn how Douglass used a black sailor's papers to escape from bondage and described his initial reaction upon attaining his freedom.

I have never approved of the very public manner, in which some of our western friends have conducted what they call the "Under-ground Railroad," but which, I think, by their open declarations, has been made, mòst emphatically, the "Upper-ground Railroad." Its stations are far better known to the slaveholders than to the slaves. I honor those good men and women for their noble daring, in willingly subjecting themselves to persecution, by openly avowing their participation in the escape of slaves; nevertheless, the good resulting from such avowals, is of a very questionable character. It may kindle an enthusiasm, very pleasant to inhale; but that is of no practical benefit to themselves, nor to the slaves escaping. Nothing is more evident, than that such disclosures are a positive evil to the slaves remaining, and seeking to escape. In publishing such accounts, the anti-slavery man addresses the slaveholder, not the slave; he stimulates the former to greater watchfulness, and adds to the facilities for capturing the slave....

My condition in the year [1838] of my escape, was, comparatively, a free and easy one, so far, at least, as the wants of the physical man were concerned; but the reader will bear in mind, that my troubles from the beginning, have been less physical than mental.... The practice, from week to week, of openly robbing me of all my earnings, kept the nature and character of slavery constantly before me. I could be robbed by indirection, but this was too open and barefaced to be endured. I could see no reason why I should, at the end of each week, pour the reward of my honest toil into the purse of any man....

Held to a strict account, and kept under a close watch – the old suspicion of my running away not having been entirely removed – escape from slavery, even in Baltimore, was very difficult. The railroad from Baltimore to Philadelphia was under regulations so stringent, that even free colored travelers were almost excluded. They must have free papers; they must be measured and carefully examined, before they were allowed to enter the cars; they only went in the day time, even when so examined. The steamboats were under regulations equally stringent. All the great turnpikes, leading northward, were beset with kidnappers, a class of men who watched the newspapers for advertisements for runaway slaves, making their living by the accursed reward of slave hunting.

My discontent grew upon me, and I was on the lookout for means of escape. With money, I could easily have managed the matter, and, therefore, I hit upon the plan of soliciting the privilege of hiring my time. It is quite common, in Baltimore, to allow slaves this privilege, and it is the practice, also in New Orleans. A slave who is considered trustworthy, can, by paying his master a definite sum regularly, at the end of each week dispose of his time as he likes. . . .

The laws of Maryland required every free Negro to carry papers describing him accurately and to pay liberally for this protection. Slaves often escaped by borrowing papers from a friend, to whom the precious documents would be returned by mail. Whenever a coloured man came with free papers to the railroad station to buy a ticket, he was always examined carefully enough to insure the detection of a runaway, unless the resemblance was very close. Our hero was not acquainted with any free Negro who looked much like him; but he found out that passengers who paid on the cars were not scrutinized so minutely as those who bought tickets, and also that sailors were treated with peculiar indulgence by the conductors. . . .

Among his friends was a sailor who was of much darker hue than he was himself, but who owned a protection, setting forth his occupation, and bearing the sacred figure of the American eagle. This was borrowed; sailor's clothes were purchased, and on Monday morning, the fugitive jumped on the train just as it started. His baggage had been put aboard by a friendly hackman. He was greatly troubled, for, as he wrote to his master, ten years later, I was making a leap in the dark. The probabilities, so far as I could by reason determine them, were stoutly against the undertaking. The preliminaries and precautions I had adopted previously, all worked badly. I was like one going to war without weapons – ten chances of defeat to one of victory. One in whom I had confided, and one who had promised me assistance, appalled by the fear at the trial hour, deserted me. However, gloomy as was the prospect, thanks be to the Most High, who is ever the God of the oppressed, at the moment which was to determine my whole earthly career, His grace was sufficient; my mind was made up.

His anxiety increased in consequence of the harshness with which the conductor questioned other passengers in the Negro car. The sailor, however, was addressed kindly and told, after a mere glance at the protection, that it was all right. Thus far he was safe; but there were several people on the train who would have known him at once in any other clothes. A German blacksmith looked at him intently, and apparently recognized him, but said nothing. On the ferry boat, by which they crossed the Susquehanna, he found an old acquaintance employed, and was asked some dangerous questions. On they went, however, until they stopped to let the train from Philadelphia pass. At the window sat a man under whom the runaway had been at work but a few days before. He might easily have recognized him, and would certainly have him arrested; but fortunately he was looking another way. The passengers went on from Wilmington by steamer to Philadelphia, where one of them took the train for New York and arrived early on Tuesday. In less than twenty-four hours the slave had made himself a free man. It was but a few months since he had become twenty-one. . . .

The flight was a bold and perilous one; but here I am, in the great city of New York, safe and sound, without loss of blood or bone. In less than a week after leaving Baltimore, I was walking amid the hurrying throng, and gazing upon the dazzling wonders of Broadway. The dreams of my childhood and the purposes of my manhood were now fulfilled. A free state around me, and a free earth under my feet! What a moment was this to me! A whole year was pressed into a single day. A new World burst upon my agitated vision.

Source: Frederick Douglass, *My Bondage and My Freedom* (New York, 1855); Frederick Holland, *Frederick Douglass* (New York, 1895).

8 Henry "Box" Brown of Virginia Escapes Slavery in a Sealed Box (1872)

"he . . . hit upon a new invention altogether"

Born into slavery in Virginia about 1815, Henry "Box" Brown decided to escape slavery after his wife and children were sold. Assisted by a white associate, he was nailed into a small box, just 2 feet wide and 2 feet long and 2 feet 8 inches high, and shipped from Richmond to Philadelphia. The 350-mile journey, by steamboat, horse cart, and railroad, took 27 hours.

He was decidedly an unhappy piece of property in the city of Richmond, Va. In the condition of a slave he felt that it would be impossible for him to remain. Full well did he know, however, that it was no holiday task to escape the vigilance of Virginia slave-hunters, or the wrath of an enraged master for committing the unpardonable sin of attempting to escape to a land of liberty. So Brown counted well the cost before venturing upon his hazardous undertaking. Ordinary modes of travel he concluded might prove disastrous to his hopes; he, therefore, hit upon a new invention altogether, which was to have himself boxed up and forwarded to Philadelphia direct by express. The size of the box and how it was to be made to fit him most comfortably, was of his own ordering. Two feet eight inches deep, two feet wide, and three feet long were the exact dimensions of the box, lined with baize. His resources in regard to food and water consisted of the following: One bladder of water and a few small biscuits. His mechanical implement to meet the death-struggle for fresh air, all told, was one large gimlet. Satisfied that it would be far better to peril his life for freedom in this way than to remain under the galling yoke of Slavery, he entered his box, which was safely nailed up and hooped with five hickory hoops, and then was addressed by his next friend, James A. Smith, a shoe dealer, to Wm. H. Johnson, Arch Street, Philadelphia, marked, "This side up with care." In this condition he was sent to Adams' Express office in a dray, and thence by overland express to Philadelphia. It was twenty-six hours from the time he left Richmond until his arrival in the city of Brotherly Love. The notice, "This side up, etc.," did not avail with the different expressmen, who hesitated not to handle the box in the usual rough manner common to this class of men. For a while they actually had the box upside down, and had him on his head for miles. A few days before he was expected, certain intimation was conveyed to a member of the Vigilance Committee that a box might be expected by the three o'clock morning train from the South, which might contain a man.

All was quiet. The door had been safely locked. The proceedings commenced. Mr. [J. M.] McKim rapped quietly on the lid of the box and called out, "All right!" Instantly came the answer from within, "All right, sir!"

The witnesses will never forget that moment. Saw and hatchet quickly had the five hickory hoops cut and the lid off, and the marvelous resurrection of Brown ensued. Rising up in the box, he reached out his hand, saying, "How do you do, gentlemen?" The little assemblage hardly knew what to think or do at the moment. He was about as wet as if he had come up out of the Delaware. Very soon he remarked that, before leaving Richmond he had selected for his arrival hymn (if he lived) the Psalm beginning with these words: "I awaited patiently for the Lord, and He heard my prayer." And most touchingly did he sing the psalm, much to his own relief, as well as to the delight of his small audience.

Source: William Still, *Underground Railroad Records* (Philadelphia, 1872).

9 Margaret Garner, a Fugitive Slave from Kentucky, Kills Her Daughter Rather Than See Her Returned to Slavery (1876)

"she would kill herself ... before she would return to bondage"

Margaret Garner, a fugitive slave from Kentucky, killed one of her children rather than permit her to be returned to slavery. Garner drowned in a shipwreck as she was being brought back to slavery.

Margaret Garner's life provided the inspiration for Toni Morrison's classic novel Beloved, *which examines how the traumas of slavery reverberated in the decades following emancipation.*

Perhaps no case that came under my notice, while engaged in aiding fugitive slaves, attracted more attention and aroused deeper interest and sympathy than the case of Margaret Garner, the slave mother who killed her child rather than see it taken back to slavery. This happened in the latter part of January, 1856. The Ohio River was frozen over at the time, and the opportunity thus offered for escaping to a free State was embraced by a number of slaves living in Kentucky, several miles back from the river. A party of seventeen, belonging to different masters in the same neighborhood, made arrangements to escape together. There was snow on the ground and the roads were smooth, so the plan of going to the river on a sled naturally suggested itself. The time fixed for their flight was Sabbath night, and having managed to get a large sled and two good horses, belonging to one of their masters, the party of seventeen crowded into the sled and started on their hazardous journey in the latter part of the night. They drove the horses at full speed, and at daylight reached the River below Covington, opposite Wester Row. They left the sled and horses here, and as quickly as possible crossed the river on foot. It was now broad daylight, and people were beginning to pass about the streets and the fugitives divided their company that they might not attract so much notice.

An old slave named Simon and his wife Mary, together with their son Robert and his wife Margaret Garner and four children, made their way to the house of a colored man named Kite, who had formerly lived in their neighborhood and had been purchased from slavery by his father, Joe Kite. They had to make several inquiries in order to find Kite's house, which was below Mill Creek, in the lower part of the city. This afterward led to their discovery; they had been seen by a number of persons on their way to Kite's, and were easily traced by pursuers. The other nine fugitives were more fortunate. They made their way up town and found friends who conducted them to safe hiding-places, where they remained until night. They were put on the Underground Railroad, and went safely through to Canada....

In a few minutes ... [Kite's] house was surrounded by pursuers – the masters of the fugitives, with officers and a posse of men. The door and windows were barred, and those inside refused to give admittance. The fugitives were determined to fight, and to die, rather than to be taken back to slavery. Margaret, the mother of the four children, declared that she would kill herself and her children before she would return to bondage. The slave men were armed and fought bravely. The window was first battered down with a stick of wood, and one of the deputy marshals attempted to enter, but a pistol shot from within made a flesh wound on his arm and caused him to abandon the attempt. The pursuers then battered down the door with some timber and rushed in. The husband of Margaret fired several shots, and wounded one of the officers, but was soon over-powered and dragged out of the house. At this moment, Margaret Garner, seeing that their hopes of freedom were in vain, seized a butcher knife that lay on the table, and with one stroke cut the throat of her little daughter, whom she probably loved the best. She then attempted to take the life of the other children and to kill herself, but she was overpowered and hampered before she could complete her desperate work. The whole party was then arrested and lodged in jail.

The trial lasted two weeks, drawing crowds to the courtroom every day.... The counsel for the defense brought witnesses to prove that the fugitives had been permitted to visit the city at various times previously. It was claimed that Margaret Garner had been brought here by her owners a number of years before, to act as nurse girl, and according to the law which liberated slaves who were brought into free States by the consent of their masters, she had been free from that time, and her children, all of whom had been born since then – following the condition of the mother – were likewise free.

The Commissioner decided that a voluntary return to slavery, after a visit to a free State, re-attached the conditions of slavery, and that the fugitives were legally slaves at the time of their escape....

But in spite of touching appeals, of eloquent pleadings, the Commissioner remanded the fugitives back to slavery. He said that it was not a question of feeling to be decided by the chance current of his sympathies; the law of Kentucky and the United States made it a question of property.

Source: Levi Coffin, *Reminiscences* (Cincinnati, 1876).

Discussion Questions

1. How did slaves resist slavery and make life in bondage more endurable?
2. What do you consider the most effective ways to resist slavery?
3. It appears that the slaves most likely to run away were young males and relatively privileged slaves, such as carriage drivers and boatmen. Why do you think this was the case?
4. Why did most fugitives flee only a relatively short distance and only temporarily?
5. Why do you think the Underground Railroad occupies such a powerful place in American national memory?
6. Why was wholesale rebellion less common in the American South than in the Caribbean?

Chapter 10   "The Walls Came Tumblin' Down": Emancipation

The slave population did not respond to Civil War with a single voice. While southern planters stressed their bondsmen's loyalty and fidelity, in Adams County, Mississippi, slave insurrectionaries plotted to burn down the city of Natchez. Other slaves served as informants to the Union army, assisted Union soldiers who escaped from Confederate prisons, or defected to Union lines or hid out in nearby woods or swamps. Wartime resistance to slavery also took the form of work stoppages, arson, sabotage, and isolated cases of murder. Enlistment in the Union army represented the most dramatic form of resistance. In August 1862, the first slave regiment was formed, the 1st South Carolina Volunteers, and by the war's end, 186,000 blacks – three-quarters of them former slaves – served in the Union army.

News of emancipation evoked a variety of responses, ranging from exuberance and exhilaration to incredulity and caution to apprehension and fear. In Choctaw County, Mississippi, former slaves whipped a planter named Nat Best to retaliate for his cruelties. In Richmond, Virginia, some 1,500 ex-slaves gathered in the Free African Church to sing hymns. A parade in Charleston attracted 10,000 spectators and featured a black-draped coffin bearing the words "Slavery is Dead." But many freedmen felt a deep uncertainty about their status and rights.

Ex-slaves expressed their newly won freedom in diverse ways. At first, many left farms or plantations for towns or cities "where freedom was free-er." Thousands sought to reunite families broken by sale and legalize marriage ties; others adopted new surnames and learned to read and write. Many black women withdrew from field labor to care for their families.

Across the South, ex-slaves left white-dominated churches and formed independent black congregations; founded schools; set up mutual aid societies; and held freedmen's conventions to air grievances, discuss pressing issues, and push for equal civil and political rights.

Reconstruction was a time of testing, when freedmen probed the boundaries and possibilities of freedom. Every aspect of southern life was subject to redefinition, from appropriate forms of racial etiquette to the systems of labor that would replace slavery.

1 Hannah Johnson, the Mother of a Black Soldier, Pleads with President Abraham Lincoln Not to Rescind the Emancipation Proclamation (1863)

"that action of yours will make the Angels sing your praises"

> *In the summer of 1863, Hannah Johnson, a resident of Buffalo, New York, and the daughter of a fugitive slave, heard rumors that President Lincoln might rescind his Emancipation Proclamation. After explaining that her son was a member of the famous 54th Massachusetts Infantry, one of the first African American Civil War regiments, she pleads with the president to stand behind his proclamation.*

July 31, 1863

Excellent Sir My good friend says I must write to you and she will send it My son went in the 54th regiment. I am a colored woman and my son was strong and able as any to fight for his country and the colored people have as much to fight for as any. My father was a Slave and escaped from Louisiana before I was born morn forty years agone I have but poor edication but I never went to schol, but I know just as well as any what is right between man and man. Now I know it is right that a colored man should go and fight for his country, and so ought to a white man. I know that a colored man ought to run no greater risques than a white, his pay is no greater his obligation to fight is the same. So why should not our enemies be compelled to treat him the same, Made to do it.

My son fought at Fort Wagoner [near Charleston, South Carolina] but thank God he was not taken prisoner, as many were I thought of this thing before I let my boy go but then they said Mr. Lincoln will never let them sell our colored soldiers for slaves, if they do he will get them back quck he will rettallyate and stop it. Now Mr Lincoln dont you think you oght to stop this thing and make them do the same by the colored men they have lived in idleness all their lives on stolen labor and made savages of the colored people, but they now are so furious because they are proving themselves to be men, such as have come away and got some edication. It must not be so. You must put the rebels to work in State prisons to making shoes and things, if they sell our colored soldiers, till they let them all go. And give their wounded the same treatment. it would seem cruel, but their no other way, and a just man must do hard things sometimes, that shew him to be a great man. They tell me some do you will take back the Proclamation, don't do it. When you are dead and in Heaven, in a thousand years that action of yours will make the Angels sing your praises I know it. Ought one man to own another, law for or not, who made the law, surely the poor slave did not. so it is wicked, and a horrible Outrage, there is no sense in it, because a man has lived by robbing all his life and his father before him, should he complain because the stolen things found on him are taken. Robbing the colored people of their labor is but a small part of the robbery their souls are almost taken, they are made bruits of often. You know all about this.

Will you see that the colored men fighting now, are fairly treated. You ought to do this, and do it at once, Not let the thing run along meet it quickly and manfully, and stop this, mean cowardly cruelty. We poor oppressed ones, appeal to you, and ask fair play.

Yours for Christs sake
Hannah Johnson

Source: Hannah Johnson to Hon. Mr. Lincoln, 31 July 1863. J-17 1863, Letters Received, ser. 360, Colored Troops Division, Adjutant General's Office, Record Group 94, National Archives.

2 Private Thomas Long Assesses the Meaning of Black Military Service During the Civil War (1870)

"we whipped down all dat"

> *It seems doubtful that Union forces could have defeated the Confederacy in the absence of black troops. In this document, Thomas Long, a former slave and a private in the 1st South Carolina Volunteers, assesses the meaning of black military service during the Civil War.*

We can remember, when we fust enlisted, it was hardly safe for we to pass by de camps to Beaufort and back, lest we went in a mob and carried side arms. But we whipped down all dat – not by going into de white camps for whip um; we didn't tote our bayonets for whip um; but we lived it down by our naturally manhood; and now de white sojers take us by de hand and say Broder Sojer. Dats what dis regiment did for de Epiopian race.

If we hadn't become sojers, all might have gone back as it was before; our freedom might have slipped through de two houses of Congress and President Linkum's four years might have passed by and notin' been done for us. But now tings can neber go back, because we have showed our energy and our courage and our naturally manhood.

Source: Thomas Wentworth Higginson, *Army Life in a Black Regiment* (Boston, 1870).

3 Corporal Jackson Cherry Appeals for Equal Opportunity for Former Slaves (1865)

"we ought to be considered as men"

> *Corporal Jackson Cherry, Company I, 35th Regiment, United States Colored Troops, appeals for equal opportunity for freedmen. There can be little doubt that African American troops' valor in battle helped erode the virulent racial prejudice that pervaded pre-Civil War America.*

We have been faithful in the field up to the present time, and think that we ought to be considered as men, and allowed a fair chance in the race of life. It has been said that a black man can not make his own living, but give us opportunities and we will show the whites that we will not come to them for any thing, if they do not come to us. We think the colored people have been the making of them, and can make something of ourselves in time. The colored people know how to work, and the whites have been dependent upon them. They can work again, and will work. A white man may talk very well, but put him to work, and what will he say? He will say that hard work is not easy. He will say that it is hard for a man who has owned so many able-bodied Negroes to have the Yankees come and taken them all away.

Source: Jackson Cherry, *South Carolina Leader*, December 16, 1865.

4 Jourdon Anderson, a Former Tennessee Slave, Declines His Former Master's Invitation to Return to His Plantation (1865)

"I thought the Yankees would have hung you long before this"

Jourdon Anderson, an ex-Tennessee slave, declines his former master's invitation to return as a laborer on his plantation. The authenticity of this letter, which was printed in a newspaper, is uncertain.

Dayton, Ohio, August 7, 1865

To My Old Master, Colonel P. H. Anderson, Big Spring, Tennessee

Sir: I got your letter and was glad to find you had not forgotten Jourdon, and that you wanted me to come back and live with you again, promising to do better for me than anybody else can. I have often felt uneasy about you. I thought the Yankees would have hung you long before this for harboring Rebs they found at your house. I suppose they never heard about your going to Col. Martin's to kill the Union soldier that was left by his company in their stable. Although you shot at me twice before I left you, I did not want to hear of your being hurt, and am glad you are still living. It would do me good to go back to the dear old home again and see Miss Mary and Miss Martha and Allen, Esther, Green, and Lee. Give my love to them all, and tell them I hope we will meet in the better world, if not in this. I would have gone back to see you all when I was working in the Nashville hospital, but one of the neighbors told me Henry intended to shoot me if he ever got a chance.

I want to know particularly what the good chance is you propose to give me. I am doing tolerably well here; I get $25 a month, with victuals and clothing; have a comfortable home for Mandy (the folks here call her Mrs. Anderson), and the children, Milly, Jane and Grundy, go to school and are learning well; the teacher says Grundy has a head for a preacher. They go to Sunday-School, and Mandy and me attend church regularly. We are kindly treated; sometimes we overhear others saying, "The colored people were slaves" down in Tennessee. The children feel hurt when they hear such remarks, but I tell them it was no disgrace in Tennessee to belong to Col. Anderson. Many darkies would have been proud, as I used to was, to call you master. Now, if you will write and say what wages you will give me, I will be better able to decide whether it would be to my advantage to move back again.

As to my freedom, which you say I can have, there is nothing to be gained on that score, as I got my free-papers in 1864 from the Provost-Marshal-General of the Department of Nashville. Mandy says she would be afraid to go back without some proof that you are sincerely disposed to treat us justly and kindly – and we have concluded to test your sincerity by asking you to send us our wages for the time we served you. This will make us forget and forgive old scores, and rely on your justice and friendship in the future. I served you faithfully for thirty-two years and Mandy twenty years. At $25 a month for me, and $2 a week for Mandy, our earnings would amount to $11,680. Add to this the interest for the time our wages has been kept back and deduct what you paid for our clothing and three doctor's visits to me, and pulling a tooth for Mandy, and the balance will show what we are in justice entitled to. Please send the money by Adams Express, in care of V. Winters, esq, Dayton, Ohio. If you fail to pay us for faithful labors in the past we can have little faith in your promises in the future. We trust the good Maker has opened your eyes to the wrongs which you and your fathers have done to me and my fathers, in making us toil for you for generations without recompense. Here I draw my wages every Saturday night, but in Tennessee there was never any pay day for the Negroes any more than for the horses and cows. Surely there will be a day of reckoning for those who defraud the laborer of his hire.

In answering this letter please state if there would be any safety for my Milly and Jane, who are now grown up and both good-looking girls. You know how it was with Matilda and Catherine. I would rather stay here and starve and die if it comes to that than have my girls brought to shame by the violence and wickedness of their young masters. You will also please state if there has been any schools opened for the colored children in your neighborhood, the great desire of my life now is to give my children an education, and have them form virtuous habits.

P.S. – Say howdy to George Carter, and thank him for taking the pistol from you when you were shooting at me.

From your old servant
Jourdon Anderson

Source: Jourdon Anderson, *Cincinnati Commercial*, reprinted in *New York Tribune*, August 22, 1865.

5 Major General Rufus Saxon Assesses the Freedmen's Aspirations (1866)

"the word 'color' should be left out of all laws"

Major General Rufus Saxton commanded the area that included Georgia's Sea Islands and later became the Freedmen's Bureau's assistant commissioner for Florida, Georgia, and South Carolina. This selection, from his testimony before Congress's Joint Committee on Reconstruction in 1866, offers his assessment of the freedmen's aspirations and the former Confederates' attitudes toward them.

[Question] What is [the freedmen's] disposition in regard to purchasing land, and what is the disposition of the landowners in reference to selling land to Negroes?

[Answer] The object which the freedman has most at heart is the purchase of land. They all desire to get small homesteads and to locate themselves upon them, and there is scarcely any sacrifice too great for them to make to accomplish this object. I believe it is the policy of the majority of the farm owners to prevent Negroes from becoming landholders. They desire to keep the Negroes landless, and as nearly in a condition of slavery as it is possible for them to do. I think that the former slaveholders know really less about the freedmen than any other class of people. The system of slavery has been one of concealment on the part of the Negro of all his feelings and impulses; and that feeling of concealment is so ingrained with the very constitution of the Negro that he deceives his former master on almost every point. The freedman has no faith in his former master, nor has his former owner any faith in the capacity of the freedman. A mutual distrust exists between them. But the freedman is ready and willing to contract to work for any northern man. One man from the North, a man of capital, who employed large numbers of freedmen, and paid them regularly, told me, as others have, that he desired no better laborers; that he considered them fully as easy to manage as Irish laborers. That was my own experience in employing several thousands of them in cultivating the soil. I have also had considerable experience in employing white labor, having, as quartermaster, frequently had large numbers of laborers under my control.

[Question] If the Negro is put in possession of all his rights as a man, do you apprehend any danger of insurrection among them?

[Answer] I do not; and I think that is the only thing which will prevent difficulty. I think if the Negro is put in possession of all his rights as a citizen and as a man, he will be peaceful, orderly, and self-sustaining as any other man or class of men, and that he will rapidly advance. . . .

[Question] It has been suggested that, if the Negro is allowed to vote, he will be likely to vote on the side of his former master, and be inveigled in the support of a policy hostile to the government of the United States; do you share in that apprehension?

[Answer] I have positive information from Negroes, from the most intelligent freedmen in those States, those who are leaders among them, that they are thoroughly loyal, and know their friends, and they will never be found voting on the side of oppression. . . . I think it vital to the safety and prosperity of the two races in the south that the Negro should immediately be put in possession of all his rights as a man; and that the word "color" should be left out of all laws, constitutions, and regulations for the people; I think it vital to the safety of the Union that this should be done.

Source: *Report of the Joint Committee on Reconstruction* (Washington, 1866).

6 Colonel Samuel Thomas Describes the Attitudes of Ex-Confederates Toward the Freedmen (1865)

"To kill a Negro they do not deem murder"

> *Overwhelming defeat in the Civil War did not lead many former Confederates to accept legal or social equality with African Americans. In this selection, Col. Samuel Thomas, a Freedmen's Bureau official, describes the attitude of ex-Confederates toward the former slaves.*

Wherever I go – the street, the shop, the house, or the steamboat – I hear the people talk in such a way as to indicate that they are yet unable to conceive of the Negro as possessing any rights at all. Men who are honorable in their dealings with their white neighbors will cheat a Negro without feeling a single twinge of their honor. To kill a Negro they do not deem murder; to debauch a Negro woman they do not think fornication; to take the property away from a Negro they do not consider robbery. The people boast that when they get freedmen affairs in their own hands, to use their own classic expression, "the niggers will catch hell."

The reason of all this is simple and manifest. The whites esteem the blacks their property by natural right, and however much they may admit that the individual relations of masters and slaves have been destroyed by the war and the President's emancipation proclamation, they still have an ingrained feeling that the blacks at large belong to the whites at large, and whenever opportunity serves they treat the colored people just as their profit, caprice or passion may dictate.

Source: Col. Samuel Thomas, Assistant Commissioner, Bureau of Refugees, Freedmen and Abandoned Lands in 39 Cong., 1 Sess., Senate Exec. Doc. 2 (1865).

7 Francis L. Cardozo of South Carolina Asks for Land for the Freedmen (1868)

"Let the lands of the South be ... divided"

Francis L. Cardozo, a black graduate of the University of Glasgow and a minister in New Haven, Connecticut, returned to his native South Carolina immediately after the Civil War to serve as a principal of a Negro school. In this selection, he calls upon the South Carolina Constitutional Convention to grant land to the freedmen. To this day, many historians believe that the only way to have ensured the rights of former slaves was to have ensured that they had productive land to farm.

One of the greatest of slavery bulwarks was the infernal plantation system, one man owning his thousand, another his twenty, another fifty thousands acres of land. This is the only way by which we will break up that system, and I maintain that our freedom will be of no effect if we allow it to continue. What is the main cause of the prosperity of the North? It is because every man has his own farm and is free and independent. Let the lands of the South be similarly divided. I would not say for one moment they should be confiscated, but if sold to maintain the war, now that slavery is destroyed, let the plantation system go with it. We will never have true freedom until we abolish the system of agriculture which existed in the Southern States. It is useless to have any schools while we maintain the stronghold of slavery as the agricultural system of the country.

Source: *Proceedings of Constitution Convention of South Carolina* (1868).

8 The Rev. Elias Hill Is Attacked by the Ku Klux Klan (1872)

"they hit me with their fists"

Efforts to intimidate African Americans through violence were widespread in the aftermath of the Civil War. Elias Hill, a black minister in York County, South Carolina, testified before a Congressional committee in 1871 about the Ku Klux Klan's aims and methods of operation.

Elias Hill is a remarkable character. He is crippled in both legs and arms, which are shriveled by rheumatism; he cannot walk, cannot help himself, has to be fed and cared for personally by others; was in early life a slave, whose freedom was purchased, his father buying his mother and getting Elias along with her, as a burden of which his master was glad to be rid. Stricken at seven years old with disease, he never was afterward able to walk, and he presents the appearance of a dwarf with the limbs of a child, the body of a man, and a finely developed intellectual head. He learned his letters and to read by calling the school children into the cabin as they passed, and also learned to write. He became a Baptist preacher, and after the war engaged in teaching colored children, and conducted the business correspondence of many of his colored neighbors. He is a man of blameless character, of unusual intelligence, speaks good English, and we put the story of his wrongs in his own language:

"On the night of the 5th of last May, after I had heard a great deal of what they had done in that neighborhood, they [the Ku Klux Klan] came. It was between 12 and 1 o'clock at night when I was awakened and heard the dogs barking, and something walking, very much like horses. ... At last they came to my brother's door, which is in the same yard, and broke open the door and attacked his wife, and I heard her screaming and mourning. ... At last I heard them have her in the yard. She was crying and the Ku-Klux were whipping her to make her tell where I lived. ... Some one then hit my door. It flew open. One ran in the house, and stopping about the middle of the house, which is a small cabin, he turned around, as it seemed to me as I lay there awake, and said, 'Who's here?' Then I knew they would take me, and I answered, 'I am here.' He shouted for joy, as it seemed, 'Here he is! Here he is! We have found him!' and he threw the bedclothes off of me and caught me by one arm, while another man took me by the other and they carried me into the yard between the houses. ... The first thing they asked me was, 'Who did the burning? Who burned our houses?' – gin-houses, dwelling-houses and such. Some had been burned in the neighborhood. I told them it was not me; I could not burn houses; it was unreasonable to ask me. Then they hit me with their fists, and said I did it, I ordered it. They went on asking me didn't I tell the black men to ravish all the white women. No, I answered them. They struck me again with their fists on my breast, and then they went on. ...

They pointed pistols at me all around my head once or twice, as if they were going to shoot me, telling me they were going to kill me; wasn't I ready to die, and willing to die? Didn't I preach? That they came to kill me – all the time pointing pistols at me. ... One said 'G-d d – n it, hush!' He had a horsewhip, and he told me to pull up my shirt, and he hit me. He told me at every lick, 'Hold up your shirt.' I made a moan every time he cut with the horsewhip. I reckon he struck me eight cuts right on the hip bone; it was almost the only place he could hit my body, my legs are so short – all my limbs drawn up and withered away with pain. ... They all had disguises on. I then thought they would kill me. One of them then took a strap, and buckled it around my neck and said, 'Let's take him to the river and drown him. ...'

They said 'Look here! Will you put a card in the paper next week like June Moore and Sol Hill?' They had been prevailed on to put a card in the paper to renounce all republicanism and never vote. I said, 'If I had the money to pay the expense, I could.' They said I could borrow, and gave me another lick. They asked me, 'Will you quit preaching?' I told them I did not know. I said that to save my life. They said I must stop the republican paper that was coming to Clay Hill. It has been only a few weeks since it stopped. The republican paper was then coming to me from Charleston. It came to my name. They said I must stop it, quit preaching, and put a card in the newspaper renouncing republicanism, and they would not kill me; but if I did not they would come back the next week and kill me.

Source: *Report of the Joint Select Committee to Inquire into the Condition of Affairs in the Late Insurrectionary States* (Washington, 1872).

9 Henry Blake, a Former Arkansas Slave, Describes Sharecropping (1937)

"After freedom, we worked on shares"

Henry Blake was born into slavery in Little Rock, Arkansas, and was approximately 80 years old when he was interviewed by the Works Progress

Administration. Here, he describes the new system of land tenure and labor that followed the Civil War. Sharecropping represented a crude compromise between white landowners who wanted to re-establish gang labor and former slaves who wanted individual farms. But sharecropping had the effect of placing ex-slaves in an economically dependent position.

After freedom, we worked on shares a while. Then, we rented. When we worked on shares, we couldn't make nothing – just overalls, and something to eat. Half went to the white man, and you would destroy your half, if you weren't careful. A man that didn't know how to count would always lose. He might lose anyhow. The white folks didn't give no itemized statements. No, you just had to owe so much. No matter how good account you kept, you had to go by their account, and – now, brother, I'm telling you the truth about this – it's been that way for a long time. You had to take the white man's words and notes on everything. Anything you wanted you could get, if you were a good hand. If you didn't make no money, that's all right; they would advance you more. But you better not try to leave and get caught. They'd keep you in debt. They were sharp. Christmas come, you could take up twenty dollars in somethin'-to-eat and much as you wanted in whiskey. You could buy a gallon of whiskey – anything that kept you a slave. Because he was always right and you were always wrong, if there was a difference. If there was an argument, he would get mad and there would be a shooting take place.

Source: George P. Rawick, *The American Slave: A Composite Autobiography* (Westport, Conn., 1972).

10 Frederick Douglass Assesses the Condition of the Freedmen (1880)

"the serfs of Russia ... were given three acres of ground"

Frederick Douglass examines the limitations of the formal, legal changes that had taken place. Despite the Constitutional amendments that abolished slavery, guaranteed citizenship rights, including due process and equal protection of the laws, and extended the vote, Douglass argues, former slaves remained reduced to a separate caste.

How stands the case with the recently emancipated millions of colored people in our own country? What is their condition to-day? What is their relation to the people who formerly held them as slaves? These are important questions, and they are such as trouble the minds of thoughtful men of all colors, at home and abroad. By law, by the constitution of the United States, slavery has no existence in our country. The legal form has been abolished. By the law and the constitution, the Negro is a man and a citizen, and has all the rights and liberties guaranteed to any other variety of the human family, residing in the United States. . . .

In pursuance of this idea, the Negro was made free, made a citizen, made eligible to hold office, to be a juryman, a legislator, and a magistrate. To this end, several amendments to the constitution were proposed, recommended, and adopted. . . . This is our condition on paper and parchment. If only from the national statute book we were left to learn the true condition of the colored race, the result would be altogether creditable to the American people. . . .

We have laid the heavy hand of the constitution upon the matchless meanness of caste, as well as upon the hell-black crime of slavery. . . . But to-day, in most of the Southern States, the fourteenth and fifteenth amendments are virtually nullified.

The rights which they were intended to guarantee are denied and held in contempt. The citizenship granted in the fourteenth amendment is practically a mockery, and the right to vote, provided for in the fifteenth amendment, is literally stamped out in face of government. The old master class is to-day triumphant, and the newly-enfranchised class in a condition but little above that in which they were found before the rebellion.

Do you ask me how, after all that has been done, this state of things has been made possible? I will tell you. Our reconstruction measures were radically defective. They left the former slave completely in the power of the old master, the loyal citizen in the hands of the disloyal rebel against the government. Wise, grand, and comprehensive in scope and desire as were the reconstruction measures, high and honorable as were the intentions of the statesmen by whom they were framed and adopted, time and experience, which try all things, have demonstrated that they did not successfully meet the case.

In the hurry and confusion of the hour, and the eager desire to have the Union restored, there was more care for the sublime superstructure of the republic than for the solid foundation upon which it could alone be upheld. . . . The old master class was not deprived of the power of life and death, which was the soul of the relation of master and slave. They could not, of course, sell their former slaves, but they retained the power to starve them to death, and wherever this power is held there is the power of slavery. He who can say to his fellow-man, "You shall serve me or starve," is a master and his subject is a slave. . . . Though no longer a slave, he is in a thralldom grievous and intolerable, compelled to work for whatever his employer is pleased to pay him, swindled out of his hard earnings by money orders redeemed in stores, compelled to pay the price of an acre of ground for its use during a single year, to pay four times more than a fair price for a pound of bacon and to be kept upon the narrowest margin between life and starvation. . . .

When the serfs of Russia were emancipated, they were given three acres of ground upon which they could live and make a living. But not so when our slaves were emancipated. They were sent away empty-handed, without money, without friends and without a foot of land upon which to stand. . . .

Greatness does not come on flowery beds of ease to any people. We must fight to win the prize. No people to whom liberty is given, can hold it as firmly and wear it as grandly as those who wrench liberty from the iron hand of the tyrant. The hardships and dangers involved in the struggle give strength and toughness to the character, and enable it to stand firm in storm as well as in sunshine.

Source: Frederick Douglass, *Life and Times of Frederick Douglass* (Boston, 1892).

Discussion Questions

1. What was the role of African Americans in securing freedom?
2. Why didn't Reconstruction, America's first attempt to create an interracial democracy, succeed?
3. How did African Americans perceive and assess the changes that had taken place during and immediately following the Civil War?

Bibliographical Essay

Although slavery is now one of the most intensively studied topics in United States history, there was a long period during which it was largely ignored. The Progressive school of interpretation, which dominated the American history profession during the first half of the twentieth century, considered slavery to be less important than conflicts between classes, sections, and industrial and agrarian interests. Except for the works of a handful of African American historians like Carter Woodson, Benjamin Quarles, and W. E. B. DuBois, and of southern historians like Ulrich B. Phillips, slavery was regarded as an extraneous aspect of American history.

This prolonged period of scholarly neglect came to an end in the mid-1950s. Since the publication of Kenneth Stampp's *The Peculiar Institution* in 1956, no topic has produced a greater outpouring of important scholarly works or provoked more controversy than the study of slavery. In part, the explosion of scholarly interest in slavery reflected the increasing public concern with civil rights and race relations; but it also reflected a recognition that slavery played an absolutely critical role in the settlement and economic development of the New World and the major political conflicts and alignments of the pre-Civil War period.

The study of slavery has contributed to a radical reshaping of the discipline of history, leading scholars to tap new sources of data and to employ new methods of analysis. Historical demographers have drawn upon census records to reconstruct slave birth and mortality rates and family and kinship patterns. Historical archeologists have studied slave quarters in order to reconstruct patterns of everyday life. Medical historians have scrutinized records of height, weight, and disease. Cultural historians have analyzed African American folklore and religious beliefs and customs. The result has been to reconstruct life under slavery in all of its complexity.

The modern boom in slavery studies began with Stampp. Contradicting the conclusions of Phillips, a much earlier authority on slavery, Stampp argued in 1956 that nineteenth-century slavery was a profitable institution; that slaves suffered severely from disease and physical maltreatment; that they were inadequately, fed, clothed, and housed; and that they expressed their discontent by breaking tools and running away, as well as through more violent forms of resistance.

Stanley Elkins's highly controversial *Slavery: A Problem in American Institutional and Intellectual Life* (1959), which came out three years after *The Peculiar Institution*, defined the issues that dominated subsequent scholarship. Drawing upon the work of two prominent Latin American historians, Gilberto Freyre and Frank Tannenbaum, Elkins argued that American slavery was much harsher and more exploitative than Latin American slavery. Indeed, Elkins likened southern slave plantations to Nazi concentration camps, and argued that slavery was so brutal and inhumane that it stripped slaves of their African heritage and transformed them into docile, submissive figures.

Much subsequent scholarship on American slavery can be viewed as a rebuttal of Elkins's arguments. Instead of portraying slaves as passive objects of oppression, later scholars focused their attention on the intricate ways that slaves resisted and accommodated to slavery; the nature of the culture and community that African Americans created within bondage; and the similarities and differences between southern slavery and bondage elsewhere. If any single theme can be said to unify the remarkable outpouring of scholarship on slavery, it is the extraordinary success of the enslaved in creating and sustaining vital kinship and cultural and religious traditions under conditions of extreme oppression.

In the half century since the publication of *The Peculiar Institution* and *Slavery: A Problem in American Institutional and Intellectual Life*, no field of history has generated works of greater methodological or substantive importance or sophistication – or received more scholarly awards – than the study of slavery. These works have corrected many myths and misconceptions that clouded our understanding of our collective past, above all, the notion that slavery was a marginal or peripheral subject, which could be confined largely to classes in African American or southern history.

In recent years, slavery studies have undergone five sweeping upheavals that have fundamentally altered our understanding. First, American slavery has been located in global and comparative perspective. Thanks to Orlando Patterson's *Slavery and Social Death* (1982), which analyzes slavery in 66societies including classical Greece and Rome, medieval Europe, China, Korea, the Islamic emirates, Africa, and the Caribbean islands, scholars now recognize that slavery in the American South was one manifestation of an institution and a system of exploitation that could be found in diverse societies and cultures at very different time periods.

Second, we have learned that slavery in the United States was only a piece in a much larger Atlantic slave system. Robin Blackburn's *The Making of New World Slavery* (1997) and David Brion Davis's *Inhuman Bondage* (2006) trace the development of the Atlantic slave system as it shifted from the Mediterranean to Atlantic islands near the west African coast and then to the western hemisphere. These works show how an emerging racial consciousness helped legitimize slavery and how the institution contributed to the emergence of modern consumer economies and to Europe's economic and military expansion.

The African side of the Atlantic slave system has attracted much attention. John Thornton's *Africa and Africans in the Making of the Modern World* (1998) and David Eltis's *The Rise of African Slavery in the Americas* (2000) underscore the crucial role that Africans played in the slave trade, including which people were enslaved and how the trade was conducted. A number of influential studies – including Michael Gomez's *Exchanging Our Country Marks* (1998), Gwendolyn Midlo Hall's *Slavery and African Ethnicities in the Americas* (2005), and James Sidbury's *Becoming African in America* (2007) – trace the gradual emergence of an African American identity out of various African nationalities and ethnicities. These books demonstrate that in colonial America, slave owners were well aware of the various national and ethnic identities of the enslaved, and that slaves from particular culture and language groups were able to sustain distinctive cultures, religions, and outlooks into the nineteenth century.

A third key development involves the recognition that North American slavery, far from being a static or monolithic institution, underwent profound transformations over time and varied widely across geographical space. Until remarkably recently, there was a tendency to treat slavery as an unchanging institution. A number of recent volumes have begun to chronicle the historical evolution of American slavery. Ira Berlin's *Many Thousands Gone* (1998) and his *Generations of Captivity* (2003) identify distinct "generations" of slaves who underwent very different experiences of bondage, and highlight regional differences in demography and labor regimes. Slavery in colonial America is no longer an understudied subject thanks to books like Philip D. Morgan's *Slave Counterpoint* (1998), which underscores the differences in the nature of slavery in the Chesapeake colonies of Maryland and Virginia and the Carolina Low Country, as well as Allan Kulikoff's *Tobacco and Slaves: The Development of Southern Cultures in the Chesapeake, 1680–1800* (1986), Mechal Sobel's *The World They Made Together: Black and White Values in Eighteenth Century Virginia* (1987); and Peter H. Wood's *Black Majority: Negroes in Colonial South Carolina* (1974).

A number of important works, including Sylvia R. Frey's *Water from the Rock: Black Resistance in a Revolutionary Age* (1991), have demonstrated slavery's centrality to the origins, meaning, course, and outcome of the American Revolution. The complex story of the abolition of slavery in the North is well told in Gary B. Nash and Jean B. Soderlund's *Freedom by Degrees: Emancipation in Pennsylvania and its Aftermath* (1991), Shane White's *Somewhat More Independent: The End of Slavery in New York City* (1991), and Arthur Zilversmit's *The First Emancipation* (1967). On the expansion of slavery into the Old Southwest, see Adam Rothman's *Slave Country* (2005).

A fourth major development is a heightened recognition of slavery's centrality to American political history and economic development. Slave-grown cotton constituted 75 percent of the value of the nation's exports in the decades before the Civil War, and paid for the capital that financed canals, railroads, and textile factories. Slave owners (who made up nine of the first fifteen presidents) occupied the presidency for approximately 50 of the nation's first 72 years. Two slaveholders served as chief justice of the Supreme Court from 1801 to the Civil War and presided over a court made up of a majority of slave owners. To learn more about slavery's role in American political history, see Don E. Fehrenbacher and Ward M. McAfee's *The Slaveholding Republic* (2001), Leonard Richards's *The Slave Power* (2000), and Garry Wills's *"Negro President": Jefferson and the Slave Power* (2003).

A fifth new direction in slavery studies involves a shift in focus. Rather than drawing largely on the records of masters, many recent works seek to recover enslaved African Americans' voices and to recognize their agency in constructing their lives and culture. Thus slavery is viewed not simply as a system of domination and submission, but as a power relationship that involved a complex, ongoing process of accommodation, resistance, and negotiation.

One of the major puzzles presented by slavery is how to reconcile two seemingly contradictory facts: the slave system's high rate of efficiency and productivity and the substantial evidence of resistance: of shirking, sabotage, flight, and physical resistance. A number of recent works have scrutinized the process by which enslaved African Americans were able to negotiate important concessions from their masters, including freedom to travel to neighboring plantations, access to garden plots, the opportunity to sell goods in local markets, and permission to hold religious services without interference. Key studies of slave resistance include John Hope Franklin and Loren Schweninger, *Runaway Slaves* (1999); Douglas R. Egerton, *Gabriel's Rebellion* (1993); Eugene D. Genovese, *From Rebellion to Revolution* (1979); Melton A. McLaurin, *Celia: A Slave* (1991); and James Sidbury, *Ploughshares into Swords* (1997).

The modern study of slave culture traces its roots back to Melville J. Herskovit's *Myth of the Negro Past* (1941), which argued that many aspects of African American culture – including art, family, folklore, language, and music – represented cultural survivals from west Africa. More recent studies have substituted the notion of syncretism – that is, a blending of African and European cultures – for Herskovit's concept of cultural survival. Michael Mullin's *Africa in America* (1992) shows that enslaved Africans were able to retain much more of their African heritage, including religious traditions and even languages, than previously thought. Other valuable studies of slaves' culture and worldviews include Daniel J. Crowley, ed., *African Folklore in the New World* (1977); Joseph E. Holloway, *Africans in American Culture* (1990); and Lawrence Levine, *Black Culture and Black Consciousness* (1977).

A focus on slave culture has overturned many long-held assumptions about African American history. For example, one important finding is how slowly Christianity was adopted by the enslaved, and how its adoption depended on the incorporation of certain concepts and practices that had an affinity with African traditions, as well as its promise of liberation. On the development of slave religion, see Albert J. Raboteau, *Slave Religion* (1978); Mechal Sobel, *Trabelin' On: The Slave Journey to an Afro-Baptist Faith* (1988); and Thomas L. Webber, *Deep Like the Rivers: Education in the Slave Quarter Community* (1978). On patterns of education and literacy in the slave quarters, see Heather Andrea Williams, *Self-Taught* (2005).

Recent scholarship has decisively demonstrated that slaves were active agents who succeeded in creating a rich and vital culture that had a profound influence on the surrounding culture, including its music and decorative arts. To learn more about slaves' impact on American culture, see Dena J. Epstein, *Sinful Tunes and Spirituals* (1977), and John Michael Vlach, *The Afro-American Tradition in Decorative Arts* (1978).

No aspect of slavery has gone unexamined. Basic reference works include Seymour Drescher and Stanley Engerman, eds., *A Historical Guide to World Slavery*

(1998); Paul Finkelman and Joseph C. Miller, eds., *Macmillan Encyclopedia of World Slavery* (1998); Peter Hinks and John McKivigan, eds., *Encyclopedia of Antislavery and Abolition* (2007); Martin A. Klein, ed., *Historical Dictionary of Slavery and Abolition* (2002); Randall M. Miller, ed., *Dictionary of Afro-American Slavery* (1997); and Junius P. Rodriguez, ed., *Encyclopedia of Slave Resistance and Rebellion* (2007), and *The Historical Encyclopedia of World Slavery* (1997).

The most profound analyses of the intellectual history of slavery are David Brion Davis, *The Problem of Slavery in Western Culture* (1988), *The Problem of Slavery in the Age of Revolution* (1975), and *Slavery and Human Progress* (1984); George M. Fredrickson, *The Black Image in the White Mind* (1971); and Winthrop D. Jordan, *White Over Black: American Attitudes Toward the Negro* (1968). Medical histories of slavery include Kenneth F. Kiple and Virginia Himmelsteib King, *Another Dimension to the Black Diaspora: Diet, Disease, and Racism* (1981), and Todd L. Savitt, *Medicine and Slavery* (1978).

On the historiography of slavery, see Charles B. Dew, "The Slavery Experience," in John B. Boles and Evelyn Thomas Nolen eds., *Interpreting Southern History* (1987), and Peter J. Parish, *Slavery: History and Historians* (1989). The law of slavery is analyzed in A. Leon Higginbotham, Jr., *In the Matter of Color* (1978); Thomas D. Morris, *Southern Slavery and the Law* (1996); Mark Tushnet, *The American Law of Slavery* (1981); and Alan Watson, *Slave Law in the Americas* (1989).

On the Middle Passage, see Marcus Rediker's *The Slave Ship* (2007), which examines the slave trade from the perspective of captains, common sailors, and slaves, and Stephanie E. Smallwood's *Saltwater Slavery* (2007), which uses letters, journals, and narratives to reconstruct the captives' experience of the Middle Passage. Hugh Thomas's *The Slave Trade* (1997) chronicles the history, financing, and suppression of the Atlantic slave trade, while Robert Harms's *The Diligent* (2002) focuses on a single slave ship. On the domestic slave trade, see Walter Johnson's *Soul by Soul* (1999) and Steven Deyle's *Carry Me Back* (2005), which demonstrates that most slave sales were local rather than interstate, and that most slaves were sold not by professional traders but by owners, following a death or to repay debts or to deal with a shortage or surplus of labor.

Slave family life is a historical battleground, with Herbert G. Gutman's *The Black Family in Slavery and Freedom* (1976) emphasizing the strength and resilience of slave family life, and Brenda E. Stevenson's *Life in Black and White: Family and Community in the Slave South* (1996) highlighting the stresses and disruptions facing families in bondage. Dylan C. Penningroth's *The Claims of Kinfolk* (2003) demonstrates that slaves were able to accumulate property and pass it on to their descendants. On the hardships and disruptions faced by slave children, see Wilma King's *Stolen Childhood* (1995) and Marie Jenkins Schwartz's *Born in Bondage* (2000).

Recent studies of slave women's lives have demonstrated that these women were resourceful and resistant, not passive victims. Women's lives under slavery are skillfully explored in Stephanie Camp, *Closer to Freedom* (2004); Jacqueline Jones, *Labor of Love, Labor of Sorrow* (1985), Jennifer L. Morgan, *Laboring Women* (2004), and Deborah Gray White, *Ar'n't I a Woman?* (1985). On the relationship between slave women and their mistresses, see Elizabeth Fox-Genovese, *Within the Plantation Household: Black and White Women of the Old South* (1988). On slave women's health and medical practices, see Marie Jenkins Schwartz's *Birthing a Slave* (2006).

For urban slavery, see Claudia D. Goldin, *Urban Slavery in the American South* (1976), and Richard C. Wade, *Slavery in the Cities* (1964). On free blacks, see Ira Berlin, *Slaves Without Masters: The Free Negro in the Antebellum South* (1974); Leonard P. Curry, *The Free Black in Urban America* (1981); Michael P. Johnson and James L. Roark, *Black Masters* (1984) and *No Chariot Let Down: Charleston's Free People of Color* (1984). On slave narratives, see Charles T. Davis and Henry Louis Gates, Jr., *The Slave's Narrative* (1985), and Marion Wilson Starling, *The Slave Narrative* (1981). Specialized studies that are especially worthy of note are Janet Sharp Hermann, *The Pursuit of a Dream* (1981); and Robert S. Starobin, *Industrial Slavery in the Old South* (1970). On slave management, see James O. Breeden, ed., *Advice Among Masters* (1980); William K. Scarborough, *The Overseer* (1966); and William L. Van Deburg, *The Slave Drivers* (1979).

Not all scholars who have studied slavery are historians. Many economists, who are interested in the impact of slavery on economic growth, have also conducted intensive research on the institution. The modern debate over the profitability of slavery and its impact on the southern economy began with an article by Alfred H. Conrad and John R. Meyer entitled "The Economics of Slavery in the Antebellum South," which appeared in the *Journal of Political Economy* in 1958. Among the scholars inspired by Conrad and Meyer's approach were Robert William Fogel and Stanley Engerman, who used sophisticated econometric and statistical techniques in their highly controversial reinterpretation of the slave economy, *Time on the Cross* (1974). Relying on a wide array of quantitative data, this book argued that slavery was a highly profitable institution; that slave labor was highly efficient; that masters promoted stable nuclear families; and that slaves were healthy, well fed, rarely whipped, and seldom sold away from spouses. The volume produced withering criticisms that challenged the book's evidence, methods, and interpretations, including those by Herbert G. Gutman, *Slavery and the Numbers Game* (1975), and Paul A. David et al., *Reckoning with Slavery* (1976). Fogel responded to his critics' charges in 1989 with a volume entitled *Without Consent or Contract*, which synthesizes much recent quantitative research on slavery.

A large number of important recent studies have explored slavery's aftermath. Among these works that focus on the black experience during the Civil War and Reconstruction are Eric Foner, *Nothing But Freedom* (1983) and *Reconstruction* (1988); Joseph T. Glatthaar, *Forged in Battle: The Civil War Alliance between Black Soldiers and White Officers* (1990); Steven Hahn, *A Nation Under Our Feet: Black Political Struggles in the Rural South from Slavery to the Great Migration* (2003); Thomas Holt, *Black Over White* (1977); Peter Kolchin, *First Freedom* (1972); Leon Litwack, *Been in the Storm So Long* (1979); Jay R. Mandle, *Not Slave, Not Free* (1992); Clarence L. Mohr, *On the Threshold of Freedom: Masters and Slaves in Civil War Georgia* (1986); George C. Rable, *But There Was No Peace* (1984); Roger L. Ransom and Richard Sutch, *One Kind of Freedom* (1977); Willie Lee Rose, *Rehearsal for Reconstruction* (1964); and Joel Williamson, *After Slavery* (1965) and *A Rage for Order* (1986).

Bibliography

Bibliographies

Boles, John B. *Interpreting Southern History*. Baton Rouge: Louisiana State University Press, 1987.

Brignano, Russell C. *Black Americans in Autobiography: An Annotated Bibliography of Autobiographies and Autobiographical Books Written since the Civil War*. Rev. and exp. edn. Durham, N.C.: Duke University Press, 1984.

Hogg, Peter C. *The African Slave Trade and its Suppression: A Classified and Annotated Bibliography of Books, Pamphlets and Periodical Articles*. Cass Library of African studies. General Studies, 137. London: Frank Cass, 1973.

Kujoory, Parvin. *Black Slavery in America: An Annotated Mediagraphy*. Lanham: Scarecrow Press, 1995.

Microfilming Corporation of America. *Slavery: A Bibliography and Union List of the Microform Collection*. Sanford, N.C.: Microfilming Corporation of America, 1980.

Miller, Joseph Calder. *Slavery: A Worldwide Bibliography, 1900–1982*. White Plains, N.Y.: Kraus International, 1985.

Miller, Joseph Calder. *Slavery and Slaving in World History: A Bibliography, 1900–1996*. Armonk, N.Y.: M. E. Sharpe, 1999.

Olson, James Stuart. *Slave Life in America: A Historiography and Selected Bibliography*. Lanham: University Press of America, 1983.

Scott, Rebecca, Thomas C. Holt, Frederick Cooper, and Aims McGuinness, eds. *Societies after Slavery: A Select Annotated Bibliography of Printed Sources on Cuba, Brazil, British Colonial Africa, South Africa, and the British West Indies*. Pittsburgh: University of Pittsburgh Press, 2002.

Smith, John David, comp. *Black Slavery in the Americas: An Interdisciplinary Bibliography, 1865–1980*. Westport, Conn.: Greenwood Press, 1982.

Williams, Ethel L. and Clifton F. Brown, comps. *The Howard University Bibliography of African and Afro-American Religious Studies*. Wilmington, Del.: Scholarly Resources, 1977.

Dictionaries

Klein, Martin A. *Historical Dictionary of Slavery and Abolition*. Lanham: Scarecrow Press, 2002.

Miller, Randall M., ed. *Dictionary of Afro-American Slavery*. Updated edn. Westport, Conn.: Praeger, 1997.

Encyclopedias

Drescher, Seymour and Stanley Engerman, eds. *A Historical Guide to World Slavery*. New York: Oxford University Press, 1998.

Finkelman, Paul and Joseph C. Miller, eds. *Macmillan Encyclopedia of World Slavery*. New York: Macmillan, 1998.

Hinks, Peter and John McKivigan, eds. *Encyclopedia of Antislavery and Abolition*. Westport, Conn.: Greenwood Press, 2007.

Rodriguez, Junius P., ed. *Encyclopedia of Slave Resistance and Rebellion*. Westport, Conn.: Greenwood Press, 2007.

Rodriguez, Junius P., ed. *The Historical Encyclopedia of World Slavery*. Santa Barbara: ABC-CLIO, 1997.

Historiography

Bragg, Gail. *An Historiography of American Slave Women*. CompuBibs, 6. Brooklyn, N.Y.: CompuBibs, 1984.

Dew, Charles B. "The Slavery Experience," in John B. Boles and Evelyn Thomas Nolen, eds., *Interpreting Southern History*. Baton Rouge: Louisiana State University Press, 1987.

Finkelman, Paul, ed. *Slavery and Historiography*. New York: Garland, 1989.

Fogel, Robert William. *The Slavery Debates, 1952–1990: A Retrospective*. Baton Rouge: Louisiana State University Press, 2003.

Olson, James Stuart. *Slave Life in America: A Historiography and Selected Bibliography*. Lanham: University Press of America, 1983.

Parish, Peter J. *Slavery: History and Historians*. New York: Harper and Row, 1989.

Smith, John David. *Slavery, Race, and American History: Historical Conflict, Trends, and Method, 1866–1953*. Armonk, N.Y.: M. E. Sharpe, 1999.

Smith, Mark M. *Debating Slavery: Economy and Society in the Antebellum American South*. New York: Cambridge University Press, 1998.

Journals

Slavery & Abolition (1980).

Films

Amazing Grace (dir. Michael Apted, 2006).
Amistad (dir. Steven Spielberg, 1997).
Andanggaman (dir. Roger Gnoan M'Bala, 2000).
Band of Angels (dir. Raoul Walsh, 1957).
Beloved (dir. Jonathan Demme, 1998).
Burn! (dir. Gilo Pontecorvo, 1968).
Ceddo (dir. Ousmane Sembene, 1977).
Cimarron (dir. Sergio Giral, 1967).
Daughters of the Dust (dir. Julie Dash, 1991).
Glory (dir. Edward Zwick, 1989).
Last Supper (dir. Tomas Gutierrez Alea, 1976).
Maluala (dir. Sergio Giral, 1979).
Middle Passage (dir. Guy Deslauriers, 2000).
NightJohn (dir. Charles Burnett, 1996).
Other Francisco (dir. Sergio Giral, 1975).
Quilombo (dir. Carlos Diegues, 1984).
Sankofa (dir. Haile Gerima, 1993).
Slave Ship (dir. Tay Garnett, 1937).
Slaves (dir. Herbert J. Biberman, 1969).
Souls at Sea (dir. Henry Hathaway, 1937).
Spartacus (dir. Stanley Kubrick, 1960).

General Works

Blackburn, Robin. *The Making of New World Slavery: From the Baroque to the Modern, 1492–1800*. London: Verso, 1997.
Blackburn, Robin. *The Overthrow of Colonial Slavery, 1776–1848*. London: Verso, 1988.
Davis, David Brion. *Inhuman Bondage: The Rise and Fall of Slavery in the New World*. New York: Oxford University Press, 2006.
Davis, David Brion. *The Problem of Slavery in the Age of Revolution*. New York: Oxford University Press, 1975.
Davis, David Brion. *The Problem of Slavery in Western Culture*. New York: Oxford University Press, 1988.
Davis, David Brion. *Slavery and Human Progress*. New York: Oxford University Press, 1984.
Horton, James Oliver and Lois Horton. *Slavery and the Making of America*. New York: Oxford University Press, 2004.
Jewett, Clayton E. and John O. Allen. *Slavery in the South: A State-by-State History*. Westport, Conn.: Greenwood Press, 2004.
Johnson, Charles Richard and Patricia Smith. *Africans in America: America's Journey Through Slavery*. New York: Harcourt Brace, 1998.
Patterson, Orlando. *Freedom in the Making of Western Culture*. New York: Basic Books, 1991.
Patterson, Orlando. *Slavery and Social Death: A Comparative Study*. Cambridge. Mass.: Harvard University Press, 1982.

Phillips, William D. *Slavery from Roman Times to the Early Transatlantic Trade*. Minneapolis: University of Minnesota Press, 1985.

Thornton, John. *Africa and Africans in the Making of the Atlantic World, 1400–1680*. 2nd edn. Cambridge: Cambridge University Press, 1998.

Walvin, James. *Slavery and the Slave Trade: A Short Illustrated History*. Jackson: University Press of Mississippi, 1983.

Primary Sources

Berlin, Ira, Marc Favreau, and Steven F. Miller. *Remembering Slavery: African Americans Talk About their Personal Experiences of Slavery and Freedom*. New York: New Press, 1998.

Blassingame, John W., ed. *Slave Testimony: Two Centuries of Letters, Speeches, Interviews, and Autobiographies*. Baton Rouge: Louisiana State University Press, 1977.

Engerman, Stanley, Seymour Drescher, and Robert Paquette, eds. *Slavery*. New York: Oxford University Press, 2001.

Rawick, George P. The *American Slave: A Composite Autobiography*. Supplement, series 1. Contributions in Afro-American and African Studies, 35. Westport, Conn.: Greenwood Press, 1977.

Rawick, George P. *The American Slave: A Composite Autobiography*. Supplement, series 2. Contributions in Afro-American and African Studies, 49. Westport, Conn.: Greenwood Press, 1979.

Rose, Willie Lee. *A Documentary History of Slavery in North America*. Athens: University of Georgia Press, 1999.

Collections of Essays

Archer, Leonie J. *Slavery and Other Forms of Unfree Labor*. New York: Routledge, 1988.

Baptist, Edward E. and Stephanie M. H. Camp, eds. *New Studies in the History of American Slavery*. Athens: University of Georgia Press, 2006.

Bieber, Judy. *Plantation Societies in the Era of European Expansion*. Aldershot: Variorum, 1997.

Boritt, Gabor and Scott Hancock, eds. *Slavery, Resistance, Freedom*. New York: Oxford University Press, 2007.

Brown, Christopher and Philip D. Morgan, eds. *Arming Slaves: From Classical Times to the Modern Age*. New Haven: Yale University Press, 2006.

Bush, M. L. *Serfdom and Slavery: Studies in Legal Bondage*. London: Longman, 1996.

Cateau, Heather and S. H. H. Carrington, eds. *Capitalism and Slavery Fifty Years Later. Eric Eustace Williams: A Reassessment of the Man and His Work*. New York: Peter Lang, 2000.

Craton, Michael. *Roots and Branches: Current Directions in Slave Studies*. Historical Reflections = Reflexions historiques. Directions, 1. Toronto and New York: Pergamon Press, 1979.

Curtin, Philip D. *The Rise and Fall of the Plantation Complex*. 2nd edn. Cambridge: Cambridge University Press, 1998.

Davis, David Brion. *Challenging the Boundaries of Slavery*. Cambridge, Mass.: Harvard University Press, 2003.

Davis, David Brion. *From Homicide to Slavery*. New York: Oxford University Press, 1986.

Davis, David Brion. *In the Image of God: Religion, Moral Values, and our Heritage of Slavery.* New Haven: Yale University Press, 2001.

Drescher, Seymour. *From Slavery to Freedom: Comparative Studies in the Rise and Fall of Atlantic Slavery.* New York: New York University Press, 1999.

Eltis, David, ed. *Coerced and Free Migration: Global Perspectives.* Stanford: Stanford University Press, 2002.

Engerman, Stanley L. *Slavery, Emancipation and Freedom: Comparative Perspectives.* Baton Rouge: Louisiana State University Press, 2007.

Engerman, Stanley. *The Terms of Labor: Slavery, Serfdom, and Free Labor.* Stanford: Stanford University Press, 1999.

Fox-Genovese, Elizabeth. *Fruits of Merchant Capital: Slavery and Bourgeois Property in the Rise and Expansion of Capitalism.* Oxford and New York: Oxford University Press, 1983.

Fredrickson, George M. *The Arrogance of Race: Historical Perspectives on Slavery, Racism, and Social Inequality.* Middletown, Conn.: Wesleyan University Press, 1988.

Frey, Sylvia R. and Betty Wood. *From Slavery to Emancipation in the Atlantic World.* Portland: Frank Cass, 1999.

Hernæs, Per and Tore Iversen, eds. *Slavery Across Time and Space: Studies in Slavery in Medieval Europe and Africa.* Trondheim: Dept. of History, 2002.

Heuman, Gad and James Walvin, eds. *The Slavery Reader.* New York: Routledge, 2003.

Lovejoy, Paul E., ed. *Unfree Labour in the Development of the Atlantic World.* London: Frank Cass, 1994.

Palmer, Colin A. *The Worlds of Unfree Labour: From Indentured Servitude to Slavery.* Aldershot: Variorum, 1998.

Peabody, Sue and Keila Grinberg, eds. *Slavery, Freedom, and the Law in the Atlantic World: A Brief History with Documents.* New York: Palgrave Macmillan, 2007.

Shepherd, Verene A., ed. *Working Slavery, Pricing Freedom: Perspectives from the Caribbean, Africa and the African Diaspora.* Oxford: James Currey, 2002.

New World Slavery: General Works

Berlin, Ira, ed. *Cultivation and Culture: Labor and the Shaping of Slave Life in the Americas.* Charlottesville: University of Virginia Press, 1993.

Berlin, Ira, ed. *The Slaves' Economy: Independent Production by Slaves in the Americas.* London: Frank Cass, 1991.

Conniff, Michael L. *Africans in the Americas: A History of the Black Diaspora.* New York: St Martin's Press, 1994.

Curtin, Philip D. *The Rise and Fall of the Plantation Complex.* New York: Cambridge University Press, 1990.

Dessens, Nathalie. *Myths of the Plantation Society: Slavery in the American South and the West Indies.* Gainesville: University Press of Florida, 2003.

Eltis, David. *The Rise of African Slavery in the Americas.* New York: Cambridge University Press, 2000.

Eltis, David, Frank D. Lewis, and Kenneth L. Sokoloff, eds. *Slavery in the Development of the Americas.* New York: Cambridge University Press, 2004.

Engerman, Stanley L. and Eugene D. Genovese, eds. *Race and Slavery in the Western Hemisphere: Quantitative Studies.* Princeton: Princeton University Press, 1975.

Geggus, David P., ed. *The Impact of the Haitian Revolution in the Atlantic World*. Columbia.: University of South Carolina Press, 2001.

Genovese, Eugene D. *From Rebellion to Revolution: Afro-American Slave Revolts in the Making of the Modern World*. Baton Rouge: Louisiana State University Press, 1979.

Genovese, Eugene D., ed. *The Slave Economies*. New York: Wiley, 1973.

Hall, Gwendolyn Midlo. *Slavery and African Ethnicities in the Americas*. Chapel Hill: University of North Carolina Press, 2005.

Hoetink, H. *Slavery and Race Relations in the Americas*. New York: Harper and Row, 1973.

Sidbury, James. *Becoming African in America*. New York: Oxford University Press, 2007.

Comparative Studies

Degler, Carl N. *Neither Black Nor White: Slavery and Race Relations in Brazil and the United States*. Madison: University of Wisconsin Press, 1986.

Klein, Herbert S. *Slavery in the Americas: A Comparative Study of Virginia and Cuba*. Chicago: University of Chicago Press, 1967.

Kolchin, Peter. *Unfree Labor: American Slavery and Russian Serfdom*. Cambridge, Mass.: Harvard University Press, 1987.

Mullin, Michael. *Africa in America: Slave Acculturation and Resistance in the American South and the British Caribbean, 1736–1831*. Urbana: University of Illinois Press, 1992.

Scott, Rebecca J. *Degrees of Freedom: Louisiana and Cuba after Slavery*. Cambridge, Mass.: Belknap Press of Harvard University Press, 2005.

Walker, Daniel E. *No More, No More: Slavery and Cultural Resistance in Havana and New Orleans*. Minneapolis: University of Minnesota Press, 2004.

United States

The following are organized by general works, then alphabetically by state.

Abzug, Robert H., ed. *New Perspectives on Race and Slavery in America*. Lexington: University Press of Kentucky, 1986.

Benes, Peter, ed. *Slavery/Antislavery in New England*. Boston: Boston University, 2005.

Blassingame, John W. *The Slave Community: Plantation Life in the Antebellum South*. Rev. and enl. edn. New York: Oxford University Press, 1978.

Boles, John B. *Black Southerners, 1619–1869*. Lexington: University Press of Kentucky, 1983.

David, Paul A., Herbert G. Gutman, Richard Sutch, Peter Temin, and Gavin Wright. *Reckoning with Slavery: A Critical Study in the Quantitative History of American Negro Slavery*. New York: Oxford University Press, 1976.

Dunaway, Wilma A. *Slavery in the American Mountain South*. New York: Cambridge University Press, 2003.

Elkins, Stanley M. *Slavery: A Problem in American Institutional and Intellectual Life*. 3rd edn., rev. Chicago: University of Chicago Press, 1976.

Farrow, Anne, Joel Lang, and Jenifer Frank. *Complicity: How the North Promoted, Prolonged, and Profited from Slavery*. New York: Ballantine Books, 2005.

Finkelman, Paul, ed. *Economics, Industrialization, Urbanization, and Slavery.* Articles on American Slavery, vol. 10. New York: Garland, 1989.

Fogel, Robert William. *Without Consent or Contract. Technical Papers: The Rise and Fall of American Slavery.* New York: Norton, 1989.

Fogel, Robert William and Stanley Engerman. *Time on the Cross: The Economics of American Negro Slavery.* New York: Norton, 1974.

Foner, Eric. *Slavery and Freedom in Nineteenth Century America.* Oxford: Clarendon Press, 1994.

Freehling, William W. *The Reintegration of American History: Slavery and the Civil War.* New York: Oxford University Press, 1994.

Genovese, Eugene D. *Political Economy of Slavery.* 2nd edn. Middletown, Conn.: Wesleyan University Press, 1989.

Genovese, Eugene D. *Roll, Jordan, Roll: The World the Slaves Made.* New York: Vintage Books, 1976.

Goodheart, Lawrence B., ed. *Slavery in American Society.* 3rd edn. Lexington, Mass.: D. C. Heath, 1993.

Greenberg, Kenneth S. *Honor and Slavery.* Princeton: Princeton University Press, 1996.

Gutman, Herbert George. *Slavery and the Numbers Game: A Critique of Time on the Cross.* Urbana: University of Illinois Press, (1975).

Hahn, Steven. *A Nation Under Our Feet: Black Political Struggles in the Rural South from Slavery to the Great Migration.* Cambridge, Mass.: Belknap Press of Harvard University Press, 2003.

Hirschfeld, Fritz. *George Washington and Slavery: A Documentary Portrayal.* Columbia: University of Missouri, 1997.

Hodges, Graham Russell. *Slavery, Freedom and Culture among Early American Workers.* Armonk, N. Y.: M. E. Sharpe, 1998.

Hudson, Larry E., Jr. *Working toward Freedom: Slave Society and Domestic Economy in the American South.* Rochester, N.Y.: University of Rochester Press, 1994.

Huggins, Nathan Irvin. *Black Odyssey: The Afro-American Ordeal in Slavery.* New York: Vintage Books, 1990.

Jones, Jacqueline. *Labor of Love, Labor of Sorrow: Black Women, Work, and the Family from Slavery to the Present.* New York: Basic Books, 1985.

Jordan, Winthrop D., ed. *Slavery and the American South: Essays and Commentaries.* Jackson: University Press of Mississippi, 2003.

Kolchin, Peter. *American Slavery, 1619–1877.* Rev. edn. New York: Hill and Wang, 2003.

Lane, Ann J. *The Debate over Slavery: Stanley Elkins and His Critics.* Urbana: University of Illinois Press, 1971.

Morgan, Kenneth. *Slavery in America: A Reader and Guide.* Athens: University of Georgia Press, 2005.

Oakes, James. *Slavery and Freedom: An Interpretation of the Old South.* New York: Knopf, 1990.

Owens, Leslie Howard. *This Species of Property: Slave Life and Culture in the Old South.* Oxford and New York: Oxford University Press, 1977.

Paquette, Robert Louis and Louis A. Ferleger, eds. *Slavery, Secession, and Southern History.* Charlottesville: University of Virginia Press, 2000.

Ransom, Roger L. *Conflict and Compromise: The Political Economy of Slavery, Emancipation, and the American Civil War.* Cambridge: Cambridge University Press, 1989.

Roediger, David and Martin Blatt. *The Meaning of Slavery in the North.* New York: Garland, 1998.

Rose, Willie Lee Nichols. *Slavery and Freedom*. Exp. ed. Oxford: Oxford University Press, 1982.

Schweninger, Loren, ed. *The Southern Debate over Slavery*. Urbana: University of Illinois Press, 2001.

Smith, Mark M. *Mastered by the Clock: Time, Slavery, and Freedom in the American South*. Chapel Hill: University of North Carolina Press, 1997.

Wiencek, Henry. *The Hairstons: An American Family in Black and White*. New York: St Martin's Press, 1999.

Wiencek, Henry. *An Imperfect God: George Washington, His Slaves, and the Creation of America*. New York: Farrar, Straus and Giroux, 2003.

Colonial and Revolutionary Era: General Interpretations

Berlin, Ira. *Generations of Captivity: A History of African-American Slaves*. Cambridge, Mass.: Belknap Press of Harvard University Press, 2003.

Berlin, Ira. *Many Thousands Gone: The First Two Centuries of Slavery in North America*. Cambridge, Mass.: Belknap Press of Harvard University Press, 1998.

Berlin, Ira, ed. *Slavery and Freedom in the Age of the American Revolution: Blacks in the New World*. Urbana: Published for the United States Capitol Historical Society by the University of Illinois Press, 1986.

Bontemps, Alex. *The Punished Self: Surviving Slavery in the Colonial South*. Ithaca: Cornell University Press, 2001.

Bradley, Patricia. *Slavery, Propaganda, and the American Revolution*. Jackson: University Press of Mississippi, 1998.

Countryman, Edward. *How Did American Slavery Begin?* Bedford: Macmillan, 1999.

Finkelman, Paul. *Slavery, Revolutionary America, and the New Nation*. New York: Garland, 1989.

Gomez, Michael Angelo. *Exchanging Our Country Marks: The Transformation of African Identities in the Colonial and Antebellum South*. Chapel Hill: University of North Carolina Press, 1998.

Gordon-Reed, Annette. *Thomas Jefferson and Sally Hemings: An American Controversy*. Charlottesville: University of Virginia Press, 1997.

Macleod, Duncan J. *Slavery, Race and the American Revolution*. New York: Cambridge University Press, 1974.

Morgan, Philip D. *Slave Counterpoint: Black Culture in the Eighteenth-Century Chesapeake and Lowcountry*. Chapel Hill: University of North Carolina Press, 1998.

Nash, Gary B. *The Forgotten Fifth: African Americans in the Age of Revolution*. Cambridge, Mass.: Harvard University Press, 2006.

Olwell, Robert and Alan Tully, eds. *Cultures and Identities in Colonial British America*. Baltimore: Johns Hopkins University Press, 2006.

Rappleye, Charles. *Sons of Providence: The Brown Brothers, the Slave Trade, and the American Revolution*. New York: Simon and Schuster, 2006.

Schama, Simon. *Rough Crossings: Britain, the Slaves, and the American Revolution*. New York: Ecco, 2006.

Silver, Timothy. *A New Face on the Countryside: Indians, Colonists, and Slaves in South Atlantic Forests, 1500–1800*. Cambridge: Cambridge University Press, 1990.

Voelz, Peter Michael. *Slave and Soldier: The Military Impact of Blacks in Colonial America*. New York: Garland, 1993.

Waldstreicher, David. *Runaway America: Benjamin Franklin, Slavery, and the American Revolution.* New York: Hill and Wang, 2004.

Walsh, Lorena S. *From Calabar to Carter's Grove: The History of a Virginia Slave Community.* Charlottesville: University of Virginia Press, 1997.

Wood, Betty. *The Origins of American Slavery: Freedom and Bondage in the English Colonies.* New York: Hill and Wang, 1997.

Wood, Peter H. *Strange New Land: Africans in Colonial America.* New York: Oxford University Press, 2003.

Wright, Donald R. *African Americans in the Colonial Era.* 2nd edn. Arlington Heights: Harlan Davidson, 2000.

Appalachia

Inscoe, John C. *Mountain Masters, Slavery, and the Sectional Crisis in Western North Carolina.* Knoxville: University of Tennessee Press, 1989.

California

Lapp, Rudolph M. *Blacks in Gold Rush California.* Yale Western Americana Series, 29. New Haven: Yale University Press, 1977.

Chesapeake

Davis, David Brion. *Slavery in the Colonial Chesapeake.* The Foundations of America. Williamsburg, Va.: Colonial Williamsburg Foundation, 1986.

Kulikoff, Allan. *Tobacco and Slaves: The Development of Southern Cultures in the Chesapeake, 1680–1800.* Chapel Hill: Published for the Institute of Early American History and Culture, Williamsburg, Virginia, by the University of North Carolina Press, 1986.

Delaware

Essah, Patience. *A House Divided: Slavery and Emancipation in Delaware, 1638–1865.* Charlottesville: University of Virginia Press, 1996.

Williams, William Henry. *Slavery and Freedom in Delaware, 1639–1865.* Wilmington: SR Books, 1996.

Florida

Landers, Jane. *Black Society in Spanish Florida.* Urbana: University of Illinois Press, 1997.

Georgia

Harris, J. William. *Plain Folk and Gentry in a Slave Society: White Liberty and Black Slavery in Augusta's Hinterlands.* Baton Rouge: Louisiana State University Press, 1998.

Lane, Mills, ed. *Neither More Nor Less Than Men: Slavery in Georgia: A Documentary History.* Library of Georgia. Savannah: Beehive Press, 1993.

Mohr, Clarence L. *On the Threshold of Freedom: Masters and Slaves in Civil War Georgia*. Athens: University of Georgia Press, 1986.

O'Donovan, Susan E. *Becoming Free in the Cotton South*. Cambridge, Mass.: Harvard University Press, 2007.

Reidy, Joseph P. *From Slavery to Agrarian Capitalism in the Cotton Plantation South: Central Georgia, 1800–1880*. Fred W. Morrison Series in Southern Studies. Chapel Hill: University of North Carolina Press, 1992.

Smith, Julia Floyd. *Slavery and Rice Culture in Low Country Georgia, 1750–1860*. Knoxville: University of Tennessee Press, 1985.

Wood, Betty. *Slavery in Colonial Georgia, 1730–1775*. Athens: University of Georgia Press, 1984.

Wood, Betty. *Women's Work, Men's Work: The Informal Slave Economies of Lowcountry Georgia*. Athens: University of Georgia Press, 1995.

Kentucky

Tallant, Harold D. *Evil Necessity: Slavery and Political Culture in Antebellum Kentucky*. Lexington: University Press of Kentucky, 2003.

Louisiana

Follett, Richard J. *The Sugar Masters: Planters and Slaves in Louisiana's Cane World, 1820–1860*. Baton Rouge: Louisiana State University Press, 2005.

Hall, Gwendolyn Midlo. *Africans in Colonial Louisiana: The Development of Afro-Creole Culture in the Eighteenth Century*. Baton Rouge: Louisiana State University Press, 1992.

Ingersoll, Thomas N. *Mammon and Manon in Early New Orleans: The First Slave Society in the Deep South, 1718–1819*. Knoxville: University of Tennessee Press, 1999.

Schafer, Judith Kelleher. *Becoming Free, Remaining Free: Manumission and Enslavement in New Orleans, 1846–1862*. Baton Rouge: Louisiana State University Press, 2003.

Maryland

Fields, Barbara Jeanne. *Slavery and Freedom on the Middle Ground: Maryland during the Nineteenth Century*. Yale Historical Publications. Miscellany, 123. New Haven: Yale University Press, 1985.

Phillips, Christopher. *Freedom's Port: The African American Community of Baltimore, 1790–1860*. Urbana: University of Illinois Press, 1997.

Preston, Dickson J. *Young Frederick Douglass: The Maryland Years*. Baltimore: Johns Hopkins University Press, 1980.

Whitman, T. Stephen. *The Price of Freedom: Slavery and Manumission in Baltimore and Early National Maryland*. Lexington: University Press of Kentucky, 1997.

Mississippi

Alford, Terry. *Prince among Slaves*. New York: Oxford University Press, 1986.

Hermann, Janet Sharp. *The Pursuit of a Dream*. New York: Oxford University Press, 1981.

Jordan, Winthrop D. *Tumult and Silence at Second Creek: An Inquiry into a Civil War Slave Conspiracy*. Baton Rouge: Louisiana State University Press, 1993.

Libby, David J. *Slavery and Frontier Mississippi, 1720–1835*. Jackson: University Press of Mississippi, 2004.

Moore, John Hebron. *The Emergence of the Cotton Kingdom in the Old Southwest: Mississippi, 1770–1860*. Baton Rouge: Louisiana State University Press, 1988.

Missouri

Frazier, Harriet C. *Slavery and Crime in Missouri, 1773–1865*. Jefferson, N.C.: McFarland, 2001.

Hurt, R. Douglas. *Agriculture and Slavery in Missouri's Little Dixie*. Columbia: University of Missouri Press, 1992.

New Jersey

Hodges, Graham Russell. *Slavery and Freedom in the Rural North: African Americans in Monmouth County, New Jersey, 1665–1865*. Madison: Madison House, 1997.

New York

Berlin, Ira and Leslie M. Harris, eds. *Slavery in New York*. New York: New Press, 2005.

Davis, Thomas J. *A Rumor of Revolt: The "Great Negro Plot" in Colonial New York*. New York: Free Press, 1985.

Foote, Thelma Wills. *Black and White Manhattan: The History of Racial Formation in Colonial New York City*. New York: Oxford University Press, 2003.

Gellman, David N. *Emancipating New York: The Politics of Slavery and Freedom, 1777–1827*. Baton Rouge: Louisiana State University Press, 2006.

Gellman, David N. and David Quigley, eds. *Jim Crow New York: A Documentary History of Race and Citizenship, 1777–1877*. New York: New York University Press, 2004.

Harris, Leslie M. *In the Shadow of Slavery: African Americans in New York City, 1626–1863*. Chicago: University of Chicago Press, 2003.

Hoffer, Peter Charles. *The Great New York Conspiracy of 1741: Slavery, Crime, and Colonial Law*. Lawrence: University Press of Kansas, 2003.

Lepore, Jill. *New York Burning: Liberty, Slavery, and Conspiracy in Eighteenth-Century Manhattan*. New York: Knopf, 2005.

McManus, Edgar J. *A History of Negro Slavery in New York*. Syracuse: Syracuse University Press, 2001.

White, Shane. *Somewhat More Independent: The End of Slavery in New York City, 1770–1810*. Athens: University of Georgia Press, 1991.

North Carolina

Hilty, Hiram H. *By Land and by Sea: Quakers Confront Slavery and its Aftermath in North Carolina*. Greensboro: North Carolina Friends Historical Society, 1993.

Inscoe, John C. *Mountain Masters, Slavery, and the Sectional Crisis in Western North Carolina*. Knoxville: University of Tennessee Press, 1989.

Kay, Marvin L. Michael. *An African Diaspora: Slavery in North Carolina, 1748–1775*. Chapel Hill: University of North Carolina Press, 1995.

Kay, Marvin L. Michael and Lorin Lee Cary. *Slavery in North Carolina, 1748–1775*. Chapel Hill: University of North Carolina Press, 1995.

Sensbach, Jon F. *A Separate Canaan: The Making of an Afro-Moravian World in North Carolina, 1763–1840*. Chapel Hill: University of North Carolina Press, 1998.

Pennsylvania

Nash, Gary B. and Jean B. Soderlund. *Freedom by Degrees: Emancipation in Pennsylvania and its Aftermath*. New York: Oxford University Press, 1991.

Rhode Island

Fitts, Robert K. *Inventing New England's Slave Paradise: Master/Slave Relations in Eighteenth Century Narragansett, Rhode Island*. New York: Garland, 1998.

South Carolina

Ball, Edward. *Slaves in the Family*. New York: Farrar, Straus and Giroux, 1998.

Creel, Margaret Washington. *A Peculiar People: Slave Religion and Community-Culture among the Gullahs*. New York: New York University Press, 1988.

Dusinberre, William. *Them Dark Days: Slavery in the American Rice Swamps*. New York: Oxford University Press, 1996.

Edelson, S. Max. *Plantation Enterprise in Colonial South Carolina*. Cambridge, Mass.: Harvard University Press, 2006.

Jones, Norrece T. *Born a Child of Freedom, Yet a Slave: Mechanisms of Control and Strategies of Resistance in Antebellum South Carolina*. Middletown, Conn.: Wesleyan University Press, 1989.

Joyner, Charles W. *Down by the Riverside: A South Carolina Slave Community*. Blacks in the New World. Urbana: University of Illinois Press, 1984.

Klein, Rachel N. *Unification of a Slave State: The Rise of the Planter Class in the South Carolina Backcountry, 1760–1808*. Chapel Hill: University of North Carolina Press, and Williamsburg, Va.: Published for the Institute of Early American History and Culture, 1990.

Koger, Larry. *Black Slaveowners: Free Black Slave Masters in South Carolina, 1790–1860*. Jefferson, N.C.: McFarland, 1985.

Littlefield, Daniel C. *Rice and Slaves: Ethnicity and the Slave Trade in Colonial South Carolina*. Baton Rouge: Louisiana State University Press, 1981.

Lofton, John. *Denmark Vesey's Revolt: The Slave Plot that Lit a Fuse to Fort Sumter*. Kent, Ohio: Kent State University Press, 1983.

Olwell, Robert. *Masters, Slaves, and Subjects: The Culture of Power in the South Carolina Low Country, 1740–1790*. Ithaca: Cornell University Press, 1998.

Saville, Julie. *The Work of Reconstruction: From Slave to Wage Laborer in South Carolina, 1860–1870*. Cambridge: Cambridge University Press, 1994.

Sinha, Manisha. *The Counterrevolution of Slavery: Politics and Ideology in Antebellum South Carolina*. Chapel Hill: University of North Carolina Press, 2000.

West, Emily. *Chains of Love: Slave Couples in Antebellum South Carolina*. Urbana: University of Illinois Press, 2004.

Wood, Peter H. *Black Majority: Negroes in Colonial South Carolina from 1670 through the Stono Rebellion*. New York: Norton, 1974.

Tennessee

Howington, Arthur F. *What Sayeth the Law: The Treatment of Slaves and Free Blacks in the State and Local Courts of Tennessee.* American Legal and Constitutional History. New York: Garland, 1986.

Texas

Campbell, Randolph. *An Empire for Slavery: The Peculiar Institution in Texas, 1821–1865.* Baton Rouge: Louisiana State University Press, 1989.

Virginia

Dew, Charles B. *Bond of Iron: Master and Slave at Buffalo Forge.* New York: Norton, 1994.
Egerton, Douglas R. *Rebels, Reformers, and Revolutionaries.* New York: Routledge, 2002.
Freehling, Alison Goodyear. *Drift toward Dissolution: The Virginia Slavery Debate of 1831–1832.* Baton Rouge: Louisiana State University Press, 1982.
Hashaw, Tim. *The Birth of Black America: The First African Americans and the Pursuit of Freedom at Jamestown.* New York: Carroll and Graf, 2007.
Link, William A. *Roots of Secession: Slavery and Politics in Antebellum Virginia.* Chapel Hill: University of North Carolina Press, 2003.
McColley, Robert. *Slavery and Jeffersonian Virginia.* 2nd edn. Urbana: University of Illinois Press, 1973.
Morgan, Edmund Sears. *American Slavery, American Freedom: The Ordeal of Colonial Virginia.* New York: Norton, 1975.
Mullin, Gerald W. *Flight and Rebellion: Slave Resistance in Eighteenth-Century Virginia.* New York: Oxford University Press, 1972.
Parent, Anthony S., Jr. *Foul Means: The Formation of a Slave Society in Virginia, 1660–1740.* Chapel Hill: University of North Carolina Press, 2003.
Rothman, Joshua D. *Notorious in the Neighborhood: Sex and Families Across the Color Line in Virginia, 1787–1861.* Chapel Hill: University of North Carolina Press, 2003.
Schwarz, Philip J. *Migrants Against Slavery: Virginians and the Nation.* Charlottesville: University of Virginia Press, 2001.
Sobel, Mechal. *The World They Made Together: Black and White Values in Eighteenth Century Virginia.* Princeton: Princeton University Press, 1987.
Takagi, Midori. *"Rearing Wolves to Our Own Destruction": Slavery in Richmond, Virginia, 1782–1865.* Charlottesville: University of Virginia Press, 1999.
Wolf, Eva Sheppard. *Race and Liberty in the New Nation: Emancipation in Virginia from the Revolution to Nat Turner's Rebellion.* Baton Rouge: Louisiana State University Press, 2006.

Topics

Abolition

Dictionaries and encyclopedias

Hinks, Peter and John McKivigan. *Encyclopedia of Antislavery and Abolition.* Westport, Conn.: Greenwood Press, 2007.

Klein, Martin A. *Historical Dictionary of Slavery and Abolition*. Lanham: Scarecrow Press, 2002.

General interpretations

Bender, Thomas. *The Antislavery Debate: Capitalism and Abolitionism as a Problem in Historical Interpretation*. Berkeley: University of California Press, 1992.

Blackburn, Robin. *The Overthrow of Colonial Slavery, 1776–1848*. London: Verso, 1988.

Fogel, Robert W. *Without Consent or Contract: The Rise and Fall of American Slavery*. New York: Norton, 1989.

Hochschild, Adam. *Bury the Chains: Prophets and Rebels in the Fight to Free an Empire's Slaves*. Boston: Houghton Mifflin, 2005.

Sklar, Kathryn Kish and James Brewer Stewart, eds. *Women's Rights and Transatlantic Antislavery in the Era of Emancipation*. New Haven: Yale University Press, 2007.

Wise, Steven M. *Though the Heavens May Fall: The Landmark Trial that Led to the End of Human Slavery*. Cambridge, Mass.: Da Capo, 2005.

American Abolition

Abbott, Richard H. *Cotton and Capital: Boston Businessmen and Antislavery Reform, 1854–1868*. Amherst: University of Massachusetts Press, 1991.

Azevedo, Celia Maria Marinho de. *Abolitionism in the United States and Brazil: A Comparative Perspective*. New York: Garland, 1995.

Bilotta, James D. *Race and the Rise of the Republican Party, 1848–1865*. New York: Peter Lang, 1992.

Blackett, R. J. M. *Building an Antislavery Wall: Black Americans in the Atlantic Abolitionist Movement, 1830–1860*. Baton Rouge: Louisiana State University Press, 1983.

Blue, Frederick J. *No Taint of Compromise: Crusaders in Antislavery Politics*. Baton Rouge: Louisiana State University Press, 2005.

Buckmaster, Henrietta. *Let My People Go: The Story of the Underground Railroad and the Growth of the Abolition Movement*. Columbia: University of South Carolina Press, 1992.

Clark, Christopher. *The Communitarian Moment: The Radical Challenge of the Northampton Association*. Ithaca: Cornell University Press, 1995.

Cook, Robert. *Baptism of Fire: The Republican Party of Iowa, 1838–1878*. Ames: Iowa State University Press, 1994.

DeBoer, Clara Merritt. *Be Jubilant My Feet: African American Abolitionists in the American Missionary Association, 1839–1861*. New York: Garland, 1994.

Dillon, Merton Lynn. *Slavery Attacked: Southern Slaves and their Allies, 1619–1865*. Baton Rouge: Louisiana State University Press, 1990.

Dixon, Chris. *Perfecting the Family: Antislavery Marriages in Nineteenth-Century America*. Amherst: University of Massachusetts Press, 1997.

Fanuzzi, Robert. *Abolition's Public Sphere*. Minneapolis: University of Minnesota Press, 2003.

Foner, Philip S. and Herbert Shapiro. *Northern Labor and Antislavery: A Documentary History*. Westport, Conn.: Greenwood Press, 1994.

Gellman, David N. *Emancipating New York: The Politics of Slavery and Freedom, 1777–1827*. Baton Rouge: Louisiana State University Press, 2006.

Goodheart, Lawrence B. and Hugh Hawkins. *The Abolitionists: Means, Ends, and Motivations*. 3rd edn. Lexington, Mass.: D. C. Heath, 1995.

Gougeon, Len. *Virtue's Hero: Emerson, Antislavery, and Reform*. Athens: University of Georgia Press, 1990.

Grimstead, David. *American Mobbing, 1828–1861*. New York: Oxford University Press, 1998.

Guy, Anita Aidt. *Maryland's Persistent Pursuit to End Slavery, 1850–1864*. New York: Garland, 1997.

Hansen, Debra Gold. *Strained Sisterhood: Gender and Class in the Boston Female Anti-Slavery Society*. Amherst: University of Massachusetts Press, 1993.

Harrold, Stanley. *The Abolitionists and the South, 1831–1861*. Lexington: University Press of Kentucky, 1995.

Harrold, Stanley. *Subversives: Antislavery Community in Washington, D.C., 1828–1865*. Baton Rouge: Louisiana State University Press, 2003.

Horton, James Oliver and Lois E. Horton. *In Hope of Liberty: Culture, Community, and Protest Among Northern Free Blacks, 1700–1860*. New York: Oxford University Press, 1997.

Howard, Victor B. *The Evangelical War Against Slavery and Caste: The Life and Times of John G. Free*. Senlinsgrove, Pa.: Susquehanna University Press, 1996.

Jacobs, Donald M. *Courage and Conscience: Black and White Abolitionists in Boston*. Bloomington: Indiana University Press, 1993.

Jeffrey, Julie Roy. *The Great Silent Army of Abolitionism: Ordinary Women in the Antislavery Movement*. Chapel Hill: University of North Carolina Press, 1998.

Jennings, Lawrence C. *French Reaction to British Slave Emancipation*. Baton Rouge: Louisiana State University Press, 1988.

Jordan, Ryan P. *Slavery and the Meetinghouse: The Quakers and the Abolitionist Dilemma, 1820–1865*. Bloomington: Indiana University Press, 2007.

Julius, Kevin C. *The Abolitionist Decade, 1829–1838: A Year-by-Year History of Early Events in the Antislavery Movement*. Jefferson, N.C.: McFarland, 2004.

McCarthy, Timothy Patrick and John Stauffer, eds. *Prophets of Protest: Reconsidering the History of American Abolitionism*. New York: New Press, 2006.

McGlynn, Frank, ed. *The Meaning of Freedom: Economics, Politics, and Culture after Slavery*. Pittsburgh: University of Pittsburgh, 1992.

McInerney, Daniel John. *The Fortunate Heirs of Freedom: Abolition and Republican Thought*. Lincoln: University of Nebraska Press, 1994.

McManus, Michael J. *Political Abolitionism in Wisconsin, 1840–1861*. Kent: Kent State University Press, 1998.

Marshall, Peter D. *Bristol and the Abolition of Slavery: The Politics of Emancipation*. Local History Pamphlets, 37. Bristol: Bristol Branch of the Historical Association, The University, 1975.

Melish, Joanne Pope. *Disowning Slavery: Gradual Emancipation and "Race" in New England, 1780–1860*. Ithaca: Cornell University Press, 1998.

Mitchell, Thomas G. *Anti-Slavery Politics in Antebellum and Civil War America*. Westport, Conn.: Praeger, 2007.

Nash, Gary B. *Race and Revolution*. Madison: Madison House, 1990.

Newman, Richard S. *The Transformation of American Abolitionism: Fighting Slavery in the Early Republic*. Chapel Hill: University of North Carolina Press, 2002.

Perry, Lewis. *Radical Abolitionism: Anarchy and the Government of God in Antislavery Thought*. Knoxville: University of Tennessee Press, 1995.

Perry, Lewis and Michael Fellman. *Antislavery Reconsidered: New Perspectives on the Abolitionists*. Baton Rouge: Louisiana State University Press, 1979.

Ripley, C. Peter. *Witness for Freedom: African American Voices on Race, Slavery, and Emancipation.* Chapel Hill: University of North Carolina Press, 1993.

Rogers, William B. *"We Are All Together Now": Frederick Douglass, William Lloyd Garrison, and the Prophetic Tradition.* New York: Garland, 1995.

Rucker, Walter C. *The River Flows On: Black Resistance, Culture, and Identity Formation in Early America.* Baton Rouge: Louisiana State University Press, 2006.

Sanchez-Eppler, Karen. *Touching Liberty: Abolition, Feminism, and the Politics of the Body.* Berkeley: University of California Press, 1993.

Sears, Richard D. *The Kentucky Abolitionists in the Midst of Slavery.* Lewiston: Edwin Mellen Press, 1993.

Sernett, Milton C. *North Star Country: Upstate New York and the Crusade for African American Freedom.* Syracuse: Syracuse University Press, 2002.

Sklar, Kathryn Kish. *Women's Rights Emerges within the Anti-slavery Movement 1830–1870: A Brief History with Documents.* Boston: St Martin's Press, 2000.

Stauffer, John. *The Black Hearts of Men: Radical Abolitionists and the Transformation of Race.* Cambridge, Mass.: Harvard University Press, 2002.

Stewart, James Brewer. *Holy Warriors: The Abolitionists and American Slavery.* Rev. edn. New York: Hill and Wang, 1996.

Strong, Douglas M. *Perfectionist Politics: Abolitionism and the Religious Tensions of American Democracy.* New York: Syracuse University Press, 1998.

Toledo, Gregory. *The Hanging of Old Brown: A Story of Slaves, Statesmen, and Redemption.* Westport, Conn.: Praeger, 2002.

Volpe, Vernon L. *Forlorn Hope of Freedom: The Liberty Party in the Old Northwest, 1838–1848.* Kent: Kent State University Press, 1990.

Vorenberg, Michael. "Final Freedom: The Civil War, the End of Slavery, and the Thirteenth Amendment." PhD thesis, Harvard University, 1995.

Wellman, Judith. *Grass Roots Reform in the Burned-Over District of Upstate New York: Religion, Abolitionism, and Democracy.* New York: Garland, 2000.

Wyly-Jones, Susan. "The Antiabolitionist Panic: Slavery, Abolition, and Politics in the U.S. South, 1835–1844." PhD thesis, Harvard, 2000.

Yee, Shirley J. *Black Women Abolitionists: A Study in Activism, 1828–1860.* Knoxville: University of Tennessee Press, 1992.

Yellin, Jean Fagan and John C. Van Horne. *The Abolitionist Sisterhood: Women's Political Culture in Antebellum America.* Ithaca: Cornell University Press, 1994.

Young, R. J. *Antebellum Black Activists: Race, Gender, and Self.* New York: Garland, 1996.

Amistad Affair

Jones, Howard. *Mutiny on the Amistad: The Saga of a Slave Revolt and its Impact on American Abolition, Law, and Diplomacy.* New York: Oxford University Press, 1987.

Osagie, Iyunolu Folayan. *The Amistad Revolt: Memory, Slavery, and the Politics of Identity in the United States and Sierra Leone.* Athens: University of Georgia Press, 2000.

Biographical Studies: Slaves and Free Blacks

Billingsley, Andrew. *Yearning to Breathe Free: Robert Smalls of South Carolina and his Families.* Columbia: University of South Carolina Press, 2007.

Blight, David W. *Frederick Douglass' Civil War: Keeping Faith in Jubilee*. Baton Rouge: Louisiana State University Press, 1989.

Carretta, Vincent. *Equiano, the African: Biography of a Self-Made Man*. Athens: University of Georgia Press, 2005.

Cheek, William F. *John Mercer Langston and the Fight for Black Freedom, 1829–65*. Urbana: University of Illinois Press, 1989.

Hamilton, Virginia. *Anthony Burns: The Defeat and Triumph of a Fugitive Slave*. New York: Knopf, 1988.

Lampe, Gregory P. *Frederick Douglass: Freedom's Voice, 1818–1945*. East Lansing: Michigan State University Press, 1998.

Larson, Kate Clifford. *Bound for the Promised Land: Harriet Tubman, Portrait of an American Hero*. New York: Ballantine Books, 2004.

Mabee, Carleton. *Sojourner Truth: Slave, Prophet, Legend*. New York: New York University Press, 1993.

Painter, Nell Irvin. *Sojourner Truth: A Life, a Symbol*. New York: Norton, 1996.

Pasternak, Martin B. *Rise Now and Fly to Arms: The Life of Henry Highland Garnet*. New York: Garland, 1995.

Sparks, Randy J. *The Two Princes of Calabar: An Eighteenth-Century Atlantic Odyssey*. Cambridge, Mass.: Harvard University Press, 2004.

Stauffer, John, ed. *The Works of James McCune Smith: Black Intellectual and Abolitionist*. New York: Oxford University Press, 2006.

Thomas, Herman Edward. *James W. C. Pennington: African American Churchman and Abolitionist*. New York: Garland, 1995.

Von Frank, Albert J. *The Trials of Anthony Burns*. Cambridge, Mass.: Harvard University Press, 1998.

Walvin, James. *An African's Life: The Life and Times of Olaudah Equiano, 1745–1797*. Washington: Cassell, 1998.

Winch, Julie. *A Gentleman of Color: The Life of James Forten*. Oxford: Oxford University Press, 2003.

Architecture

Vlach, John Michael. *Back of the Big House: The Architecture of Plantation Slavery*. Fred W. Morrison Series in Southern Studies. Chapel Hill: University of North Carolina Press, 1993.

Art and Slavery

Davis, Natalie Zemon. *Slaves on Screen: Film and Historical Vision*. Cambridge, Mass.: Harvard University Press, 2000.

Heneghan, Bridget T. *Whitewashing America: Material Culture and Race in the Antebellum Imagination*. Jackson: University Press of Mississippi, 2003.

Vlach, John Michael. *The Planter's Prospect: Privilege and Slavery in Plantation Paintings*. Chapel Hill: University of North Carolina Press, 2002.

Wood, Marcus. *Blind Memory: Visual Representations of Slavery in England and America, 1780–1865*. New York: Routledge, 2000.

Black Slaveowners

Johnson, Michael P. and James L. Roark. *Black Masters: A Free Family of Color in the Old South.* New York: Norton, 1984.

Johnson, Michael P. and James L. Roark. *No Chariot Let Down: Charleston's Free People of Color on the Eve of the Civil War.* Chapel Hill: University of North Carolina Press, 1984.

Koger, Larry. *Black Slaveowners: Free Black Slave Masters in South Carolina, 1790–1860.* Columbia: University of South Carolina Press, 1994.

Whitten, David O. *Andrew Durnford: A Black Sugar Planter in the Antebellum South.* New Brunswick: Transaction, 1995.

Civil War and Slavery

Berlin, Ira, ed. *Black Military Experience.* Freedom: A Documentary History of Emancipation, 1861–1867. Cambridge: Cambridge University Press, 1982.

Berlin, Ira, ed. *The Destruction of Slavery.* Freedom: A Documentary History of Emancipation, 1861–1867. Cambridge: Cambridge University Press, 1985.

Berlin, Ira, ed. *Free at Last.* Freedom: A Documentary History of Emancipation, 1861–1867. Cambridge: Cambridge University Press, 1985.

Berlin, Ira, ed. *Slave No More: Three Essays on Emancipation and the Civil War.* Cambridge: Cambridge University Press, 1985.

Berlin, Ira, ed. *The Wartime Genesis of Free Labor: The Upper South.* Freedom: A Documentary History of Emancipation, 1861–1867. Cambridge and New York: Cambridge University Press, 1993.

Durden, Robert Franklin. *The Gray and the Black: The Confederate Debate on Emancipation.* Baton Rouge: Louisiana State University Press, 1972.

Gerteis, Louis S. *From Contraband to Freedman: Federal Policy toward Southern Blacks, 1861–1865.* Westport, Conn.: Greenwood Press, 1977.

Glatthaar, Joseph. *Forged in Battle: The Civil War Alliance between Black Soldiers and White Officers.* New York: Free Press, 1990.

Manning, Chandra. *What this Cruel War Was Over: Soldiers, Slavery, and the Civil War.* New York: Knopf, 2007.

Colonization

Burin, Eric. *Slavery and the Peculiar Solution: A History of the American Colonization Society.* Gainesville: University Press of Florida, 2005.

Lapsansky-Werner, Emma J. and Margaret Hope Bacon. *Back to Africa: Benjamin Coates and the Colonization Movement in America, 1848–1880.* University Park, Pa.: Pennsylvania State University Press, 2005.

McDaniel, Antonio. *Swing Low, Sweet Chariot: The Mortality Cost of Colonizing Liberia in the Nineteenth Century.* Chicago: University of Chicago Press, 1995.

Staudenraus, P. J. *The African Colonization Movement, 1816–1865.* New York: Octagon Books, 1980.

Yarema, Allan E. *The American Colonization Society: An Avenue to Freedom?* Lanham: University Press of America, 2006.

Economics of Slavery

Aitken, Hugh G. J., comp. *Did Slavery Pay? Readings in the Economics of Black Slavery in the United States*. New Perspectives in History. Boston: Houghton Mifflin, 1971.

Appiah, Kwame Anthony and Martin Bunzl, eds. *Buying Freedom: The Ethics and Economics of Slave Redemption*. Princeton: Princeton University Press, 2007.

Martin, Jonathan D. *Divided Mastery: Slave Hiring in the American South*. Cambridge, Mass.: Harvard University Press, 2004.

Schwartz, Stuart B., ed. *Tropical Babylons: Sugar and the Making of the Atlantic World, 1450–1680*. Chapel Hill: University of North Carolina Press, 2004.

Tomich, Dale W. *Through the Prism of Slavery: Labor, Capital, and World Economy*. Lanham: Rowman and Littlefield, 2004.

Wright, Gavin. *Slavery and American Economic Development*. Baton Rouge: Louisiana State University Press, 2006.

Education

Albanese, Anthony Gerald. *The Plantation School*. New York: Vantage, 1976.

Cornelius, Janet Duitsman. *"When I Can Read my Title Clear": Literacy, Slavery, and Religion in the Antebellum South*. Columbia: University of South Carolina Press, 1991.

Stone, Jeffrey C. *Slavery, Southern Culture, and Education in Little Dixie, Missouri, 1820–1860*. New York: Routledge, 2006.

Webber, Thomas L. *Deep Like the Rivers: Education in the Slave Quarter Community, 1831–1865*. New York: Norton, 1978.

Williams, Heather Andrea. *Self-Taught: African American Education in Slavery and Freedom*. Chapel Hill: University of North Carolina Press, 2005.

Emancipation

Guelzo, Allen C. *Lincoln's Emancipation Proclamation*. New York: Simon and Schuster, 2004.

Kerr-Ritchie, Jeffrey R. *Rites of August First: Emancipation Day in the Black Atlantic World*. Baton Rouge: Louisiana State University Press, 2007.

McKissack, Pat and Fredrick L. McKissack. *Days of Jubilee: The End of Slavery in the United States*. New York: Scholastic Press, 2003.

Zilversmit, Arthur. *The First Emancipation*. Chicago: University of Chicago Press, 1967.

Expressive Culture

Abrahams, Roger D. *Singing the Master: The Emergence of African American Culture in the Plantation South*. 1st edn. New York: Pantheon Books, 1992.

Buchanan, Thomas C. *Black Life on the Mississippi: Slaves, Free Blacks, and the Western Steamboat World*. Chapel Hill: University of North Carolina Press, 2004.

Campbell, Edward D. C., Jr. *Before Freedom Came: African-American Life in the Antebellum South. To Accompany an Exhibition Organized by the Museum of the Confederacy*. Richmond: The Museum, and Charlottesville: University of Virginia Press, 1991.

Crowley, Daniel J., ed. *African Folklore in the New World*. Austin: University of Texas Press, 1977.

Epstein, Dena J. *Sinful Tunes and Spirituals.* Urbana: University of Illinois Press, 1977.

Gomez, Michael Angelo. *Black Crescent: The Experience and Legacy of African Muslims in the Americas.* New York: Cambridge University Press, 2005.

Holloway, Joseph E. *Africans in American Culture.* Bloomington: Indiana University Press, 1990.

Levine, Lawrence. *Black Culture and Black Consciousness.* New York: Oxford University Press, 1977.

Palmie, Stephan, ed. *Slave Cultures and the Cultures of Slavery.* Knoxville: University of Tennessee Press, 1995.

Reiss, Benjamin. *The Showman and the Slave: Race, Death, and Memory in Barnum's America.* Cambridge, Mass.: Harvard University Press, 2001.

Rucker, Walter C. *The River Flows On: Black Resistance, Culture, and Identity Formation in Early America.* Baton Rouge: Louisiana State University Press, 2006.

Thornton, John. *Africa and Africans in the Making of the Modern World.* New York: Cambridge University Press, 1998.

Vlach, John Michael. *The Afro-American Tradition in Decorative Arts.* Cleveland: Cleveland Museum of Art, 1978.

White, Shane and Graham White. *The Sounds of Slavery: Discovering African American History through Songs, Sermons, and Speech.* Boston: Beacon Press, 2005.

White, Shane and Graham White. *Stylin': African American Expressive Culture from its Beginnings to the Zoot Suit.* Ithaca: Cornell University Press, 1998.

Families and Children

Dunaway, Wilma A. *The African-American Family in Slavery and Emancipation.* New York: Cambridge University Press, 2003.

Franklin, John Hope and Loren Schweninger. *In Search of the Promised Land: A Slave Family in the Old South.* New York: Oxford University Press, 2006.

Gutman, Herbert. *The Black Family in Slavery and Freedom.* New York: Pantheon, 1976.

Hunefeldt, Christine. *Paying the Price of Freedom: Family and Labor among Lima's Slaves, 1800–1854.* Berkeley: University of California Press, 1994.

King, Wilma. *African American Childhoods: Historical Perspectives from Slavery to Civil Rights.* New York: Palgrave Macmillan, 2005.

King, Wilma. *Stolen Childhood: Slave Youth in Nineteenth-Century America.* Bloomington: Indiana University Press, 1995.

Malone, Ann Patton. *Sweet Chariot: Slave Family and Household Structure in Nineteenth Century Louisiana.* Chapel Hill: University of North Carolina Press, 1992.

Miles, Tiya. *Ties that Bind: The Story of an Afro-Cherokee Family in Slavery and Freedom.* Berkeley: University of California Press, 2005.

Penningroth, Dylan C. *The Claims of Kinfolk: African American Property and Community in the Nineteenth-Century South.* Chapel Hill: University of North Carolina Press, 2003.

Schwartz, Marie Jenkins. *Birthing a Slave: Motherhood and Medicine in the Antebellum South.* Cambridge, Mass.: Harvard University Press, 2006.

Schwartz, Marie Jenkins. *Born in Bondage: Growing Up Enslaved in the Antebellum South.* Cambridge, Mass.: Harvard University Press, 2000.

Stevenson, Brenda E. *Life in Black and White: Family and Community in the Slave South.* New York: Oxford University Press, 1996.

West, Emily. *Chains of Love: Slave Couples in Antebellum South Carolina.* Urbana: University of Illinois Press, 2004.

Free Blacks

Berlin, Ira. *Slaves Without Masters: The Free Negro in the Antebellum South*. New York: New Press, 1974.

Curry, Leonard P. *The Free Black in Urban America*. Chicago: University of Chicago Press, 1981.

White, Shane. *Somewhat More Independent: The End of Slavery in New York City, 1770–1810*. Athens: University of Georgia Press, 1991.

White, Shane. *Stories of Freedom in Black New York*. Cambridge, Mass.: Harvard University Press, 2002.

Genealogy

Streets, David H. *Slave Genealogy: A Research Guide with Case Studies*. Bowie, Md.: Heritage Books, 1986.

Intellectual History

Ericson, David F. *The Debate over Slavery: Antislavery and Proslavery Liberalism in Antebellum America*. New York: New York University Press, 2000.

Lott, Tommy L. *Subjugation and Bondage: Critical Essays on Slavery and Social Philosophy*. Lanham: Rowman and Littlefield, 1998.

Lowance, Mason I., Jr., ed. *A House Divided: The Antebellum Slavery Debates in America, 1776–1865*. Princeton: Princeton University Press, 2003.

McGary, Howard. *Between Slavery and Freedom: Philosophy and American Slavery*. Blacks in the Diaspora. Bloomington: Indiana University Press, 1992.

Papenfuse, Eric Robert. *The Evils of Necessity: Robert Goodloe Harper and the Moral Dilemma of Slavery*. Philadelphia: American Philosophical Society, 1997.

Spiegel, Marjorie. *The Dreaded Comparison: Human and Animal Slavery*. New York: Mirror Books, 1996.

Stanley, Amy Dru. *From Bondage to Contract: Wage Labor, Marriage, and the Market in the Age of Slave Emancipation*. Cambridge: Cambridge University Press, 1998.

Jews and Slavery

Faber, Eli. *Jews, Slaves and the Slave Trade*. New York: New York University Press, 1998.

Friedman, Saul S. *Jews and the American Slave Trade*. New Brunswick: Transaction, 1998.

Goldenberg, David. *The Curse of Ham: Race and Slavery in Early Judaism, Christianity, and Islam*. Princeton: Princeton University Press, 2003.

Hezser, Catherine. *Jewish Slavery in Antiquity*. New York: Oxford University Press, 2005.

Labor

Breeden, James O., ed. *Advice Among Masters*. Westport, Conn.: Greenwood Press, 1980.

Dew, Charles B. *Bond of Iron: Master and Slave at Buffalo Forge*. New York: Norton, 1994.

Fogel, Robert William and Stanley L. Engerman. *Slave Hires, 1775–1865*. ICPSR, 7422. Ann Arbor, Mich.: Inter-university Consortium for Political and Social Research, 1976.

Fogel, Robert William and Stanley L. Engerman. *Slave Sales and Appraisals, 1775–1865.* ICPSR, 7421. Ann Arbor, Mich.: Inter-university Consortium for Political and Social Research, 1976.

Jernegan, Marcus Wilson. *Laboring and Dependent Classes in Colonial America, 1607–1783.* Westport, Conn.: Greenwood Press, 1980.

Lewis, Ronald L. *Coal, Iron, and Slaves: Industrial Slavery in Maryland and Virginia, 1715–1865.* Westport, Conn.: Greenwood Press, 1979.

Mandel, Bernard. *Labor, Free and Slave: Workingmen and the Anti-Slavery Movement in the United States.* Urbana: University of Illinois Press, 2007.

Mintz, Sidney J. *Was the Plantation Slave a Proletarian?* Binghamton: State University of New York at Binghamton, 1977.

Scarborough, William Kauffman. *The Overseer: Plantation Management in the Old South.* Athens: University of Georgia, 1966.

Shepherd, Verene A., ed. *Slavery Without Sugar: Diversity in Caribbean Economy and Society since the 17th Century.* Gainesville: University Press of Florida, 2002.

Starobin, Robert S. *Industrial Slavery in the Old South.* New York: Oxford University Press, 1970.

Van Deburg, William L. *The Slave Drivers: Black Agricultural Labor Supervisors in the Antebellum South.* Contributions in Afro-American and African Studies, 43. Westport, Conn.: Greenwood Press, 1979.

The Law of Slavery

Allen, Austin. *Origins of the Dred Scott Case: Jacksonian Jurisprudence and the Supreme Court, 1837–1857.* Athens: University of Georgia Press, 2006.

Brandon, Mark E. *Free in the New World: American Slavery and Constitutional Failure.* Princeton: Princeton University Press, 1998.

Cover, Robert M. *Justice Accused: Antislavery and the Judicial Process.* New Haven: Yale University Press, 1975.

DeLombard, Jeannine Marie. *Slavery on Trial: Law, Abolitionism, and Print Culture.* Chapel Hill: University of North Carolina Press, 2007.

Fehrenbacher, Don Edward. *The Dred Scott Case: Its Significance in American Law and Politics.* New York: Oxford University Press, 1978.

Fehrenbacher, Don Edward. *Slavery, Law, and Politics: The Dred Scott Case in Historical Perspective.* New York: Oxford University Press, 1981.

Finkelman, Paul. *Dred Scott v. Sandford: A Brief History with Documents.* Boston: Bedford Books, 1997.

Finkelman, Paul. *An Imperfect Union: Slavery, Federalism, and Comity.* Studies in Legal History. Chapel Hill: University of North Carolina Press, 1981.

Finkelman, Paul. *The Law of Freedom and Bondage: A Casebook.* New York University School of Law Series in Legal History. Ingram Documents in American Legal History. New York: Oceana, 1986.

Finkelman, Paul. *Slavery in the Courtroom: An Annotated Bibliography of American Cases.* Washington, D.C.: Library of Congress, for sale by the Supt. of Docs., US GPO, 1985.

Finkelman, Paul. *Slavery and the Founders: Race and Liberty in the Age of Jefferson.* Armonk, N.Y.: M. E. Sharpe, 1995.

Finkelman, Paul. *Slavery and the Law.* Madison: Madison House, 1997.

Finkelman, Paul. *Southern Slaves in Free State Courts: The Pamphlet Literature.* Slavery, Race, and the American Legal System, 1700–1872, ser. 1. New York: Garland, 1988.

Gross, Ariela Julie. *Double Character: Slavery and Mastery in the Antebellum Southern Courtroom.* Princeton: Princeton University Press, 2000.

Hall, Kermit L. *The Law of American Slavery: Major Historical Interpretations.* United States Constitutional and Legal History, vol. 9. New York: Garland, 1987.

Higginbotham, A. Leon, Jr. *In the Matter of Color.* New York: Oxford University Press, 1978.

Lively, Donald E. *The Constitution and Race.* New York: Praeger, 1992.

Maltz, Earl M. *Dred Scott and the Politics of Slavery.* Lawrence: University Press of Kansas, 2007.

McLaurin, Melton Alonza. *Celia: A Slave.* Athens: University of Georgia Press, 1991.

Morris, Thomas D. *Southern Slavery and the Law, 1619–1860.* Chapel Hill: University of North Carolina Press, 1996.

Schwarz, Philip J. *Twice Condemned: Slaves and the Criminal Laws of Virginia, 1705–1865.* Baton Rouge: Louisiana State University Press, 1988.

Shaw, Robert B. *A Legal History of Slavery in the United States.* Potsdam, N.Y.: Northern Press, 1991.

Tsesis, Alexander. *The Thirteenth Amendment and American Freedom: A Legal History.* New York: New York University Press, 2004.

Tushnet, Mark V. *The American Law of Slavery, 1810–1860: Considerations of Humanity and Interest.* Princeton: Princeton University Press, 1981.

Tushnet, Mark V. *Slave Law in the American South: State v. Mann in History and Literature.* Lawrence: University Press of Kansas, 2003.

Wahl, Jenny Bourne. *The Bondsman's Burden: An Economic Analysis of the Common Law of Southern Slavery.* Cambridge: Cambridge University Press, 1998.

Waldrep, Christopher and Donald G. Nieman, eds. *Local Matters: Race, Crime, and Justice in the Nineteenth-Century South.* Athens: University of Georgia Press, 2001.

Watson, Alan. *Slave Law in the Americas.* Athens: University of Georgia Press, 1989.

Weiner, Mark Stuart. *Black Trials: Citizenship from the Beginnings of Slavery to the End of Caste.* New York: Knopf, 2004.

Wiecek, William M. *The Sources of Antislavery Constitutionalism in America, 1760–1848.* Ithaca: Cornell University Press, 1977.

Wiethoff, William E. *A Peculiar Humanism: The Judicial Advocacy of Slavery in High Courts of the Old South, 1820–1850.* Athens: University of Georgia Press, 1996.

Williams, Oscar R. *African Americans and Colonial Legislation in the Middle Colonies.* New York: Garland, 1998.

Medicine and Demography

Bankole, Katherine Kemi. *Slavery and Medicine: Enslavement and Medical Practices in Antebellum Louisiana.* New York: Garland, 1998.

Kiple, Kenneth F. *The African Exchange: Toward a Biological History of Black People.* Durham, N.C.: Duke University Press, 1987.

Kiple, Kenneth F. and Virginia Himmelsteib King. *Another Dimension to the Black Diaspora: Diet, Disease, and Racism.* Cambridge: Cambridge University Press, 1981.

Kiple, Kenneth F. *The Caribbean Slave: A Biological History.* Cambridge: Cambridge University Press, 1984.

McClelland, Peter D. *Demographic Dimensions of the New Republic: American Interregional Migration, Vital Statistics, and Manumission, 1800–1860*. Cambridge: Cambridge University Press, 1982.

Numbers, Ronald, ed. *Science and Medicine in the Old South*. Baton Rouge: Louisiana State University Press, 1989.

Postell, William Dosite. *The Health of Slaves on Southern Plantations*. Louisiana State University Studies: Social Science Series, 1. Gloucester, Mass.: P. Smith, 1970.

Savitt, Todd Lee, ed. *Disease and Distinctiveness in the American South*. Knoxville: University of Tennessee Press, 1988.

Savitt, Todd Lee. *Medicine and Slavery: The Diseases and Health Care of Blacks in Antebellum Virginia*. Blacks in the New World. Urbana: University of Illinois Press, 1978.

Schwartz, Marie Jenkins. *Birthing a Slave: Motherhood and Medicine in the Antebellum South*. Cambridge, Mass.: Harvard University Press, 2006.

Sheridan, Richard B. *Doctors and Slaves: A Medical and Demographic History of Slavery in the British West Indies, 1680–1834*. New York: Cambridge University Press, 1985.

Stowe, Steven M. *Doctoring the South: Southern Physicians and Everyday Medicine in the Mid-Nineteenth Century*. Chapel Hill: University of North Carolina Press, 2004.

Memory and Slavery

Blight, David W. *Race and Reunion: The Civil War in American Memory*. Cambridge, Mass.: Harvard University Press, 2002.

Braxton, Joanne M. and Maria I. Diedrich, eds. *Monuments of the Black Atlantic: Slavery and Memory*. New Brunswick: Transaction, 2004.

Eichstedt, Jennifer and Stephen Small. *Representations of Slavery: Race and Ideology in Southern Plantation Museums*. Washington, D.C.: Smithsonian Institution Press, 2002.

Fleischner, Jennifer. *Mastering Slavery: Memory, Family, and Identity in Women's Slave Narratives*. New York: New York University Press, 1996.

French, Scot. *The Rebellious Slave: Nat Turner in American Memory*. Boston: Houghton Mifflin, 2004.

Horton, James Oliver and Lois E. Horton. *Slavery and Public History*. New York: New Press, 2006.

Kerr-Ritchie, Jeffrey R. *Rites of August First: Emancipation Day in the Black Atlantic World*. Baton Rouge: Louisiana State University Press, 2007.

Kowaleski-Wallace, Elizabeth. *The British Slave Trade and Public Memory*. New York: Columbia University Press, 2006.

Larson, Pier Martin. *History and Memory in the Age of Enslavement: Becoming Merina in Highland Madagascar, 1770–1822*. Portsmouth, N.H.: Heinemann, 2000.

Nudelman, Franny. *John Brown's Body: Slavery, Violence, and the Culture of War*. Chapel Hill: University of North Carolina Press, 2004.

Oldfield, J. R. *Chords of Freedom: Commemoration, Ritual and British Transatlantic Slavery*. Manchester: Manchester University Press, 2007.

Native Americans and Slavery

Brooks, James F. *Captives and Cousins: Slavery, Kinship, and Community in the Southwest Borderlands*. Chapel Hill: University of North Carolina Press, 2002.

Gallay, Alan. *The Indian Slave Trade: The Rise of the English Empire in the American South, 1670–1717*. New Haven: Yale University Press, 2002.

Halliburton, R. *Red over Black: Black Slavery among the Cherokee Indians*. Westport, Conn.: Greenwood Press, 1977.

Leland, Donald. *Aboriginal Slavery on the Northwest Coast of North America*. Berkeley: University of California Press, 1997.

Littlefield, Daniel F. *Africans and Seminoles: From Removal to Emancipation*. Contributions in Afro-American and African Studies, 32. Westport, Conn.: Greenwood Press, 1977.

Magnaghi, Russell M. *Indian Slavery, Labor, Evangelization, and Captivity in the Americas: An Annotated Bibliography*. Lanham: Scarecrow Press, 1998.

Minges, Patrick N. *Slavery in the Cherokee Nation: The Keetoowah Society and the Defining of a People, 1855–1867*. New York: Routledge, 2003.

Perdue, Theda. *Slavery and the Evolution of Cherokee Society, 1540–1866*. Knoxville: University of Tennessee Press, 1979.

North African "White Slavery"

Baepler, Paul. *White Slaves, African Masters: An Anthology of American Barbary Captivity Narratives*. Chicago: University of Chicago Press, 1999.

Colley, Linda. *Captives: Britain, Empire and the World, 1600–1850*. London: Jonathan Cape, 2002.

Davis, Robert C. *Christian Slaves, Muslim Masters: White Slavery in the Mediterranean, the Barbary Coast, and Italy, 1500–1800*. New York: Palgrave Macmillan, 2003.

Vitkus, Daniel J. *Piracy, Slavery, and Redemption: Barbary Captivity Narratives from Early Modern England*. New York: Columbia University Press, 2001.

Politics of Slavery

Anbinder, Tyler. *Nativism and Slavery: The Northern Know Nothings and the Politics of the 1850s*. New York: Oxford University Press, 1992.

Ashworth, John, *Slavery, Capitalism and Politics in the Antebellum Republic*. Cambridge: Cambridge University Press, 1995.

Bilotta, James D. *Race and the Rise of the Republican Party, 1848–1865*. New York: Peter Lang, 1992.

Cooper, William J. *Liberty and Slavery: Southern Politics to 1860*. Columbia: University of South Carolina Press, 2000.

Cooper, William J. *The South and the Politics of Slavery, 1828–1856*. Baton Rouge: Louisiana State University Press, 1978.

Davis, David Brion. *Slave Power Conspiracy and the Paranoid Style*. Baton Rouge: Louisiana State University Press, 1986.

Earle, Jonathan Halperin. *Jacksonian Antislavery and the Politics of Free Soil, 1824–1854*. Chapel Hill: University of North Carolina Press, 2004.

Einhorn, Robin L. *American Taxation, American Slavery*. Chicago: University of Chicago Press, 2006.

Etcheson, Nicole. *Bleeding Kansas: Contested Liberty in the Civil War Era*. Lawrence: University Press of Kansas, 2004.

Fehrenbacher, Don Edward, completed and ed. Ward M. McAfee. *The Slaveholding Republic: An Account of the United States Government's Relations to Slavery.* New York: Oxford University Press, 2001.

Finkelman, Paul. *Slavery and the Founders: Race and Liberty in the Age of Jefferson.* 2nd edn. Armonk, N.Y.: M. E. Sharpe, 2001.

Forbes, Robert Pierce. *The Missouri Compromise and its Aftermath: Slavery and the Meaning of America.* Chapel Hill: University of North Carolina Press, 2007.

Freehling, William W. *The Reintegraiton of American History: Slavery and the Civil War.* New York: Oxford University Press, 1994.

Goldstone, Lawrence. *Dark Bargain: Slavery, Profits, and the Struggle for the Constitution.* New York: Walker, 2005.

Horne, Gerald. *The White Pacific: U.S. Imperialism and Black Slavery in the South Seas after the Civil War.* Honolulu: University of Hawai'i Press, 2007.

Johannsen, Robert Walter. *Lincoln, the South, and Slavery: The Political Dimension.* Baton Rouge: Louisiana State University Press, 1991.

Kennedy, Roger G. *Mr. Jefferson's Lost Cause: Land, Farmers, Slavery, and the Louisiana Purchase.* New York: Oxford University Press, 2003.

Klingaman, William K. *Abraham Lincoln and the Road to Emancipation, 1861–1865.* New York: Viking, 2001.

Lightner, David L. *Slavery and the Commerce Power: How the Struggle Against the Interstate Slave Trade Led to the Civil War.* New Haven: Yale University Press, 2006.

Lynd, Staughton. *Class Conflict, Slavery, and the United States Constitution.* Westport, Conn.: Greenwood Press, 1980.

Mason, Matthew. *Slavery and Politics in the Early American Republic.* Chapel Hill: University of North Carolina Press, 2006.

Matthewson, Tim. *A Proslavery Foreign Policy: Haitian–American Relations during the Early Republic.* Westport, Conn.: Praeger, 2003.

Miller, William Lee. *Arguing About Slavery: The Great Battle in the United States Congress.* New York: Knopf, 1996.

Mitchell, Thomas G. *Anti-Slavery Politics in Antebellum and Civil War America.* Westport, Conn.: Praeger, 2007.

Morrison, Michael A. *Slavery and the American West: The Eclipse of Manifest Destiny and the Coming of the Civil War.* Chapel Hill: University of North Carolina Press, 1997.

Oakes, James. *The Radical and the Republican: Frederick Douglass, Abraham Lincoln, and the Triumph of Antislavery Politics.* New York: Norton, 2007.

Richards, Leonard L. *The Slave Power: The Free North and Southern Domination, 1780–1860.* Baton Rouge: Louisiana State University Press, 2000.

Robinson, Armstead L. *Bitter Fruits of Bondage: The Demise of Slavery and the Collapse of the Confederacy, 1861–1865.* Charlottesville: University of Virginia Press, 2005.

Robinson, Donald L. *Slavery in the Structure of American Politics, 1765–1820.* New York: Norton, 1979.

Siddali, Silvana R. *From Property to Person: Slavery and the Confiscation Acts, 1861–1862.* Baton Rouge: Louisiana State University Press, 2005.

Striner, Richard. *Father Abraham: Lincoln's Relentless Struggle to End Slavery.* New York: Oxford University Press, 2006.

Wills, Garry. *"Negro President": Jefferson and the Slave Power.* Boston: Houghton Mifflin, 2003.

Pro-Slavery Argument

Ambrose, Douglas. *Henry Hughes and Proslavery Thought in the Old South*. Baton Rouge: Louisiana State University Press, 1997.

Finkelman, Paul. *Defending Slavery. Proslavery Thought in the Old South: A Brief History with Documents*. Boston: St Martin's Press, 2003.

Fox-Genovese, Elizabeth and Eugene Genovese. *Mind of the Master Class*. New York: Cambridge University Press, 2005.

Greenberg, Kenneth S. *Honor and Slavery*. Princeton: Princeton University Press, 1996.

Young, Jeffrey Robert. *Proslavery and Sectional Thought in the Early South, 1740–1829: An Anthology*. Columbia: University of South Carolina Press, 2006.

Psychological Aspects of Slavery

Hartman, Saidiya V. *Scenes of Subjection: Terror, Slavery, and Self-Making in Nineteenth-Century America*. New York: Oxford University Press, 1997.

Patterson, Orlando. *Rituals of Blood: Consequences of Slavery in Two American Centuries*. New York: Basic Civitas, 1998.

Race

Fredrickson, George M. *The Black Image in the White Mind*. New York: Harper and Row, 1971.

Freimarck, Vincent, ed., *Race and the American Romantics*. New York: Schocken Books, 1971.

Goldenberg, David. *The Curse of Ham: Race and Slavery in Early Judaism, Christianity, and Islam*. Princeton: Princeton University Press, 2003.

Jordan, Winthrop D. *The White Man's Burden: Historical Origins of Racism in the United States*. New York: Oxford University Press, 1974.

Jordan, Winthrop D. *White Over Black: American Attitudes Toward the Negro, 1550–1812*. Chapel Hill: University of North Carolina Press, 1968.

Miller, John Chester. *The Wolf by the Ears: Thomas Jefferson and Slavery*. New York: Free Press, 1977.

Peterson, Thomas Virgin. *Ham and Japheth: The Mythic World of Whites in the Antebellum South*. Metuchen, N.J.: Scarecrow Press, 1978.

Smedley, Audrey. *Race in North America: Origin and Evolution of a Worldview*. 2nd edn. Boulder: Westview Press, 1999.

Tise, Larry E. *Proslavery: A History of the Defense of Slavery in America, 1701–1840*. Athens: University of Georgia, 1987.

Reconstruction

Foner, Eric. *Nothing But Freedom*. Baton Rouge: Louisiana State University Press, 1983.

Foner, Eric. *Reconstruction: America's Unfinished Revolution*. New York: HarperCollins, 1988.

Holt, Thomas. *Black Over White: Negro Political Leadership in South Carolina during Reconstruction*. Urbana: University of Illinois Press, 1977.

Kolchin, Peter. *First Freedom: The Responses of Alabama's Blacks to Emancipation and Reconstruction*. Westport, Conn.: Greenwood Press, 1972.

Litwack, Leon. *Been in the Storm So Long: The Aftermath of Slavery*. New York: Knopf, 1979.

Mandle, Jay R. *Not Slave, Not Free: The African American Economic Experience since the Civil War*. Durham, N.C.: Duke University Press, 1992.

Rable, George C. *But There Was No Peace*. Athens: University of Georgia Press, 1984.

Ransom, Roger L. and Richard Sutch. *One Kind of Freedom*. 2nd edn. Cambridge: Cambridge University Press, 1977.

Rose, Willie Lee. *Rehearsal for Reconstruction*. Indianapolis: Bobbs-Merrill, 1964.

Williamson, Joel. *After Slavery*. Chapel Hill: University of North Carolina Press, 1965.

Williamson, Joel. *A Rage for Order*. Chapel Hill: University of North Carolina Press, 1986.

Religion

Boles, John B. *Masters and Slaves in the House of the Lord: Race and Religion in the American South, 1740–1870*. Lexington: University Press of Kentucky, 1988.

Cornelius, Janet Duitsman. *Slave Missions and the Black Church in the Antebellum South*. Columbia: University of South Carolina Press, 1999.

Diouf, Sylviane. *Servants of Allah: African Muslims Enslaved in the Americas*. New York: New York University Press, 1998.

Essig, James D. *The Bonds of Wickedness: American Evangelicals against Slavery, 1770–1808*. Philadelphia: Temple, 1982.

Finkelman, Paul, ed. *Religion and Slavery*. Articles on American Slavery, vol. 16. New York: Garland, 1989.

Haynes, Stephen R. *Noah's Curse: The Biblical Justification of American Slavery*. New York: Oxford University Press, 2002.

Lesick, Lawrence Thomas. *The Lane Rebels: Evangelicalism and Antislavery in Antebellum America*. Studies in Evangelicalism, 2. Metuchen, N.J.: Scarecrow Press, 1980.

McKivigan, John R. *The War against Proslavery Religion: Abolitionism and the Northern Churches, 1830–1865*. Ithaca: Cornell University Press, 1984.

McKivigan, John R. and Mitchell Snay. *Religion and the Antebellum Debate Over Slavery*. Athens: University of Georgia Press, 1998.

Raboteau, Albert J. *Slave Religion: The "Invisible Institution" in the Antebellum South*. New York: Oxford University Press, 1978.

Sobel, Mechal. *Trabelin' On: The Slave Journey to an Afro-Baptist Faith*. Princeton: Princeton University Press, 1988.

Resistance

Alpers, Edward, Gwyn Campbell, and Michael Salman, eds. *Resisting Bondage in Indian Ocean Africa and Asia*. New York: Routledge, 2007.

Aptheker, Herbert. *Negro Slave Revolts in the United States, 1526–1860*. New York: International, 1939.

Bracey, John H., comp. *American Slavery: The Question of Resistance*. Explorations in the Black Experience. Belmont, Calif.: Wadsworth, (1971).

Egerton, Douglas R. *Gabriel's Rebellion: The Virginia Slave Conspiracies of 1800 and 1802*. Chapel Hill: University of North Carolina Press, 1993.

Frey, Sylvia R. *Water from the Rock: Black Resistance in a Revolutionary Age*. Princeton: Princeton University Press, 1991.

Genovese, Eugene D. *From Rebellion to Revolution: Afro-American Slave Revolts in the Making of the Modern World*. Walter Lynwood Fleming Lectures in Southern History, Louisiana State University. Baton Rouge: Louisiana State University Press, 1979.

Hinks, Peter P. *To Awaken My Afflicted Brethren: David Walker and the Problem of Antebellum Slave Resistance*. University Park: Pennsylvania State University Press, 1997.

Matthews, Gelien. *Caribbean Slave Revolts and the British Abolitionist Movement*. Baton Rouge: Louisiana State University Press, 2006.

Oates, Stephen B. *The Fires of Jubilee: Nat Turner's Fierce Rebellion*. New York: Harper Perennial, 1990.

Okihio, Gary Y. *In Resistance: Studies in African, Caribbean, and Afro-American History*. Amherst: University of Massachusetts Press, 1986.

Rossbach, Jeffery S. *Ambivalent Conspirators: John Brown, the Secret Six, and a Theory of Slave Violence*. Philadelphia: University of Pennsylvania Press, 1982.

Sidbury, James. *Ploughshares into Swords: Race, Rebellion and Identity in Gabriel's Virginia, 1730–1810*. Cambridge: Cambridge University Press, 1997.

Whitman, T. Stephen. *Challenging Slavery in the Chesapeake: Black and White Resistance to Human Bondage, 1775–1865*. Baltimore: Maryland Historical Society, 2007.

Slave Narratives: Criticism and Interpretation

Andrews, William L. *To Tell a Free Story: The First Century of Afro-American Autobiography, 1760–1865*. Urbana: University of Illinois Press, 1986.

Brignano, Russell C. *Black Americans in Autobiography: An Annotated Bibliography of Autobiographies and Autobiographical Books Written since the Civil War*. Rev. and exp. edn. Durham, N.C.: Duke University Press, 1984.

Davis, Charles T. and Henry Louis Gates, Jr. *The Slave's Narrative*. New York: Oxford University Press, 1985.

Fisch, Audrey, ed. *The Cambridge Companion to the African American Slave Narrative*. New York: Cambridge University Press, 2007.

Foster, Frances Smith. *Witnessing Slavery: The Development of Ante-Bellum Slave Narratives*. Wisconsin Studies in American Sutobiography. Madison: University of Wisconsin Press, 1994.

Starling, Marion Wilson. *The Slave Narrative: Its Place in American History*. 2nd edn. Washington, D.C.: Howard University Press, 1981.

Slave Trade

Atlantic slave trade

Curtin, Philip D. *The Atlantic Slave Trade: A Census*. Madison: University of Wisconsin Press, 1969.

Davidson, Basil. *Black Mother: The Years of the African Slave Trade*. Boston: Little, Brown, 1961.

Diouf, Sylviane A. *Dreams of Africa in Alabama: The Slave Ship Clotilda and the Story of the Last Africans Brought to America*. New York: Oxford University Press, 2007.

Diouf, Sylviane A., ed. *Fighting the Slave Trade: West African Strategies*. Athens: Ohio University Press, 2003.

Dresser, Madge. *Slavery Obscured: The Social History of the Slave Trade in an English Provincial Port*. New York: Continuum, 2001.

Elder, Melinda. *The Slave Trade and the Economic Development of Eighteenth-Century Lancaster*. Krumlin, Halifax: Ryburn, 1992.

Eltis, David, ed. *The Abolition of the Atlantic Slave Trade: Origins and Effects in Europe, Africa, and the Americas*. Madison: University of Wisconsin Press, 1981.

Eltis, David. *Economic Growth and the Ending of the Transatlantic Slave Trade*. New York: Oxford University Press, 1987.

Eltis, David and David Richardson. *Routes to Slavery: Direction, Ethnicity, and Mortality in the Transatlantic Slave Trade*. London: Frank Cass, 1997.

Harms, Robert. *The Diligent*. New York: Basic Books, 2002.

Horne, Gerald. *The Deepest South: The United States, Brazil, and the African Slave Trade*. New York: New York University Press, 2007.

Inkori, Joseph E. *The Abolition of the Atlantic Slave Trade: Origins and Effects in Europe, Africa, and the Americas*. Madison: University of Wisconsin Press, 1981.

Klein Herbert S. *The Atlantic Slave Trade*. New York: Cambridge University Press, 1999.

Klein, Herbert S. *The Middle Passage: Comparative Studies in the Atlantic Slave Trade*. Princeton: Princeton University Press, 1978.

Manning, Patrick. *Slave Trades, 1500–1800*. Aldershot: Variorum, 1996.

Miller, Joseph Calder. *Way of Death: Merchant Capitalism and the Angolan Slave Trade, 1730–1830*. Madison: University of Wisconsin Press, 1988.

Northrup, David. *The Atlantic Slave Trade*. Problems in World History. Lexington, Mass.: D. C. Heath, 1994.

Palmer, Colin A. *Human Cargoes: The British Slave Trade to Spanish America, 1700–1739*. Blacks in the New World. Urbana: University of Illinois Press, 1981.

Rawley, James A. *The Transatlantic Slave Trade: A History*. New York: Norton, 1981.

Rediker, Marcus. *The Slave Ship: A Human History*. New York: Viking, 2007.

Smallwood, Stephanie E. *Saltwater Slavery: A Middle Passage from Africa to American Diaspora*. Cambridge, Mass.: Harvard University Press, 2007.

Taylor, Eric Robert. *If We Must Die: Shipboard Insurrections in the Era of the Atlantic Slave Trade*. Baton Rouge: Louisiana State University Press, 2006.

Thomas, Hugh. *The Slave Trade*. New York: Simon and Schuster, 1997.

Wright, John. *The Trans-Saharan Slave Trade*. New York: Routledge, 2007.

Domestic slave trade

Deyle, Steven. *Carry Me Back: The Domestic Slave Trade in American Life*. New York: Oxford University Press, 2005.

Gudmestad, Robert H. *A Troublesome Commerce: The Transformation of the Interstate Slave Trade*. Baton Rouge: Louisiana State University Press, 2003.

Johnson, Walter, ed. *The Chattel Principle: Internal Slave Trades in the Americas*. New Haven: Yale University Press, 2004.

Johnson, Walter. *Soul by Soul: Life Inside the Antebellum Slave Market*. Cambridge, Mass.: Harvard University Press, 1999.

Obadele-Starks, Ernest. *Freebooters and Smugglers: The Foreign Slave Trade in the United States after 1808*. Fayetteville: University of Arkansas Press, 2007.

Rothman, Adam. *Slave Country: American Expansion and the Origins of the Deep South.* Cambridge, Mass.: Harvard University Press, 2005.

Tadman, Michael. *Speculators and Slaves: Masters, Traders, and Slaves in the Old South.* Madison: University of Wisconsin Press, 1989.

Slavery in the Contemporary World

Bales, Kevin. *Disposable People: New Slavery in the Global Economy.* Berkeley: University of California Press, 2004.

Bales, Kevin. *New Slavery: A Reference Handbook.* 2nd edn. Santa Barbara: ABC-CLIO, 2004.

Bales, Kevin. *Understanding Global Slavery: A Reader.* Berkeley: University of California Press, 2005.

Miers, Suzanne. *Slavery in the Twentieth Century: The Evolution of a Global Pattern.* Walnut Creek, Calif.: AltaMira Press, 2003.

Sawyer, Roger. *Slavery in the Twentieth Century.* London and New York: Routledge and Kegan Paul, 1986.

van den Anker, Christien, ed. *The Political Economy of New Slavery.* New York: Palgrave Macmillan, 2004.

Underground Railroad

Baker, H. Robert. *The Rescue of Joshua Glover: A Fugitive Slave, the Constitution, and the Coming of the Civil War.* Athens: Ohio University Press, 2006.

Blight, David W. *Passages to Freedom: The Underground Railroad in History and Memory.* Washington, D.C.: Smithsonian Books in association with the National Underground Railroad Freedom Center, 2004.

Bordewich, Fergus M. *Bound for Canaan: The Underground Railroad and the War for the Soul of America.* New York: Amistad, 2005.

Brandt, Nat. *The Town that Started the Civil War.* Syracuse: Syracuse University Press, 1990.

Buckmaster, Henrietta. *Let My People Go: The Story of the Underground Railroad and the Growth of the Abolition Movement.* Columbia: University of South Carolina Press, 1992.

Franklin, John Hope and Loren Schweninger. *Runaway Slaves.* New York: Oxford University Press, 1999.

Gara, Larry. *The Liberty Line: The Legend of the Underground Railroad.* Lexington: University Press of Kentucky, 1961.

Griffler, Keith P. *Front Line of Freedom: African Americans and the Forging of the Underground Railroad in the Ohio Valley.* Lexington: University Press of Kentucky, 2004.

Grover, Kathryn. *The Fugitive's Gibraltar: Escaping Slaves and Abolitionism in New Bedford, Massachusetts.* Amherst: University of Massachusetts Press, 2001.

Hudson, J. Blaine. *Encyclopedia of the Underground Railroad.* Jefferson, N.C.: McFarland, 2006.

Hunter, Carol M. *To Set the Captives Free: The Reverend Jermain Loguen and the Struggle for Freedom in Central New York, 1835–1872.* New York: Garland, 1993.

Pacheco, Josephine F. *The Pearl: A Failed Slave Escape on the Potomac.* Chapel Hill: University of North Carolina Press, 2005.

Pybus, Cassandra. *Epic Journeys of Freedom: Runaway Slaves of the American Revolution and their Global Quest for Liberty.* Boston: Beacon Press, 2006.

Ricks, Mary Kay. *Escape on the Pearl: The Heroic Bid for Freedom on the Underground Railroad*. New York: William Morrow, 2007.

Ruggles, Jeffrey. *The Unboxing of Henry Brown*. Richmond: Library of Virginia, 2003.

Windley, Lathan A. *Runaway Slave Advertisements: A Documentary History from the 1730s to 1790*. Westport, Conn.: Greenwood Press, 1983.

Urban Slavery

Finkelman, Paul. *Economics, Industrialization, Urbanization, and Slavery*. Articles on American Slavery, vol. 10. New York: Garland, 1989.

Goldin, Claudia Dale. *Urban Slavery in the American South, 1820–1860: A Quantitative History*. Chicago: University of Chicago Press, 1976.

Wade, Richard C. *Slavery in the Cities: The South, 1820–1860*. London and New York: Oxford University Press, 1964.

Women

Camp, Stephanie M. H. *Closer to Freedom: Enslaved Women and Everyday Resistance in the Plantation South*. Chapel Hill: University of North Carolina Press, 2004.

Finkelman, Paul, ed. *Women and the Family in a Slave Society*. Articles on American Slavery, vol. 9. New York: Garland, 1989.

Fox-Genovese, Elizabeth. *Within the Plantation Household: Black and White Women of the Old South*. Chapel Hill: University of North Carolina Press, 1988.

Gaspar, David Barry and Darlene Clark Hine, eds. *Beyond Bondage: Free Women of Color in the Americas*. Urbana: University of Illinois Press, 2004.

Gaspar, David Barry and Darlene Clark Hine, eds. *More than Chattel: Black Women and Slavery in the Americas*. Bloomington: Indiana University Press, 1996.

Jones, Jacqueline. *Labor of Love, Labor of Sorrow: Black Women, Work, and the Family from Slavery to the Present*. New York: Basic Books, 1985.

Morgan, Jennifer L. *Laboring Women: Reproduction and Gender in New World Slavery*. Philadelphia: University of Pennsylvania Press, 2004.

Morton, Patricia, ed. *Discovering the Women in Slavery: Emancipating Perspectives on the American Past*. Athens: University of Georgia Press, 1996.

Scully, Pamela and Diana Paton, eds. *Gender and Slave Emancipation in the Atlantic World*. Durham, N.C.: Duke University Press, 2005.

White, Deborah G. *Ar'n't I a Woman? Female Slaves in the Plantation South*. New York: Norton, 1985.

Wood, Betty. *Women's Work, Men's Work: The Informal Slave Economies of Lowcountry Georgia*. Athens: University of Georgia, 1995.

Index